Thornton Wilder and Amos Wilder

Thornton Wilder
& Amos Wilder

Writing Religion in Twentieth-Century America

CHRISTOPHER J. WHEATLEY

University of Notre Dame Press

Notre Dame, Indiana

Published in the United States of America

Library of Congress Cataloging-in-Publication Data

Wheatley, Christopher J., 1955–
Thornton Wilder and Amos Wilder : writing religion in
twentieth-century America / Christopher J. Wheatley.
    p. cm.
Includes bibliographical references and index.
ISBN-13: 978-0-268-04424-4 (pbk. : alk. paper)
ISBN-10: 0-268-04424-4 (pbk. : alk. paper)
1. Wilder, Thornton, 1897–1975—Criticism and interpretation.
2. Wilder, Thornton, 1897–1975—Religion. 3. Wilder, Thornton,
1897–1975—Family. 4. Wilder, Amos N. (Amos Niven), 1895–1993.
5. Religion in literature. 6. Social values in literature. 7. Social change
in literature. 8. Religion and literature—United States—History—20th century.
I. Title.   II. Title: Writing religion in twentieth-century America.
PS3545.I345Z978 2011
818'.5209—dc23

2011025684

To Megan

Contents

Acknowledgments

Some of the research for this book was made possible by a grant from the Foley Fund of the English Department at The Catholic University of America to read in Amos Wilder's papers at the Andover-Harvard Theological Library. I thank Frances E. O'Donnell, curator of Manuscripts and Archives, for her assistance. The Thornton Wilder Fellowship from the Beinecke Library at Yale allowed me to read in the Thornton Wilder collection there. I thank Priscilla Holmes and the staff of the Beinecke for their help.

Individual chapters were read by Ernest Suarez and Virgil Nemoianu. I am grateful for their thoughtful criticism and suggestions. Tappan Wilder and Jackson Bryer also provided helpful advice. Lincoln Konkle read the entire manuscript and gave a detailed critique upon which I relied extensively when revising the manuscript. I have benefited as well from many discussions over the years with the Drama Dogs, William Demastes and Michael Vanden Heuvel.

I must also thank the students in the senior seminars on Thornton Wilder whom I have taught over the years. They assumed (willingly, I hope) the role of unpaid research assistants, and their insights, while not explicitly cited in this book, are incorporated throughout. My thanks go to Cathy Borla, James Brooks, Molly Bryson, Matthew Burke, Kerry Carew, Sue Anne Cassidy, Nolan Deibert, Sheila Dempsey, Marie Desobeau, Danielle Donovan, Kristen Doyle, Alison Dunlop, Julie Eichstedt, Jessica Gallagher, Toni Gallo, Anne Giammatteo, Katie Gloninger, George Heery, Mendie Hoffman, Elizabeth

Jurkowski, Natalia Kellum, Mary Kelly, Kathryn Kramer, Glynnis La-Garde, Siobhan McLaughlin, Tami McNamara, Maria Malkiewicz, Debra Marshall, Christina Murphy, Carole Nazzaro, Joanna Pulcini, Robyn Rebollo, Patrick Reed, Douglas Rowe, Rosemarie Ruddy, Mary Russell, Joseph Schmitt, Christina Sherry, Leah Silver, Michelle Smith, Meghan Steele, Christopher Ulisse, Robert Vaccarino, Jennifer Villano, and Alexander Walker. Fine kids all, and I am sure that they are now valuable members of the community.

Abbreviations

The following editions of works by Thornton Wilder are cited parenthetically in the text with these abbreviations:

Bridge *The Bridge of San Luis Rey.* New York: Harper & Row, 1986.

Cabala *The Cabala.* In *The Cabala; and, The Woman of Andros.* New York: HarperCollins, 2006.

CP *Thornton Wilder: Collected Plays and Writings on Theater.* New York: Library of America, 2007.

ED *The Eighth Day.* New York: Carroll & Graf, 1987.

Heaven's *Heaven's My Destination.* New York: HarperCollins, 2003.

Ides *The Ides of March.* New York: Harper & Brothers, 1948.

SL *The Selected Letters of Thornton Wilder.* Edited by Robin G. Wilder and Jackson R. Bryer. New York: Harper, 2008.

TN *Theophilus North.* New York: HarperCollins, 2003.

TSS *The Trumpet Shall Sound.* Printed in four issues, *Yale Literary Magazine* (October 1919): 9–26; (November 1919): 78–92; (December 1919): 128–46; and (January 1920): 192–207.

W of A *The Woman of Andros.* In *The Cabala; and, The Woman of Andros.* New York: HarperCollins, 2006.

Introduction

Brothers in Arms

The plays and novels of Thornton Wilder have often attracted religious interpretations. These interpretations, however, are profoundly ahistorical and have ignored significant elements of the nineteenth- and twentieth-century context of Wilder's work as well as their historical settings. In doing so, such explications have failed to reveal Wilder's pervasive sense that religious themes are always contested and always shaped by historical forces. In other words, an individual's apprehension of the sacred is dynamic rather than static, and the manifestations of the sacred are plural rather than monist. Further, most critics have ignored the most immediate religious context for Wilder's work: the scholarship of his brother, Amos Niven Wilder, Hollis Professor of Divinity at Harvard, an ordained minister, a biblical scholar, and a published poet. Both brothers saw themselves in a battle, not against the modern age, but against those who would, consciously or not, reduce faith to antiquarian interest.

In his introduction to *The Angel That Troubled the Waters and Other Plays* (1928), Thornton Wilder describes how he began to come up with titles for the plays in the collection while he was in his teens and wrote many of them while still an undergraduate at Oberlin and Yale. This not only indicates how early Wilder discovered his vocation as a writer, but it also shows his initial and ongoing interest in diverse religious traditions; among the early titles that turned into plays are

1

"Brother Fire" (featuring Brother Francis, a character obviously derived from Saint Francis) and "Proserpina and the Devil" (a puppet show that synthesizes Greek and Christian mythology).[1] Many of the plays seem anachronistic for the 1920s, and Wilder's description of some of the subject matter is presented as a challenge to accepted literary and social practices of the time:

> The last four plays here ["Mozart and the Gray Steward," "Hast Thou Considered My Servant Job?" "The Flight into Egypt," "The Angel That Troubled the Waters"] have been written within a year and a half. Almost all the plays in this book are religious, but religious in that dilute fashion that is a believer's concession to a contemporary standard of good manners. But these four plant their flag as boldly as they may.... I hope, through many mistakes, to discover the spirit that is not unequal to the elevation of the great religious themes, yet which does not fall into a repellant didacticism. (*CP*, 653–54)

This statement provides an explicit justification for critics interested in Wilder's religious beliefs. One biographer, Richard Goldstone, sees Wilder as ultimately a nineteenth-century man who, despite his enormous erudition, world travels, and literary experimentalism, was very much the product of his father's earnest New England, Congregationalist background: "We must remember that Wilder's world was essentially the world of the nineteenth century; he was born before 1900 and the old century conditioned his moral and spiritual Weltanschauung, together with that of all his intimates."[2] Exactly why being born in 1897 restricts one to a nineteenth-century worldview is unclear. But even more important, Goldstone ignores elements of the nineteenth century that, for better or worse, shape most of us in important ways even in the twenty-first century: the nineteenth century of Darwin, Marx, Frazer, Nietzsche, and, at the turn of the century, Freud; the nineteenth century in which the developing sciences of astronomy and geology threatened to turn humanity into a meaningless cosmic accident, and in which the individual felt himself dwarfed by the immensity of space and time.

Moreover, Lincoln Konkle also argues that Goldstone's characterization of Wilder as a Puritan is both ill informed and pejorative. Nevertheless, Konkle, too, insists that "the tradition Wilder's drama and fiction stem from is heavily doctrinal, Puritan, and didactic."[3] Konkle is surely right to see traces of the Puritan heritage in Wilder's work; few American writers escape the Puritan legacy, just as few can escape the philosophical traditions of pragmatism. Both are simply part of the culture, absorbed by osmosis; and this is true whether one was raised Protestant, Catholic, Jew, agnostic, or atheist. Wilder himself identified in 1931 a pervasive Puritan belief that Americans feel themselves to be "permanently, directly, and responsibly bound to world destiny."[4] But Konkle's version of Puritanism is very much that of the seventeenth-century settlers of Massachusetts. And, as Amos Wilder has shown, "There are many differing aspects and amalgams of the Calvinist and wider Protestant heritage in our society"; a part of this heritage was avowedly progressive.[5] In any case, Wilder's introduction to *The Angel That Troubled the Waters* specifically repudiates didacticism in literature: "Didacticism is an attempt at the coercion of another's free will, even though one knows in these matters beyond logic, beauty is the only persuasion" (*CP*, 654).

Yet another critic commenting on *The Angel That Troubled the Waters*, David Garrett Izzo, claims that "Wilder rejected the Christianity of his youth, even to the point of considering its dogmatic aspects ultimately deleterious to Western Civilization"; Wilder was, in fact, "a Karmi Yogi" who "believed in the Vedantic unicity of one/many, east/west, many faiths into one faith, the all in the *All* concurrently accounted for in the *eternal now* which obviates the artifice of time."[6] All of Wilder's works, in Izzo's view, are parables of the path to "goodness." Without much effort, one could multiply examples of scholars who have explicated Wilder's works in relation to different religious or spiritual traditions. Rhea B. Miller detects the influence of the Russian Christian existentialist Nicolai Berdyaev in Wilder's later works.[7] Thomas E. Porter sees Northrop Frye's "apocalyptic myth" in *Our Town*.[8] And many have pointed out Wilder's close reading of Kierkegaard, with Paul Lifton and Donald Haberman offering particularly good exegeses of Kierkegaard's influence.[9]

Wilder might well have been surprised by this wide variation. In a letter to Stanley J. McCord on May 3, 1962, he confesses, "I'm always embarrassed—astonished and embarrassed—when anyone proposes doing a thesis—or a mere paper—on me. This is not from modesty but simply that I don't see my work as sufficiently complex to afford material; it all seems sort of self-evident to me."[10] But what is striking about these divergent readings of Wilder is how compelling most of them seem, even when they are contradictory. The poetic density of his language very much repays rereading. Nor is it difficult from Wilder's published and unpublished works to make a case for his familiarity with almost any writer one can think of. Fluent in French, German, Italian, and Spanish, he read the major works of those cultures in their original languages, and he certainly knew all the major literary and philosophical works of classical Greek and Roman civilization. He adapted Ibsen for the Broadway stage and translated Sartre for Off-Broadway. He published scholarly articles on dating the plays of the Spanish Golden Age playwright Lope de Vega in *Romance Philology* and annotated Joyce's *Finnegans Wake* obsessively. Thus, Wilder can be seen both as a central figure in an American literary tradition and as an American interacting with world literature. Indeed, he lectured on the topic of Goethe and World Literature. Few readers can share Wilder's enormous erudition. Moreover, his career was both lengthy and productive. His first full-length play, *The Trumpet Shall Sound,* was published serially in the *Yale Literary Magazine* beginning in 1919, and his last novel, *Theophilus North,* was published in 1973. If there were a unifying trope that covered all of Wilder's career, then his works would be a great deal less interesting than they in fact are.

While Wilder's works may unconsciously reflect an American Puritan tradition, he was very much an avowed modernist, at least formally.[11] In his sister Isabel's quasi-autobiographical novel *Mother and Four,* Spencer may well be a portrait of the young Thornton at Yale:

> Spencer, Carlo, and their friends lived in a busy world they had created for themselves under the patronage of the university. They were snobs in and out of term time and they were tyrants. They judged a man by his knowledge of Proust and James Joyce and D. H. Law-

rence. Spengler and *The American Mercury*—that big squarish book and that bright green magazine—were their badges. They made and broke reputations through their mouthpiece, *The Newton Literary Magazine,* known as the *Newt.*[12]

This cannot be taken as an unqualified picture of Wilder since *The American Mercury,* founded by George Jean Nathan and H. L. Mencken, did not begin publication until 1924, and Wilder graduated from Yale in 1920. But the rest of the list certainly sounds like what Wilder (and many other bright young men and women) would be reading at the time.

Certainly, Wilder's English themes at Yale reflect a young man's condescension toward the American intellectual and literary tradition. About Ben Franklin's *Autobiography,* the beginning of the pragmatist tradition in America, he sneers, "He is the dreadful man who would be glad to lead his life over again, 'with minor alterations.'" Wilder is just as hard on Hawthorne, clearly an important voice in the Puritan literary tradition: "As a matter of principle I view the story that is half story and half allegory with aversion; and when, proportionately, the story tends toward the realistic, and the allegory toward the heavily didactic, like the lovers in Dante, 'in that book I read no more.'"[13] The instructor graded that theme a B. And Wilder insists on the primacy of the aesthetic in works of fiction. About *Uncle Tom's Cabin* he writes, "There are two factors that ought not to influence a critic in the appreciation of a novel. Its economic or moral effects; the extent of its popularity" (B+).[14]

In the 1920s, Wilder was very much *au courant* with literary trends. Edmund Wilson discovered while riding in a taxi with Wilder that he had read Proust closely and not uncritically. He subsequently wrote a review detailing the influence of Proust on Wilder.[15] Proust, in *Within a Budding Grove,* satirizes those who call for a literature that upholds social and moral standards. M. de Norpois, the earnest purveyor of moral uplift, criticizes Bergotte for his emphasis on form because "we may be overwhelmed at any moment by a double tide of barbarians, those from without and those from within our borders." M. de Norpois' criticism of "Art for Art's Sake" is that "it is all very precious, very thin, and altogether lacking in virility." Proust, of course, is well aware that such criticisms will be made of his own work, but he allows the reader more than a hundred pages to reflect on the claim before he dismisses it: "The arguments of M. de Norpois (in the matter of art) were unanswerable simply because they were devoid of reality."[16] All considerations in art must be secondary to aesthetic imperatives. Thus, while I believe that Wilder's works allow us to reflect on the religious issues therein, they must be examined in the context of the modernist moment in literature, when skepticism toward conventional pieties, both religious and artistic, forced writers into new forms inspired by new ideas from economics, sociology, and psychology. Wilder was, according to Wilson writing in the late 1920s, in the first rank of American writers, along with Hemingway, Fitzgerald, and Dos Passos.[17] Although Wilder writes of historical subjects in a way that none of those writers do, they are his intellectual contemporaries, rather than New England Puritans or Eastern mystics.

I shall argue that no single religious or philosophic system can account for the variety and complexity of Wilder's works, which are too often seen as independent of the debates over meaning and value that have raged since the decay of the great medieval synthesis in the seventeenth century. To explain what I mean by that, I would like to address the ways that Wilder sees an interest in, or focus on, religious themes as an authorial position increasingly regarded as irrelevant by the modern world, or, at least, by its educated members. Wilder admits in the quotation from *The Angel That Troubled the Waters* cited above that a "contemporary standard of good manners" requires that most of his plays be religious only in a dilute, attenuated sense. The four explicitly religious plays fly a flag that invites battle. And, later in the introduction, Wilder suggests that the battle will be difficult, perhaps hopeless: "The revival of religion is almost a matter of rhetoric. The work is difficult, perhaps impossible (perhaps all religions die out with the exhaustion of the language), but it at least reminds us that Our Lord asked us in His work to be not only as gentle as doves but as wise as serpents" (*CP*, 654). "Rhetoric" here keeps its traditional sense; it is the art concerned with persuasion or for communication on subjects where logic is inappropriate because the subject is incapable of demonstration. But the persuasion used for religious subjects faces an uphill fight. The language of religion is almost exhausted, and the reference to Matthew 10:16—"Behold, I send you forth as sheep in the midst of wolves; be ye therefore wise as serpents, and harmless as doves"[18]—indicates that the religious writer, like the apostles, faces powerful opposition.

Wilder often specifically incorporates a modern skeptical attitude toward religion and religious beliefs in his works. While there are multiple examples, one will suffice to indicate the breadth of his awareness of the assault waged by some in the social sciences on the foundations of religion. In his novel *Heaven's My Destination* (1935), Burkin, the itinerant film director, convinces the hero, George Brush, to let him have half an hour so he can explain what George would know if he had gone to a decent college. Burkin is an unattractive character, but he nevertheless allows Wilder to introduce the intellectual traditions that ultimately Brush's naïve Puritanism must confront: "Burkin plunged into primitive man and the jungle; he came down through nature myths; he hung the earth in astronomical time. He then exposed the absurdity of conflicting prayers, man's egoistic terror before extinction" (*Heaven's,* 163). Freud, whom Wilder knew and whose work he respected,[19] claimed in *Totem and Taboo* (1913) that "the beginnings of religion, ethics, society, and art meet in the Oedipus complex."[20] This is not a metaphor: Freud thought that some sons had murdered their father and then recreated the father as a totem to expiate their guilt, and that all religion flowed from this act. In *The Future of an Illusion* (1927), Freud insisted that religion is a product of man's ignorance, analogous to the mental states of a child:

> Religion would thus be the universal obsessional neurosis of humanity; like the obsessional neurosis of children, it arose out of the Oedipus complex, out of the relation to the father. If this view is right, it is to be supposed that a turning-away from religion is bound to occur with the fatal inevitability of a process of growth, and that we find ourselves at this very juncture in the middle phase of development.[21]

Here the modern age is the point where man turns from his childhood neurosis onto a necessary path to maturity. Any attempt to hang on to religious belief is therefore not only immature; it also shows a maladjustment to reality.

But Burkin's deconstruction of religious belief does not just rely on psychoanalysis. He also, through his reference to primitive man and nature myths, introduces anthropology and Sir James Frazer's explanation of religious ritual in the immensely influential *The Golden Bough* (1890). In a letter to his mother, for which the editors of *Selected Letters* suggest a date of 1925, Wilder elaborates on Frazer's assault on religious belief:

> I'm reading the Golden Bough, the one volume edition abridged from twelve. Tons of folklore, witch doctors, how to make it rain, May day myths, Spring ceremonies, resurrection legends . . . . the evidence accumulating like a great Juggernaut trying to flatten out any particular importance that might be reserved for Christian doctrine. But the theoretical interludes are a little pompous and repetitive and there remains a chance that the notions I learned at your knee may survive.[22]

The tone of the letter indicates both Wilder's interest in religious skepticism and his own intellectual balance, which his character Burkin lacks.

In Frazer's analysis of nature myths, he traces an intellectual development in humanity from magic to religion to science. Originally, man believes that he can manipulate nature by imitating its actions. Thus, man sacrifices because he sees that the corn must die to be reborn every year. When he sees that he cannot manipulate nature, he posits higher beings who arrange natural events and whom he must propitiate. Finally, he recaptures the magical belief in cause and effect, but now through scientific observation:

> Thus the keener minds, still pressing forward to a deeper solution of the mysteries of the universe, come to reject the religious theory of nature as inadequate, and to revert in a measure to the older stand-

point of magic by postulating explicitly, what in magic had only been implicitly assumed, to wit, an inflexible regularity in the order of natural events, which, if carefully observed, enables us to foresee their course with certainty and to act accordingly. In short, religion, regarded as an explanation of nature, is displaced by science.[23]

Frazer subsequently develops this into an analogy of history as tapestry, with magic a black thread, religion a red one, and science a white one. White, he is quite sure, will come to dominate.

Burkin moves back historically from Freud to Frazer in his critique of religion; and when he hangs man in astrological time, he has moved back to the discoveries of the nineteenth century that so troubled Tennyson after the death of his dearest friend. Sorrow tells Tennyson of an empty, meaningless universe in *In Memoriam*:

"The stars," she whispers, "blindly run;
    A web is woven across the sky;
    From out waste places comes a cry,
And murmurs from the dying sun;

"And all the phantom, Nature, stands—
    With all the music in her tone,
    A hollow echo of my own,—
A hollow form with empty hands."[24]

The dinosaurs have come and gone, and nineteenth-century physics has discovered the concept of entropy as symbolized here by the dying sun. Tennyson has to win back his faith in the face of grief and the destabilizing vision of modern science. That he does so indicates that the march of science is not quite so irresistible as perhaps Freud and Frazer believed it to be. Even the vegetation cults that Frazer analyzed retained acolytes in the twentieth century. The startling fact of Jessie L. Weston's 1920 analysis of the myth of the Holy Grail in *From Ritual to Romance* (which T. S. Eliot described as a book of great interest in his notes to *The Wasteland*) is that Weston believes that the "Grail is a living force" that "will rise to the surface again."[25]

But granted the recurrent skeptical characters in Wilder's work, Wilder's claim in the introduction to *The Angel That Troubled the Waters* that he is a believer cannot be separated from his sense that belief itself is in danger of exhaustion with the exhaustion of religious language. To an American reader in the twenty-first century, this seems like an odd statement. It is a commonplace that Americans remain far more religious than, for instance, Europeans. Moreover, Finke and Stark have argued (somewhat controversially, I should add, granted the nature of the evidence) that despite recurring claims of religious crisis, America became progressively more religious from the rough-and-tumble colonial days to the settled twentieth century, reaching perhaps a peak in the 1920s, at least as measured by church attendance, with most of the growth occurring in conservative churches at the expense of the liberalizing mainline congregations such as the Congregationalists and Episcopalians.[26] Nor is there any shortage of writers in the English language in the twentieth century who were working in a wide variety of fields and genres and in whose works religious issues take a significant role: W. H. Auden, G. K. Chesterton, T. S. Eliot, Graham Greene, C. S. Lewis, Flannery O'Connor, Walker Percy, Alan Tate, and J. R. R. Tolkien were all unapologetic about their faith. The writers Philip K. Dick, Walter Miller Jr., and Clifford Simak all produced science fiction involving religious issues. If one includes once best-selling authors who perhaps no longer claim many readers, such as the historical novelists Lloyd C. Douglas (*The Robe,* 1942) or Thomas B. Costain (*The Silver Chalice,* 1952), the list could be extensively lengthened.

But I would guess that many of these writers saw themselves, like Wilder, fighting a rearguard action "against principalities, against powers" that sought to render a religious understanding of life a historical curiosity.[27] In Tom Stoppard's *Jumpers* (1972), George, a philosopher working on a lecture "Is God?" muses, "There is presumably a calendar date—a *moment*—when the onus of proof passed from the atheist to the believer, when, quite suddenly, secretly, the noes had it."[28] Skepticism about the existence of God, or at least about God's interest in human affairs, goes back to antiquity: most famously perhaps in Lucretius' *De Rerum Naturam,* which Wilder mentions reading in a letter to his father in 1912.[29] But Stoppard is surely right: in the last three hundred years the skeptics have come to dominate, in intellectual circles at least. To trace the rising tide of skepticism through the Enlightenment is beyond the scope of this introduction, but it would not be difficult to document. And, of course, as Dostoyevsky had laid out by 1880, the "Higher Criticism" of the nineteenth century threatened a literal-minded faith. Father Paissy warns Alyosha "that the science of this world, which has become a great power, has, especially in the last century, analysed everything divine handed down to us in the holy books. After this cruel analysis the learned of this world have nothing left of all that was sacred of old."[30]

Albert Schweitzer's *The Quest of the Historical Jesus,* originally published in 1906 and available in English translation in 1910, explores relentlessly the analysis that so troubles Father Paissy. David Friedrich Strauss, Bruno Bauer, and many others over the course of the nineteenth century had shown in enormous detail and with great scholarship the incompatibility of the Synoptic Gospels (Matthew, Mark, and Luke) with the Gospel of John—the inevitable and mutually exclusive choice between supernatural and historical interpretations of the ministry of Jesus, and the eschatological character of Jesus' teachings and the problem of the delay of the Parousia (the Second Coming). For an intellectually honest man, the historical Jesus "will not be a Jesus Christ to whom the religion of the present can ascribe, according to its long-cherished custom, its own thoughts and ideas, as it did with the Jesus of its own making. . . . The historical Jesus will be to our time a stranger and an enigma." This does not mean the end of faith for Schweitzer: "Not the historical Jesus, but the spirit which goes forth from Him and in the spirit of men strives for new influence and rule, is that which overcomes the world."[31] Nevertheless, the history of biblical criticism and its identification of contradictions and accretions within the Gospel doubtless troubled many who lacked Schweitzer's comprehensive vision. In the Irish playwright and novelist George Moore's *The Passing of the Essenes* (1930), Paul actually meets Jesus, who has survived his crucifixion twenty years earlier. Paul is not ultimately dissuaded from his own Christianity since he believes that he has heard the word of God, and Jesus says tolerantly,

"It may be, as I have said, that my name hath crept into these reports, and that my sufferings, which were great, have been used by God for his own glory. (*He smiles.*) Paul, I would not rob thee of my namesake."[32] Moore, who had become interested in German biblical criticism as early as 1898, presents early Christianity as a tripartite spiritual struggle between the Essenes, Paul's insistence on the miraculous Resurrection, and Egyptian allegorical wisdom. Early versions of Moore's exploration of the thesis appear in 1910 ("The Apostle"), 1916 (*The Brook Kerith*), and 1923 (*The Apostle*). My point here is that the doubts introduced by historical analysis had worked their way into literary circles.[33]

Some of the philosophically inclined, whether pious or not, saw the loss of God, or, at least, of Christianity, as virtually accomplished from an early date. Kierkegaard writes in his diary in 1851, "I must admit that I have never seen a Christian in the strict sense of the word."[34] Kierkegaard's standards may have been impossibly high; it is not clear that Thomas Aquinas would have counted as a Christian in his view. Yet in America, Henry Adams, reflecting on his youth in and near Boston at about the same time as Kierkegaard's entry, wondered whence religious belief had disappeared:

> The boy went to church twice every Sunday; he was taught to read his Bible, and he learned religious poetry by heart; he believed in a mild deism; he prayed; he went through all the forms; but neither to him nor to his brothers and sisters was religion real. . . . The religious instinct had vanished, and could not be revived, although one made in later life many efforts to recover it.[35]

Ultimately in Adams's conception, increasing physical prowess ("the dynamo") minus the binding force of religion ("the Virgin") would lead to social disintegration. Although his autobiography was published in 1907, the 1918 reprint made Adams, in the words of Michael E. Parrish, "a posthumous member of the lost generation."[36] In Europe, Max Weber, Adams's contemporary, in 1905 traced the relationship between economics and Puritan theology and deduced that the final product was a cage of materialism: "The modern man is in general, even with the best will, unable to give religious ideas a significance for culture and national character which they deserve."[37] For both authors, the machine has swallowed the spirit.

From this perspective, even Nietzsche's famous vatic utterances in *Thus Spake Zarathustra* (1883–1885) about the death of God take on less of a revolutionary coloring and emphasize the relatively unthreatening idea of existence in this world:

> God is a conjecture: but I do not wish your conjecturing to reach beyond your creating will.
> Could ye *create* a God?—Then, I pray you, be silent about all Gods! But ye could well create the Superman.
> Not perhaps ye yourselves, my brethren! But into fathers and forefathers of the Superman could ye transform yourselves: and let that be your best creating!—
> God is a conjecture: but I should like your conjecturing restricted to the conceivable.
> Could ye *conceive* a God?—But let this mean Will to Truth unto you, that everything be transformed into the humanly conceivable, the humanly visible, the human sensible. Your own discernment shall ye follow out to the end![38]

In fact, in *Beyond Good and Evil,* Nietzsche claims that most industrious Germans "simply have no time left for religion." While they participate in religious customs when it is required, they do so "with a patient and modest seriousness and without much curiosity and discomfort: they simply live too much apart and outside to feel any need for pro and con in such matters." Those connected with universities fall into this category, but also "those indifferent in this way include today the great majority of German middle-class Protestants, especially in the great industrious centers of trade and traffic."[39] Utilitarianism, philistinism, and the vestiges of the slave morality left by Christianity are the foes that Nietzsche sees himself fighting, because God has already left the stage of history.

H. L. Mencken, the American popularizer of Nietzsche, has a similar attitude. He is not ardently opposed to religion. Writing in

1920, he claims, "I am anything but a militant atheist and haven't the slightest objection to church-going, so long as it is honest. I have gone to church myself many times honestly seeking to experience the great inward exaltation that religious persons speak of. Not even at St. Peter's in Rome have I sensed the least trace of it." Mencken illustrates that the true enemy of religious faith in the modern age is not atheism but indifference, in that he feels no indignation that religious faith still exists. Like Nietzsche, Mencken thinks that Christian morality is a significant problem: "In other words, systems of morality almost always outlive their usefulness, simply because the gods upon whose authority they are grounded are hard to get rid of."[40] But that is largely a problem of the fact that most people, in Mencken's view, are uneducable.

Thorstein Veblen in *The Theory of the Leisure Class* (1899) is careful to stress that he is not talking about the "truth or beauty" of the prominent creeds in America; nevertheless, "economic causes work towards a secularization of men's habits of thought." The poor and the stupid remain religious, while the "artisan class" is moving away from the major creeds. In the middle and upper classes, religion is, to some extent, an opportunity to demonstrate conspicuous consumption. But in each case, it is clear to Veblen, that an anthropomorphic deity is a survival of archaic habits of thought.[41] Unlike Veblen, Upton Sinclair makes no pretense of disinterested analysis. For him, organized religion is "a great capitalist interest, an integral and essential part of a predatory system."[42] In this quotation, Sinclair is speaking specifically of the Anglican Communion, but all of the creeds exist to prop up an unjust social order. Sinclair does not deny the numinous, but in a capitalist society every religion, he claims, turns into an instrument of oppression.

Not surprisingly, then, if one turns to the significant American novels of the 1920s and early 1930s, one will find no shortage of authors now freed to comment on the abuses of organized religion. On *Main Street* (1920), according to Sinclair Lewis (like Wilder a Yale man) in the novel of the same name, religion is a mechanism to enforce conformity as well as a mark of social respectability, much as Veblen argued. Dr. Kennicott is not a villain, merely the product of

Midwestern provincialism when he proclaims: "Sure, religion is a fine influence—got to have it to keep the lower classes in order—fact, it's the only thing that appeals to a lot of those fellows and makes 'em respect the rights of property. And I guess this theology is O.K.; lot of wise old coots figured it all out, and they knew more about it than we do."[43] Kennicott and his wife Carol rarely attend services themselves, since Carol is something of a rebel and Kennicott, after all, is the height of respectability and does not need religion to show his status. There is not much evidence of passionate conviction for or against religion in Gopher Prairie, at least among the propertied.

In Lewis's direct attack on American religion, *Elmer Gantry* (1927)—dedicated to Mencken—he is closer to Upton Sinclair. The film version with Burt Lancaster, while great, depicts only a small section of the novel, Elmer's sojourn as an evangelist, and ignores, for the most part, Lewis's fascination with nineteenth-century biblical criticism and his rehearsals of the "contradictions" of the New Testament. The novel satirizes not only tent-show revivals but also small-town Baptist churches, big-city Methodism, the Catholic Church, Episcopalians, and the Rotary Club. All, in one way or another, are in the business of religion and profiting off the frightened and ignorant. Worse, religion responds with violence when threatened. Frank, the honest minister, is savagely beaten when he defends evolution. Still, the small-town skeptic, Lem Staples, suggests to Frank the same sort of slow decline of religion that Nietzsche and Veblen describe:

> Then can you tell me why it is that nine-tenths of the really sure-enough, on-the-job membership of the churches is made up of two classes: the plumb ignorant, that're scared of hell and that swallow any fool doctrine, and, second, the awfu' respectable folks that play the church so's to seem more respectable? Why is that? Why is it the high-class skilled workmen and the smart professional men usually snicker at the church and don't go near it once a month?[44]

Religion, as Nietzsche suggested and as Lewis presents it, has already become irrelevant to the artisan and professional classes.

One can see the twentieth century's aversion to old answers in writers outside the mainstream Protestant sects. James Farrell's *Studs Lonigan* trilogy (1932–1935) was published while Thornton Wilder was teaching at the University of Chicago. In the story, Danny O'Neill, a student at Chicago, finally sees through the Catholic Church when snubbed by a priest with whom he tries to discuss his doubts: "It had made him feel that it was not merely ignorance and superstition. It was perhaps not merely a vested interest. It was a downright hatred of truth and honesty. He conceived the world, the environment he had known all his life, as lies." In Farrell's Chicago, immigrants in cafés talk about Nietzsche and Bolshevism, thus indicating the spread of antireligious views. Danny finally comes to see that "God was a mouldering corpse within his mind."[45]

Michael Gold, who attacks Wilder in 1930 as the "Prophet of the Genteel Christ," respects the faith of his mother in his 1930 novel *Jews Without Money,* although he no longer believes in anything except the revolution. But the temple itself has been corrupted by the New World. The orthodox Jews of the ghetto deprive themselves and their children of food for five years to bring a true rabbi from Europe who will fight the pernicious influence of America. A conversion does occur, but not the one that the pious had in mind: "The climax came a year after his arrival. One day the Rabbi deserted his congregation. He had been offered a better-paying job by a wealthy and un-Chassidic congregation in the Bronx."[46] The rabbi himself is simply a religious entrepreneur. In Henry Roth's 1934 novel *Call It Sleep,* Reb Yidel Pankower, enraged by the children who do not respect him and who are becoming Americanized, vindictively reveals David's dubious parentage and thereby creates a near catastrophe.[47] David's father, in a relentless struggle with the harshness of life on New York's Lower East Side, has no time for religion at all.

Of course, religion is present in American literature not only among charlatans and pharisees. The African Americans of William Faulkner's *The Sound and the Fury,* and the decent, poor Southerners of *As I Lay Dying* who do what they can for the egregious Anse, have a faith that enables them to endure the pain of the world. But those are precisely the people whom savants such as Mencken regarded with contempt. The former minister Hightower in *Light in August* (1932) identifies petrified churches as a central part of the problem: "He seems to see the churches of the world like a rampart, like one of those barricades of the middle ages planted with dead and sharpened stakes, against truth and against that peace in which to sin and be forgiven which is the life of man." Hightower has been driven away from the church: "I am not a man of God. And not through my own choice."[48] The educated characters in Faulkner long for a faith they no longer possess. Further, in Theodore Dreiser's 1925 best-seller *An American Tragedy,* the faith of Clyde Griffiths's mother and the Reverend Mc-Millan is real, although shaken by the execution of Clyde, but it is also clear that a part of Clyde's fall is related to his faulty education as the son of a pair of street preachers. Society as a whole is much like the jury who convict him of murder, "with but one exception, all religious if not moral, and all convinced of Clyde's guilt before ever they sat down."[49]

Granted this intellectual milieu, it is not hard to understand why Wilder's letters show, if not estrangement from his inherited faith, at least a sense that he does not accept that faith uncritically. In 1920 he writes to his father from Paris, "When you have counted your troubles with a certain Puritan satisfaction in the reflection that the inexplicable Disposer of things has thought you worthy of trials beyond the endurance or even sympathy of most men,—leave me out."[50] His letters to his father show both antagonism and acceptance of the older man's views, but above all that he cannot be indifferent to religious practices. He complains to his sister Charlotte about a sermon in 1922: "Lots of foolish things were said in the sermon, but no one got up and yelled that it was too sacred a place to tell lies in, so I sat still too."[51] Most important for my purposes, Wilder insists that religion must adjust to the modern age. In 1925 he writes to his father about rereading William Law's *A Serious Call to a Devout and Holy Life:*

It's pretty good but God had better hurry up and raise a new devotional literature for an age of Bessemer and Radiotelegraphy—the impress of machines is more than skin-deep. My generation can no longer exclaim in the purple light of an eclipse that the heavens declare the glory of God; eclipses aren't at all strange; we have found that space is finite and we have chased the unknowable down into the kernels of an atom. If that explodes tomorrow I shall have nothing to pin my faith to except the music of Schubert, the prose style of George Santayana, and the disinterested affection of people in New Haven. (*SL,* 177)

There are a number of elements here, including Henry Adams's thesis that the world has passed into the age of the dynamo, and an attempt to link faith to an aesthetic response to music and prose. Even the latter, however, is complicated by the reference to Santayana. In a letter to William Nichols on February 16, 1927, Wilder says that he has been reading Santayana's "*Character and Opinion in the United States—* the devil's own intelligence playing around the Puritans and other institutions . . . . All sorts of beautiful things wilt at the breath of that damned Spaniard" (*SL,* 206). Wilder is, I believe, being ironic here, and I will argue in subsequent chapters that Santayana sees a significant role for religion in American life. But the most salient point is that some new devotional literature must be created because the old rests upon an entirely different, and no longer compelling, set of assumptions.

When Thornton writes to his brother Amos in a letter probably from 1929, he admonishes him, "You better do something about churches, honey. I've just about been for the last time. . . . I *don't* ask a good sermon. Just a little instinctive spiritual discretion. And everywhere I go I am about the only young man in the house, a few old colonels, a few old profs, a few old grocers. It's serious."[52] Thornton's bluntness to Amos, an ordained minister, is significant; unless something is done, organized religion, threatened by old age, is endangered. Wilder did not stop attending services, nor did he stop writing about the conflicting emotions that those services inspired in him. In 1937 he writes about attending the celebrity evangelist Aimee Semple McPherson's church: "But summed up: not a grain of real religious feeling, I think. Not one. But not vulgar insincerity either. It's merely that it [is] an entirely different thing: hominess, cheer, breezy cant, trite uplift poetizing, and a lot of grand style coquetry. But perhaps I should have gone in the evening when the hysteria takes place!"[53] This quotation is more sympathetic than it appears. Without a sense of the sacred, the media-savvy evangelist nevertheless speaks of something sacred for which her congregation longs.

Wilder longs for it, too. He writes to Amos in a letter dated September 28, 1942:

> "Simple" church attendance is very hard on me because of the hymns. City churches don't sing those hymns. They're the Chefoo hymns and Papa's hymns and some Oberlin hymns. And the past rushes up and I'm unstrung. And then the "messages" begin and I turn to stone they're so bad, and then a hymn begins and I'm turned to water. Nobody ought to be made to oscillate like that. Ain't human.[54]

The intellectual in Wilder can barely stand the sermon, but the child and young man are drawn by the music back to his religious roots. Nevertheless, before going off to service in North Africa with the Army Air Corps in 1943, Wilder writes to a friend, Bill Layton, "Went to church and was revolted with what passes for church these days (Yale University Chapel, too)."[55]

A recurring theme in Wilder's letters to his brother Amos in the 1920s is spiritual ennui. On March 7, 1927, he writes that he is reading Rilke and Spengler: "We live in an autumnal age—the ebb of joy and faith has parched the writers."[56] The ebb of faith alludes to Matthew Arnold's "Dover Beach" (1867), where "The Sea of Faith / Was once, too, at the full"; now, that has receded, and the poet hears only "Its melancholy, long withdrawing roar." I do not know exactly which works by Rilke that Wilder was reading, and it should be mentioned that Rilke is not ultimately a pessimist. But melancholy pervades many of Rilke's poems, and a sense of the loss of the numinous: "Once again let it be your morning, gods. / We keep repeating. You alone are source. / With you the world arises, and your dawn / gleams on each crack and crevice of our failure."[57] The wish for the morning of the gods comes from the midst of the ruins of the modern age. Spengler, in his widely read work of cultural morphology, *The Decline of the West* (1918–1923), claimed that Western civilization had reached the end of its "Faustian" age and was about to enter an age of caesars. Western "culture," which in Spengler's view had been alive and organic, had turned into Western "civilization," which is dead. At such historical moments, the vibrant town is replaced by the dead city, and great art or music is no longer possible. Religion was just one of the manifestations of the now-dead Gothic spirit, and the tolerance of the modern city shows its lifelessness:

> The spiritual in every living Culture is religious, has religion, whether it be conscious of it or not. It is not open to a spirituality to be irreligious; at most it can play with the idea of irreligion as Medicean Florentines did. But the megalopolitan *is* irreligious; this is part of his being, a mark of his historical position. The degree of piety of which a period is capable is revealed in its attitude toward toleration. One tolerates something either because it seems to have some relation to what according to one's experience is the divine or else because one is no longer capable of such experience and is indifferent.[58]

As in Mencken, tolerance is possible because of indifference, for Spengler the sure sign of a society about to collapse from its petrification.

In a subsequent undated letter to Amos, Wilder writes about the "extraordinary harmony & reverberation from Golden Bough to Spengler to Keyserling to Whitehead. A sad, autumnal world."[59] The pairing of Spengler and Frazer's *The Golden Bough* with Keyserling and Whitehead is a little odd, since neither of the latter sees religion as dead, but merely as something under enormous pressure to change. Alfred North Whitehead in the Lowell Lectures of 1925 does observe that "there has been a gradual decay of religious influence in European civilization. Each revival touches a lower peak than its predecessor, and each period of slackness a lower depth." Without reference to Veblen, Whitehead makes a somewhat similar point: "Religion is tending to degenerate into a decent formula wherewith to embellish a comfortable life."[60]

It should be stressed that Whitehead sees the advent of science as by no means incompatible with the religious spirit, but that science does require that religion discard medieval fancies. Count Hermann Keyserling, something of a cult figure in the 1920s, also is not ultimately pessimistic and sees mankind as capable of combining Western individualism with Eastern spirituality. But the American is the most Western of all Western men, and at his worst represents the depths to which man can sink: "What is terrible in Americanism is that it makes a man a pauper. Just as it reduces all values to one of quantity, so it reduces the whole soul to one apparatus for the purpose of making money. It thus pushes man back to the level of the lowest animal."[61] Behaviorism in psychology and pragmatism in philosophy and education (which Keyserling sees as uniquely American approaches to their subjects) both treat man as an animal to be conditioned to appropriate behavior. Western society can either go forward or backward, but forward only if it realizes that progress in ideas must take precedence over material accumulation.

Bearing in mind the elements of irreligion in the *zeitgeist,* and with evidence from Wilder's letters that he perceived signs of religious crisis, I would suggest that while *The Angel That Troubled the Waters* is, as Wilder claimed, a series of religious plays, thematically they represent more suffering than consolation, and they are by no means consistent.[62] Some of the collection are unproblematic in that they represent Romantic and Victorian idealism of the sort with which any American schoolboy growing up in the early twentieth century would have been familiar; Paul Lifton is surely correct when he claims that Neoplatonic concepts inform much of the collection.[63] In "Nascuntur Poetae," the yet unborn poet is told the price of his gift: "For you there shall be ever beyond the present a lost meaning and a more meaningful love" (*CP,* 6); this obviously recalls Wordsworth's ode "Intimations of Immortality." A similar Romantic Platonism is present in "Centaurs" and will recur many years later in *The Skin of Our Teeth.* The character Shelley explains that Ibsen's *The Master Builder* is really derived from one of his unwritten poems: "Well it is not a strange idea, or a new one, that the stuff of which masterpieces are made drifts about the world waiting to be clothed with words. It is a truth that

Plato would have understood that the mere language, the words of a masterpiece are the least of its offerings" (*CP*, 31). And "Childe Roland to the Dark Tower Came" is Wilder's play on the same subject as Robert Browning's poem. Because Roland has so busied himself with the great affairs of life, the enigmatic character of the Dark Girl plays with him before allowing him entrance: "Take courage, high heart. How slow you have been to believe well of us. You gave us such little thought while living that we have made this little delay at your death" (*CP*, 29). But Roland's belief that there are consolations in death (the dark tower)—"They say that on the outside you are dark and unlovely, but that within every hero stands with his fellows and the great queens step proudly on the stair" (*CP*, 28–29)—is unchallenged if unconfirmed.

On the other hand, many of the playlets lack nineteenth-century optimism about stable Platonic forms and life as a strenuous but surmountable test. Human nature both mocks and is drawn to the divine in other plays. Satan tells Christ in "Hast Thou Considered My Servant Job?" that mankind will always turn to him: "Learn again, Prince, that if I were permitted to return to the earth in my own person, not for thirty years, but for thirty hours, I would seal all men to me and all the temptations in Heaven's gift could not persuade one to betray me. For I build not on intermittent dreams and timid aspirations, but on the unshakable passions of greed and lust and self-love" (*CP*, 49). Whether one is religious and sees the passions as a consequence of sin, or simply as facts of human nature (as would the seventeenth-century philosopher Thomas Hobbes), the truth is that these passions surely exist. Satan's error and the cause of his hubris is his belief that these passions constitute the totality of human motivations. Judas recants and says to Satan, "Accursed be thou, from eternity to eternity" (*CP*, 50). Moreover, the love of Christ for "my beloved son" Judas stands as a reproach to Satan, who remains "uncomprehending"—that even Judas is drawn to God is beyond Satan's assertion that mankind is driven entirely by motives of self-interest. This is a conventional statement of the transformational force of divine love.

But elsewhere Wilder enacts the anthropologist's conception of the invention of worship. In "The Angel on the Ship," three characters dying of thirst confess their sins to the vessel's figurehead, which they have named "the Gawd of the Atlantic"; the figurehead stares forward, but in desperation they turn it aft to face the deck and kneel before it. Fear makes them seek forgiveness for their sins, but when another ship sails into sight, they begin to repudiate their idol:

> VAN (*His eye falls on the angel*): What'll they say to the figgerhead here?
> SAM (*Sententiously*): But that's the great God Lily. Her's saved us. You ain't goin' to do anything to her?
> VAN (*Starting to beat the angel forward with his hammer*): They'll call us heathen, bowin' down to wood and stone. Get the rope, Sam. We'll put her back. (*CP*, 22–23)

On one level this is the commonplace that man seeks the divine when it suits him and recants when he reaches safety. As such, it is similar to the Hemingway vignette in *In Our Time* (1925). Under shelling the soldier prays, "*Christ please please please christ. If you'll only keep me from getting killed I'll do anything you say. I believe in you and I'll tell every one in the world that you are the only one that matters. Please please dear jesus.*" The shelling stops. "*The next night back at Mestre he did not tell the girl he went upstairs with at the Villa Rossa about Jesus. And he never told anyone.*"[64] The vestiges of religious belief may remain, however, because of the purely coincidental arrival of the desired result. In "The Angel on the Ship," not only does Sam wish to continue to venerate the idol, but Minna says, "But I can't never forget her and her great starey eyes. Her I've prayed to" (*CP*, 23). In this playlet the reader sees how gods are created and why people are loath to discard them.

Wilder also dramatizes the messy historical process of syncretism. The puppet show of "Proserpina and the Devil," which takes place in Venice in 1640, is a miniature of the phenomenon and shows how heterogeneous elements conglomerate in the Renaissance. Hermes and the Archangel Gabriel are one character, as are Pluto and the medieval Satan. Proserpina offers a pomegranate to her lord "*With an odd recollection of the Garden of Eden*" (*CP*, 9). The Manager regards the chaos with indifference: "Hurry through with it," he tells the manipulators, "I'm off for a cup of wine" (*CP*, 8). Rather than showing the similarity of religious systems, which could conceivably imply "unicity" of beliefs, the playlet suggests the loss of belief itself. As the stage collapses at the end, "*The Archangel falls upon the pavement and is cherished by gamins unto the third generation; the Devil rolls into the lake; Proserpina is struck by a falling cloud, and lies motionless on her face; Demeter by reason of the stiffness of her brocade stands upright, viewing with staring eyes the ills of her daughter*" (*CP*, 9–10). Religious icons are reduced to unmoved and unmoving puppets. Wilder's artistic lineage here extends back to Browning's dying bishop, who sees no distinction between the classical icons and Christian texts that will decorate his tomb. Venice in Wilder's playlet represents a mercantile culture appropriating classical and Christian symbolism in an inept puppet show for children. For religion to survive this, it would have to be reinvented. Nor do established churches fare well in the collection. In "Fanny Otcott," George Atcheson, the bishop of Westholmstead, visits the title character, a former actress and former lover. He, an arrant hypocrite, wants to make a public confession of his sin and comes to consult with her because of her reputation at court and in the church. She is disappointed and contemptuous: "You have borrowed your ideas from those who have never begun to live and who dare not" (*CP*, 13).

And even when Wilder bases a play (or its title anyway) on an overtly religious text, "And the Sea Shall Give Up Its Dead"—from the Anglican Book of Common Prayer for burial at sea—he challenges conventional piety. The dead, in a clear precursor of *Our Town*, lose their personalities at the Last Judgment. The Empress reflects:

> We still cling obstinately to our identity, as though there were something valuable in it. This very moment I feel relics of pleasure in the fact that I am myself and no one else. Yet in a moment, if there is a moment, we shall all be reduced to our quintessential matter, and you, Mr. Nissem, will be exactly indistinguishable from me. God himself will not be able to tell the Empress of Newfoundland from the Reverend Dr. Cosroe. (*CP*, 39)

The souls are "panic-stricken." This does not mean that the collection as a whole denies an afterlife: the plays of Malchus and Childe Roland imply the immortality of the individual soul. Nor is the idea that the soul dissolves into the cosmos a particularly new one. Edgar Allan Poe in *Eureka* (1848) rhapsodizes about just such an event: "Think that the sense of individual identity will be gradually merged in the general consciousness—that Man, for example, ceasing imperceptibly to feel himself Man, will at length attain that awfully triumphant epoch when he shall recognize his existence as that of Jehovah."[65] That is, the universe, both man and matter, is the diffused God, and God will cyclically reunite in one supreme consciousness.

Nevertheless, it is a painful idea for many. Tennyson is horrified in *In Memoriam* to think that his dear friend A. H. H. might be swallowed up in some oversoul: "Remerging in the general Soul / Is faith as vague as all unsweet" (Section 47). And the great Catholic existentialist Miguel de Unamuno, whose work Wilder knew, dismissed the entire idea: "All this talk of a man surviving in his children, or in his works, or in the universal consciousness, is but vague verbiage which satisfies only those who suffer from affective stupidity, and who, for the rest, may be persons of cerebral distinction. For it is possible to possess great talent, or what we call great talent, and yet be stupid as regards the feelings and even morally imbecile."[66] "And the Sea Shall Give Up Its Dead" may well provoke religious meditation, but it is not of a comforting sort. Of course, if the world is only material, then the ego is extinguished in death. But this playlet suggests that even if the world is not reducible to the material, the ego may *still* be extinguished.

The conventional piety of playlets such as "Hast Thou Considered My Servant Job?" and the implicit skepticism of ones closer to "The Angel on the Ship" are compatible within the paradox of Christianity. That is, the scandal of the Cross, where the Son of God dies like the lowest criminal, is by its nature both absurd and redemptive. In "Now the Servant's Name Was Malchus," Malchus requests that his name be removed from the Bible because he feels ridiculous whenever someone reads about his ear being cut off. Our Lord responds that he is himself ridiculous:

OUR LORD: Ridiculous because I suffered from the delusion that after my death I could be useful to men.

MALCHUS: They don't say that!

OUR LORD: And that my mind lay under a malady that many a
doctor could cure. And that I have deceived and cheated millions of souls who in their extremity called on me for the aid
that I had promised. They did not know that I died like any
other man and their prayers mounted into vain air, for I no longer exist. My promises were so vast that I am either divine or
ridiculous. (*Pause*) Malchus, will you stay and be ridiculous with
me? (*CP*, 42)

The accusations that Our Lord makes against himself are those of the
modern age diagnosing Jesus' delusions. And the playlet begins with
Our Lord being told by Gabriel of prayers seeking his aid; and one of
those praying at the beginning will be arriving soon, we are told at the
end, indicating that Our Lord decided not to answer them. But far
from seeing the playlet as commenting on Our Lord's irrelevance, or
denying his own divinity, the obvious echo here is of 1 Corinthians
1:25: "Because the foolishness of God is wiser than men; and the
weakness of God is stronger than men." To modern doubt, the response is only that of faith. Belief has nothing to do with prayer, at
least not in the sense of receiving divine aid.

The difficulty of faith is expressed by the ordinary donkey carrying Mary and the infant Jesus in "The Flight into Egypt." Hepzibah,
the donkey, brings up the problem of evil: "I always say to the girls;
Girls, even in faith we are supposed to use our reason. No one is intended to swallow hook, line, and sinker, as the saying is. Now these
children that Herod is killing, Why were they born since they must
die so soon? Can anyone answer that? Or put it another way; Why is
the little boy in your arms being saved while others must perish?" (*CP*,
52). Mary interjects that Herod's soldiers are gaining and that "my
child will be slain while you argue about Faith," but the donkey wants
her to concede that this is a purely personal motive and in no way addresses the Problem of Evil: "Of course, your child is dearer to you
than others, but *theologically speaking*, there's no possible reason why
you should escape safely into Egypt while the others should be put to
the sword, as the Authorized Version has it. When the Messiah comes
these writings will be made clear, but until then I intend to exercise

my reasoning faculty" (*CP*, 52). Hepzibah does come to see that she must put forth her best efforts to save the child, but she also marvels at the strangeness of creation: "Well, well, it's a queer world where the survival of the Lord is dependent upon donkeys, but so it is." The donkey asks Mary for help—"It's this matter of faith and reason, madam. I'd love to carry back to our group of girls whatever you have to say about it"—and Mary can only respond, "Dear Hepzibah, perhaps someday. But for the present just do as I do, and bear your master on" (*CP*, 53). We can only hope for knowledge, taking it on faith that the works required to serve the Lord do make sense.

And true faith requires an unworldliness that most people cannot face, as exemplified in "Brother Fire" and its central character, Brother Francis. Wilder, writing to his sister on March 10, 1922, complains that their father had given $35 to a "chinaman" at a time when both Thornton and Charlotte were contributing to their parents' upkeep: "Providence was honestly vexed at some of the self-deprivations of St. Francis; it always drove her to exhausting ingenuities, ways of providing him with material things of which he presently and gaily dispossessed himself."[67] In the playlet, Brother Francis holds his cloak in the flames until it catches fire. Annunziata rips it from him and throws it on the fire before Brother Francis is burned. She points out that it is illogical to kill animals for their pelts and then toss them in the fire, to which Brother Francis responds, "Bring me not logic, sister. She is the least of the handmaids of Love. I am often troubled when she speaks" (*CP*, 17). That he is "troubled" by logic is a two-edged sword. On the one hand, logic makes it hard for him to hear Love. On the other, it points out that there is a cost to his search for divine Love.

Even where the playlets suggest, for instance, the operation of divine providence, doing the right thing is rarely pleasant. In "The Message and Jehanne," a ring inscribed with verses is misdelivered to a young woman about to marry "a great German with fierce eyebrows" (*CP*, 24), who is obviously jealous and possessive. The verses, meant for the jeweler's sweetheart, make the young woman realize that her marriage would be loveless and so she flees: "It has broken my will. I am in flight for Padua. My family are truly become nothing but sparrows and God will feed them" (*CP*, 26). If this is providence, then it comes with a high price for Jehanne and her family. The play is set in Renaissance Paris; she has broken a marriage agreement at a time when marriage defines a woman's place in society. Her family will be destroyed by the flight unless there is divine intervention, and the play ends with foreboding.

To sum up, *The Angel That Troubled the Waters* and its title playlet are about the suffering of the believer, his doubt, and the pain that enables him to help others because he understands them. The angel asks the Newcomer in the title playlet, "Without your wound, where would your power be?" (*CP*, 56), and the wounds of apparent chaos, obstacles to faith, and weak human nature are dramatized but not healed. No doctrine, whether Puritan or some version of Eastern mysticism, is affirmed. The playlets are about great religious themes, but they do not provide any pat answers. In fact, one might say that they affirm doubt as a part of spiritual growth. Difficult and demanding, they are very much at home in the intellectual landscape of the 1920s.

Beyond locating Wilder in the context of the angst of the believer in what appeared to be an increasingly secular age, we need to examine Wilder's ideas alongside those of his brother Amos. Indeed, Amos Niven Wilder is immensely interesting in his own right.[68] Ordained as a Congregationalist minister, he finished his doctorate at Yale in 1933; a version of his thesis was subsequently published under the title *Eschatology and Ethics in the Teachings of Jesus* (1939; rev. 1950 and 1978). This was just the beginning of a prolific and distinguished academic career. He taught at Hamilton College, Andover-Newton Theological School, and Chicago Theological Seminary (which was affiliated with the University of Chicago), and he was named Hollis Professor of Divinity at Harvard, the oldest endowed chair in the United States. He was an important scholar of the New Testament and also a pioneer in the use of the techniques of literary criticism to analyze the Bible. He published four individual volumes of poetry as well as a collection of his poetic works. And, perhaps most interesting for my purposes, Amos wrote a number of books on religion and modern literature from the perspective of a poet, a Christian, and a very much up-to-date critic and scholar.[69] As a critic he was a sensitive interpreter of modern poetry. As a scholar he was intimately familiar with the revolution in biblical studies that occurred in the nineteenth and twentieth centuries, which forced a reinterpretation of the Bible in terms of its historical context.[70]

His experiences in the First World War forced Amos to think about religious and literary transformations. While a student at Yale, he volunteered for the American Ambulance Hospital in Paris in 1916. After service in Paris, he transferred to the American Field Service, where he drove ambulances at the front in the Argonne and in Macedonia. When the United States entered the war, he enlisted in the Army and served in the field artillery, seeing action in a number of major battles.[71] In the context of a discussion of the new poetry, Amos describes how he felt in biblical terms: "For our part, it seems to us that we met Leviathan in the thickets of the Villers-Cotterets in 1918."[72]

Virginia Woolf famously asked in *A Room of One's Own,* "When the guns fired in August 1914, did the faces of men and women show so plain in each other's eyes that romance was killed?" For Woolf and her circle, the poetry of Tennyson and Christina Rossetti speaks in a language and of a world that is gone. Amos Wilder shared this experience. In an interview in 1977 he told Kendig Brubaker Cully that "as a World War I ambulance driver and private I began to be dissatisfied with the genteel Victorian tradition we were brought up in, an experience shared by many of that generation."[73] Certainly, the war left an emotional mark on Amos that lasted for years after he was mustered out. By August 1918, he recollected decades later, "I must have had some kind of radical depletion, made up of battle fatigue, sleeplessness, and nervous strain. Duties had to be pursued under a kind of cloud and excessive burden. Apart from those who censored my letters and any routine medical checkup, none could suspect what was a kind of chronic anguish in my condition."[74] The effects of the nervous exhaustion—which would probably be diagnosed now as post-traumatic stress disorder—lasted for years. Their father writes to Thornton, in a letter dated February 13 but without a year, while Thornton was teaching at Lawrenceville, "The war has left a mark, apparently—he [Amos] does his work, is pleasant, but apart from his studies no action as yet." In a letter dated April 17, probably from the same year, their father again writes to Thornton about Amos:

Dr. Blumer looked Amos over and says he is all right, barring war effects and will be all right. He says some intimation that Ojai Valley Church may want him—that looks good to me. Of course it confuses me that the boy seems to lack interest in many of the conventional things of the ministers' calling; yet he is so bed-rock in character that all must be right: and will come out right.[75]

Amos's father could not see how much of an adjustment that his son had to make to reintegrate himself into American life. Reflecting on his first experience of seeing troops on the way to the front and the dehumanizing experience of war, Amos remembered: "Our reactions of the time did, indeed, anticipate, what became general in the sequel of World War I, a recognition of how superficially and fraudulently the rhetoric of patriotism and heroism and sacrifice had been invoked."[76] Doubt was a part of the legacy of the war, and any response to central issues required an honest recognition that attitudes had changed.

The war brought religion close to the minds of Amos and those with whom he served, and sometimes it was a revelation of ignorance. In December 1917 he writes, "A fellow about here is prophesying the end of the war in February, based on Revelation xiii [sic], which he expounds with huge superstition. I am astounded at the combination of ignorance and moldy superstition one finds if Christianity is raised in company like this."[77] Amos, an alumnus of Oberlin and Yale, was an educated Christian, and the war revealed to him that that group was a smaller one than he had supposed. But at the same time he writes home in September 1918 that some religious virtues are strengthened by combat experience: "There is little religion in the armies but one of the most Christian qualities is widely attained among those who fight and that is humility—a sanity of self-conception that gives a tremendous amount of sincerity and expressiveness."[78]

And there is a recurrent sense that beyond the inevitable cynicism, his fellow soldiers were nevertheless fighting to save civilization, and that this ennobled their cause. Amos quotes his own poem (published in 1923) inspired by the Battle of Belleau Wood fought on June 1, 1918, about how the victory had a cosmic significance:

We, bearing in us the decree of God,
The *ne plus ultra* to the mindless urge
Of the unordered universe, the surge
Of Chaos, to the shelving border trod.
Halted and turned the tide, and saw emerge,
Again the flowering valleys from the flood.[79]

The soldiers have reaffirmed God's fruitful creation against the impulse to primeval chaos. Order is God's decree, but it is the responsibility of man to preserve it. As an old man reflecting on the poem, Amos dryly admits, "No doubt any such theological reading of our actions would have been far from the thoughts of those engaged. Yet it is remarkable how generally the soldiery of all wars are persuaded that higher powers, if only fate or some vague idea of nemesis, overrule the fortunes of battle."[80] Thus, the First World War was not the death of religion for Amos as it was for some men, but it forced a reexamination of his sense of the individual's relationship to his society and his faith in a purposive universe: "The complacent premises of a settled society had been undermined and we knew that we needed an armistice in the aggressions and conflicts of our peacetime existence as well as the one we had attained."[81] One difficulty, he wrote to Thornton in a letter dated June 16 and probably from 1919, was hanging on to the conviction of purpose created by the war. About the experience of reading a collection of letters written by a French soldier to his mother from the front, Amos laments: "Reading a book of letters like this reminds one of the high spirituality of danger and endurance, and makes one disgusted and discouraged with the lowering of the sky and cheapening of one's disposition even so early in the peacetime. Truly one hates comfort and luxury, for what they kill of one's high belonging."[82]

It is possible to see Amos and Thornton's desire to write about serious things as a part of their Puritan heritage. But at the same time, both brothers share a profound vision of a changing role for religion and for literature about religion, because of the damage done to the existing structures; as Amos quotes Mary Colum, "We are living in the ruins of a world, our duty is to study the ruins."[83] Neither was satisfied with the anatomy of a corpse, but both thought it necessary to know what was lost before they could create a new expression for the religious impulse in the modern world.

Throughout this book I will be using Amos Wilder's work as a gloss on Thornton Wilder's plays and novels. Amos said in an interview for a documentary that when Thornton's works are examined for religious or philosophical themes, it is unfair to hold him to the standards of a theologian. Nevertheless, those works show his intellectual background—and parts of that background are the works of Amos, although he modestly did not mention that to the interviewer.[84] Of course, this kind of thematic reading must be subordinate to the formal demands of Wilder's works, and this is especially true since so many of them were written during the ascendancy of the New Critics. I borrow unapologetically Amos's own defense of his analysis of modern poetry for its religious elements: about the New Critics he says,

> I would try to keep in their good graces, first, by constantly insisting that viewed as *poetry* this material must always be judged by the aesthetic canons of poetry and not by the alleged superior spirituality or truth of its contents. But we will add that whether for better or worse this poetry abundantly evidences basic viewpoints or convictions. Such data we should be able to use for our purpose, being careful, however, as to how far we identify the particular author under consideration with the given viewpoint.[85]

As long as the analysis of a writer's religious beliefs is done in the context of his intellectual milieu and formal creation, it is therefore legitimate. Thornton Wilder is a storyteller first, but a part of the story he has to tell is the place of faith, hope, and love in the modern world.

The overarching theme of this book is to understand Thornton Wilder's works historically, just as Amos Wilder's works insist that Christianity must be understood historically. In an undated letter to Thornton, Amos writes about the difficulties of ecumenical dialogue:

> The basic model lies here—when Paul sees Christ on the road to Damascus (or any other initial revelation of religion) the whole

"event" can be appropriately "described" in terms of social [and] then psychological conditions, i.e. it can be empirically accounted for in *large part*. The Catholic says "sheer revelation". The positivist says "epilepsy" or "compensation". We should say "The Spirit finding opportunity in such [and] such social and psychic condition to make answer to an agonizing need—not of an individual only but of a social or even a racial crisis etc. etc."[86]

In Amos's view, both the Catholic and the Positivist are reductive: the Catholic denies history, and the Positivist denies any spiritual component whatsoever. Amos believes that to understand Paul's conversion fully, one needs also to understand when and where it occurred and the conditions that made it possible. My argument throughout this book is that Thortnon Wilder's works can be understood more fully if attention is paid to the when and where present in the works themselves, and to the historical moment in which he wrote them.

In a lecture at Wellesley on November 18, 1981, Amos recalled reactions to his works on modern literature: "I remember how puzzled people were in the church circles when I as a churchman sought to show the importance for them of the new writers." In those works Amos Wilder repeatedly argued that nineteenth-century literary forms could not speak to the new age, and that even secular modernists spoke to the spiritual crisis of America: "I felt that these voices were kinds of prophets of the age, by whom we could read our omens plain."[87] In the works of Thornton Wilder and Amos Wilder, we see the omens of the age in which they lived. Through their "conversation," I would like to explore their version of the religious impulse in twentieth-century America.

Chapter One

Historical Religious Crises in Wilder's Early Novels

Penelope Niven, in the introduction to a recent edition of *The Cabala* and *The Woman of Andros,* claims that "in Wilder's fiction as in his drama, time and place are not fundamental to the story." This seems odd on the face of it: Wilder's first three novels—*The Cabala* (1926), *The Bridge of San Luis Rey* (1927), and *The Woman of Andros* (1930)— all take place far from the United States, and all except *The Cabala* take place long ago. Moreover, Niven includes evidence that the setting is significant; about *The Cabala,* she quotes a letter from Wilder to his mother that emphasizes a historical transition: "The whole memoirs are to be a sort of adieu to the romance and medievalism that barely survived the war."[1] In this letter, Wilder is clearly providing a framework in which to understand the novel; the last vestiges of an older culture are memorialized after the catalyst of war has begun their dissolution. I shall argue that time and place are essential to all three of Wilder's early novels.

In *The Woman of Andros,* Wilder presents a classical, Hellenic civilization soon to be transformed by Christianity. In *The Bridge of San Luis Rey,* a colony in the New World is the site of the struggle between Baroque Christianity and the Enlightenment. And in *The Cabala,* both the classical heritage and Catholicism are depicted as exhausted remnants of once vital systems. In short, while forms of love may be the subject of all three novels, the events therein cannot be separated from the epoch in which Wilder places them. Nor is this surprising when we consider that in fields as diverse as economics (Marxism) and philosophy (existentialism), theory in the nineteenth and twentieth centuries sought to understand man as an actor in history. In biblical studies, Amos Niven Wilder argued throughout his career that while the actions of the Holy Spirit cannot be reduced to historical phenomena, they also cannot be understood independently from the practices and forms in which they are embodied historically. Thornton Wilder starts from a contemporary crisis in the European Catholic Church, works back to the dissolution of the medieval synthesis in the Enlightenment, and finally finishes his analysis of the Christian faith in history with the context for its creation at the end of the Hellenic era. I will examine the novels in reverse order of composition: first, because that is the chronological order in terms of setting and indicates Wilder's conception of how religion changes over time in response to social forces; and second, because the end of *The Cabala* provides a neat transition into Wilder's works of the 1930s, which are set in the United States and are the subject of the next two chapters. I argued in my introduction that Thornton Wilder sees religion in crisis in 1928. In this chapter I shall show that in Wilder's first three novels, that is always the case.

The Woman of Andros is framed by value claims about cultures in a particular time and place.[2] In the first paragraph of the novel we are told that "Triumph had passed from Greece and wisdom from Egypt, but with the coming of night they seemed to regain their lost honors, and the land that was soon to be called Holy prepared in the dark its wonderful burden" (*W of A,* 137). Moonlight aside, the events of the book will take place in a Greece rendered insignificant because of the rise of Rome. The reference to wisdom passing from Egypt probably recalls Plutarch's claim that the great repository of classical learning, the library at Alexandria, was destroyed accidentally by Caesar in 48 BC. The island Brynos, the setting for the novel, is bereft politically and intellectually: in Hellenic terms, the barbarians have won. The end of the novel reminds us that its events took place against a background of a history more important than that of the lives of the characters: "And in the East the stars shone tranquilly down upon the land that was soon to be called Holy and that even then was preparing its precious burden" (*W of A,* 203). The Incarnation will be a transformative event.

Superficially this suggests no more than a straightforward transition from the virtues of the classical world to Christian virtues and the Golden Rule. Indeed, Edmund Wilson rather snidely explicated the novel in this way: "*The Woman of Andros,* though it is very well done, strikes me as being a kind of thing that there is no longer much point in doing. . . . I assume that in *The Woman of Andros* he is trying to show us the sorrows and doubts that we ourselves must experience if we live without the Christian religion."[3] Wilson is on the right track, albeit dismissive: Wilder writes to Norman Fitts on October 15, 1929, that "The Woman of Andros asks whether Paganism had any solution for the hopeful enquiring sufferer and—by anticipation—whether the handful of maxims about how to live that entered the world with the message of Christ were sufficient to guide one through the maze of experience" (*SL,* 241). Chrysis, a prostitute and the title character, worries about Pamphilus, the son of the island's leading citizen and the most admirable of the young men whom she entertains and instructs at philosophical banquets. She prays for him: "Let him rest some day, O ye Olympians, from pitying those who suffer. Let him learn to look the other way. This is something new in the world, this concern for the unfit and the broken. Once he begins that, there's no end to it, only madness. It leads nowhere. That is some god's business" (*W of A,* 167). Implicitly, here a crucial difference is proposed between the approaching Christianity and the receding classical ethic. A Greek turns from suffering except when watching dramatic tragedy, where the emotions engendered can be safely purged. Under normal circumstances, pity and fear are unhealthy and hinder a person's ability to act as a responsible citizen. The unfit and broken are by definition imperfect, while the true Hellene seeks to contemplate that which recalls the ideal.

Despite her misgivings, Chrysis is drawn to Pamphilus because she herself maintains a house of "sheep," modeled after the vexatious household whom Samuel Johnson supported, because they have nowhere else to go (and who are for the most part sold into slavery after

she dies, since as non-citizens they have no rights). But the true classical ethos is apparent when she comes to Simo, Pamphilus' father,
asking for his aid in bringing to the island an insane sea captain.[4] The
normal action would be to place the captain on an island with other
lunatics where food is brought occasionally. Simo embodies his society when he says, "since your friend has lost the use of his reason,
and since he cannot realize the conditions under which he lives, it is
best you leave him on the island with the others. Is that not so?" (*W
of A,* 145). In the classical view presented here, without reason and
therefore without occupation, or the means to run a household, or to
participate in the *polis,* there is no purpose in taking care of the captain
at all. Ultimately, he is only the shell of a man. It is impious for a
Greek to kill him, but perfectly logical to put him on an island where
in the course of events he will die, just as it is impious for a father to
kill his infant son, but legitimate to expose him on a hillside so that
nature (the gods) can do that for him. Although Chrysis resists this
proposal, she has no vocabulary or paradigm that can refute it: "'I have
no answer for that,' she replied. 'It may be true for you, but it is not
true for me'" (*W of A,* 145). The great classical scholar C. M. Bowra
sums up what is missing for the modern sensibility from the Greek religious experience:

> Religion stressed the dignity of action and gave an inspiring impetus
> to it. But in this it neglected something which we associate with re-
> ligion, and indeed demand from it. It was not till their civilization
> began to collapse that the Greeks formed their first glimmerings of
> the brotherhood of men, and even then it was more of an abstract
> ideal than a purposeful conviction. What we miss in Greek religion
> is love.[5]

Simo sees the captain as incapable of action and therefore insignificant. Chrysis struggles to explain why she feels a responsibility toward
him, but her impulse is, at this time in history, ineffable.

The novel etches the presuppositions of the classical world even as
that world fades. One works to live: "Simo was more tired than usual:
whereas the law of moderation teaches us that the mind cannot be

employed for more than three hours daily over merchandise and numerals with soilure; he had that day spent five hours in argument and traffic" (*W of A*, 138). Business is not wrong, per se, but it must have only a limited hold on the mind, or else the mind becomes debased. Classical standards of judgment are apparent in the islanders' evaluation of Chrysis, who is both hated and admired but not because she is a prostitute: "The whole race was haunted by a passionate admiration for poise and serenity and slow motion, and now for an hour the Andrian's every move was followed by the furtive glances of the islanders, with mingled awe and hatred." Beauty, presented in life as it might be rendered on a vase, involuntarily calls for admiration and envy because "when she appeared" the islanders "felt themselves to be provincial and commercial" and consequently aware of their distance from the classical ideal (*W of A*, 153). Even Chrysis judges herself against the ideal and gives herself failing marks: "It was true, true, beyond a doubt, tragically true, that the world of love and virtue and wisdom was the true world and her failure in it all the more overwhelming" (*W of A*, 160). The Platonic conception of the beautiful, the true, the just, the magnanimous, of which life is only a shadow on the wall of a cave, is something that the people of Brynos still hold to, but it is something that they are evermore aware they cannot attain.

And not attaining these ideals, aware of their decline from the Golden Age, they suffer. Simo attempts a bargain with Chrysis: if she discourages Pamphilus from visiting her house, he will help her with the captain. She refuses and points out his failure in magnanimity; the great-souled spirit does not treat a request for a favor as an opportunity for bargaining. Chastened, Simo agrees to assist her, and when she leaves he "suddenly realized that he lived among people of thin natures and that he was lonely; he was out of practice in conversing with sovereign personalities whose every speech arose from resources of judgment and inner poise" (*W of A*, 146). Like calls to like when Chrysis talks to Simo, but he is the most significant citizen on the island, while she is a prostitute; and since they are their roles in society, there is in this reality no possible relationship for them, even friendship. She reads plays brilliantly: "he would like to hear her read a play; he used to be interested in such things" (*W of A*, 147), but that is not possible in a community ordered by traditional roles. Chrysis, too, after her conversation with Simo, awakens the next day and thinks: "I am alone. Why have I never seen that before?" (*W of A,* 151). And her isolation is not only personal or social but also cosmic: "'I suppose there is no god,' she whispered. 'We must do these things ourselves. We must drag ourselves through life as best we can'" (*W of A,* 168–69).

The death of Chrysis is treated with sympathetic irony:

> She saved her strength to fulfill a last desire, one that may perhaps seem unworthy to persons of a later age. Her mind had been moulded by formal literature, by epics and odes, by tragedies and heroic biography, and from this reading she had been imbued with the superstition that one should die in a noble manner, and in this high decorum even the maintenance of her beauty played a part. The only terror left in the world was the fear that she might leave it with cries of pain, with a torn mind, and with discomposed features. (*W of A,* 176)

To approach the ideal as much as possible, even in death, is Chrysis' goal: beauty, composure, and stoic indifference are the signs of her character, or, rather, these actions are her character since the figures of classical literature do not have interiority in the modern sense. Further, life must be seen as a whole: the Greek maxim, "Count no man happy until he is dead," means that a life can only be judged after it is completed, the way that one judges a work of art. That is, if one suffers great unhappiness, or even a failure of deportment, at the end of one's life, the rest is disfigured. From a Christian view, this is a kind of superstition: God judges the heart, not the appearance. But, for Chrysis, judgment is aesthetic, a comparison of the individual's life with the ideal of what a life should be. Very few people can achieve even an approximation of this. Chrysis repeats for the young men at one of her banquets Socrates' prayer from Plato's *Phaedrus:* "Beloved Pan, and all ye other gods who haunt this place, grant that I may become beautiful in the inner man and may whatever I possess without be in harmony with that which is within. May I esteem the wise man alone to be rich. And may my store of gold be such as none but the good may bear" (*W of A*, 159–60). Socrates' prayer for inner beauty (virtue), harmony, and moderation encapsulates the highest kind of life that the classical philosopher can envision. This proper, reflective life for a Greek man, however, cannot be attained by women, slaves, or even the male citizens who are aware of the deficiencies of their society.

Pamphilus, as we have seen, is the man most concerned for losers. When he impregnates Glycerium, Chrysis' sister, he finds himself in a difficult situation: "Without the support of his parents, and without a residence in their home a young man was a mere adventurer, without social, economic, or civil standing. A marriage was only possible if Simo declared it to be so" (*W of A*, 183). In Terence's play, the source of the novel, the problem is solved by making Glycerium the long-lost daughter of Chremes, the second citizen of Brynos. Without Terence's happy coincidence, the fundamental issue for the novel is that Pamphilus sees Glycerium's pregnancy as a problem when there is no social reason why he should. Some arrangement could be made to take care of Glycerium, but she has no standing whatsoever: no family to insist on a marriage, no brother or father to avenge her. Glycerium's only option is to become a prostitute like her sister.

Pamphilus' tendency to see obligation where there is none is mirrored not only by Chrysis but also by the celibate priest of Aesculapius and Apollo, odd doubles for a young man of family. Chremes is not happy about Pamphilus seeing Chrysis because he wants Pamphilus to marry his daughter, a marriage that makes perfect sense socially and economically. Chremes brings up these points in conversation with Simo, who thinks "how vulgar, how unhellene. How unphilosophic." Nevertheless, while Chremes represents the decline of their society from the Greek city-state to that of a merchant community, he also acutely sees that Pamphilus, like the priest, lacks the self-interested personality to prosper in this society: "Do you know the young priest of Aesculapius and Apollo? Well, there is something of the priest in Pamphilus. Such people aren't interested in putting their foot forward. They haven't yet come to see what life is about" (*W of A*, 143). Simo admits to himself that the comparison is valid. And the priest's concern for the unwell, while sanctioned in his case by religion, is essentially perverse to the classical mind. When Simo and his wife have to bring their unwell daughter to the priest and see the sick people in his care, they almost walk out: "Simo and Sostrata had passed their lives without ailments. They regarded them, like poverty, like unseemliness, as mere bad citizenship; they were on the point of returning home, so great was their distaste for the manifestation" (*W of A*, 188).

Christianity represented something quite different from the historical classical tradition that Wilder depicts in *The Woman of Andros*. Amos Wilder rejects "Nietzsche's crude alternatives of 'Apolline' and 'Dionysian,'" and the Platonic vision of man, in favor of the "realism" that Christianity establishes in Western thought: "Now it is precisely the 'earthly' realistic note which Christianity introduced into Western literature. Man is treated empirically, as creature among creatures, in his psychosomatic unity. He is defined by his heart not by his spirit. His fate is defined by history and not by a changeless order of ideas or being."[6] We exist not as shadowy reflections of an ideal order, but as mental and physical beings coping with the circumstances of the world. Time and place are therefore essential for a writer after the advent of Christianity. The difficulties felt (rather than recognized) by Chrysis, Simo, and Pamphilus are specific to a dying classical civilization.

While writing about kerygma (the proclamation of the mighty works of God), Amos Wilder stresses the historical specificity of the message:

> When we speak of the Good News of God we mean an action of God which has concrete antecedents and a long history. If the kerygma as the preached word is abstracted as revelation from its social-historical context, with all its relativities, or from the long story of salvation, it takes on too much the character of metaphysical enlightenment. We must take the doctrine of Incarnation here with full seriousness. The revelation takes place in the flesh; that is, the disclosure of God and his will is inseparable from particular cultural circumstances.[7]

Jesus, Amos insists, was a Jew living in Palestine; and his teachings, while relevant outside that context, are shaped by it nonetheless. The words of the prophets, the history of Israel, and the Roman occupation are all a part of Jesus' understanding of his task. Ultimately, Amos argues, an ahistorical reading of the New Testament is intellectually and spiritually impoverished. Historically, Christianity forces a change in the classical world, and Thornton Wilder's novel depicts the malaise that made Christianity so successful. In *The Woman of Andros,* what Simo desires is not a new path, but rather the same path cleared of the purely temporal flaws of his society and conforming to the unchanging ideal vision of, for instance, Plato's *Republic.* Christianity, on the other hand, brings not only a radical revision in the way one thinks about facts of the world, such as the poor and the distressed, but also an insistence that a new message requires a transformation of the world—an ongoing message that does not privilege stasis and poise.

The shift from the classical to the Jewish-Christian conception of the world recurs in Amos Wilder's works. In *Early Christian Rhetoric* he returns to it:

> It is one thing to picture a deity as fashioning the world and its creatures with his hands. It is still another to think, as the Greeks did, of the soul as a kind of copy of an eternal mind: this represents a more refined kind of anthropomorphism. But to hold that God created man by a word of command and address, this is something more. A creature that is *called* into being, by *name,* along with nature, this creature belongs to a more personal order. In the idea of the creative word not only is reason implicit but mutuality and dialogue.[8]

The consequences of this shift are profound. Since the individual is a "person" independent from his or her role in society, the possession of a soul confers a dynamic relationship with God, and a creativity that is related to God's own since we are made in his image. We are not just copies of eternal forms, different only as a diminution or a defect, but something that exists of itself, in time, and capable of shaping the world.

And it follows that we can yearn for more than Socrates prays for. Indeed, we are entitled to more. Love in the Socratic sense, as we know from Plato's *Symposium,* is a statement of absence, an awareness of defects. Socrates demonstrates to Agathon that "love is of that which a man wants and has not."[9] The divine love of Christian-Jewish thought is a statement of community between God and his creation. Pamphilus has a prophetic moment when he sees that Chrysis and Simo love him as he loves them, but that none of them can express this clearly, bound as they are by the words "prostitute," "father," and "son." The inability to find creative language for what they feel keeps them all lonely:

> a sad love that was half hope, often rebuked and waiting to be assured of its truth. But why then a love so defeated, as though it were waiting for a voice to come from the skies, declaring that therein lay the secret of the world? The moonlight is intermittent and veiled, and it was under such a light that they lived; but his heart suddenly declared to him that a sun would rise and before that sun the timidity and hesitation would disappear. (*W of A,* 198)

Pamphilus does take Glycerium home, and Simo accepts her; she then dies in childbirth, as does her child. But Pamphilus' vision of a world held together by love is validated by the act of kindness involved in the acceptance of the sister of a prostitute by Simo's family. The value of a life is not in its final form, but in its loving, and the classical world will be transformed by this view.

The Woman of Andros, then, is Thornton Wilder's examination of a cultural crisis where the older order yields to Christianity because the status quo is exhausted. This is not a rejection of classical values; in an act of creative syncretism, Christianity will rapidly incorporate Platonic, Aristotelian, and Stoic ideas. But those ideas are revitalized because of Jewish-Christian concepts of history, God, and love. The classical thesis and the Christian antithesis form a new thesis in a dialectical process. This same dialectical process can happen within Christianity as well. In *The Bridge of San Luis Rey,* Wilder examines a second historical struggle, Catholicism's attempt to cope with the Enlightenment. Of particular interest is his use of Madame de Sévigné's correspondence as a source and his examination of attempts to find a mathematical model for divine providence.

Wilder had not been to Peru prior to writing *The Bridge of San Luis Rey*, but he is specific about the date of the collapse of the bridge and the fall of the five victims: July 20, 1714. As it happens, he does not limit himself to material from the early eighteenth century but draws from the adjacent centuries. The letters of the Marquesa de Montemayor to her dismissive daughter take their inspiration from the letters of Madame de Sévigné, who died in 1696. Camila is based on a historical Peruvian actress who lived from 1748 to 1819, was the mistress of the viceroy, and was the subject of an opera by Offenbach. But the place and time of the novel are carefully chosen to allow an examination of a colony enthusiastically experiencing the dawn of Enlightenment culture. The people of Peru "never submitted to the boredom of a misplaced veneration" (*Bridge,* 92). Their love of music and literature is unfeigned:

> When the Archbishop returned from a short trip to Spain, all Lima kept asking; "What has he brought?" The news finally spread that he had returned with tomes of masses and motets by Palestrina, Morales and Vittoria, as well as thirty-five plays by Tirso de Molina and Ruiz de Alarçon and Moreto. There was a civic fête in his honor. The choirboys' school and the green room of the Comedia were swamped with the gifts of vegetables and wheat. All the world was eager to nourish the interpreters of so much beauty. (*Bridge,* 92)

Camila is brought by Uncle Pio to be the best actress in the Spanish-speaking world, although the people of Lima do not know this because they have no grounds for comparison: "Uncle Pio and Camila Perichole were tormenting themselves in an effort to establish in Peru the standards of the theatres in some Heaven whither Calderón had preceded them" (*Bridge,* 103). The Marquesa is also a genius: "Within a century of her death her letters had become one of the monuments of Spanish literature and her life and times have ever since been the subject of long studies" (*Bridge,* 13). The Abbess Madre María del Pilar is also a great woman, who founds a hospital and longs for women's rights.

Alongside the Peru of Spanish Golden Age theater, brilliant religious music, and scintillating epistolary prose is the suffering inevitable in a harsh world, as symbolized in the novel by the Abbess's hospital where the sick and deserted go to die. She comforts those "who had no one to turn to, for whom the world was more than difficult, without meaning" (*Bridge*, 148). Moreover,

> in that country those catastrophes which lawyers shockingly call the "acts of God" were more than usually frequent. Tidal waves were continually washing away cities; earthquakes arrived every week and towers fell upon good men and women all the time. Diseases were forever flitting in and out of the provinces and old age carried away some of the most admirable citizens. (*Bridge*, 4)

The narrator's ironic detachment, very much in the eighteenth-century mode and worthy of Mandeville, reminds the reader that life is for many, in Hobbes's phrase from the seventeenth century, "poor, solitary, nasty, brutish and short," and there is little that the nascent sciences can do about it. But part of the cruelty of life in eighteenth-century Peru is religious, that of an older order fighting against the Enlightenment. Uncle Pio supports the Inquisition early in his career, "but when he has seen several of his victims led off in hoods he felt that he might be involving himself in an institution whose movements were not evenly predictable" (*Bridge*, 95). In the last section of the novel, pious Brother Juniper is burned at the stake for heresy. In short, *The Bridge of San Luis Rey* portrays a society struggling between the Baroque and the Enlightenment.

Madame de Sévigné's letters embody this conflict unconsciously and offer a fascinating insight into the mind of a woman completely at home with the great writers of that age, with *mores* that would shock a nineteenth-century housewife and yet profoundly, if conventionally, religious. In a lecture about the great letter writers given at Yale on May 4, 1928, Wilder says about de Sévigné, "And time after time the letter rises beyond the understanding of the daughter and becomes an *aria* where the overloaded heart sings to itself for the sheer comfort of its felicity, sings perhaps to the daughter such as she might have been."[10] Wilder is probably overstating the indifference and lack of intellect of Madame de Grignan, the daughter, but he correctly expresses the dazzling virtuosic variety of the correspondence. As he says of the Marquesa's letters in *The Bridge,* "Night after night in her baroque palace she wrote and rewrote from her despairing mind those miracles of wit and grace, those distilled chronicles of the vice regal court" (*Bridge,* 18). For instance, Madame de Sévigné can write of romantic love and death coolly to her close friend the great novelist Madame de Lafayette: "But you must know that Mme des N— is dead, and that Trévigny, her lover, nearly died of grief. For my part I would have preferred him really to die of it for the honour of the ladies." But her grief when their mutual friend La Rochefoucauld dies is presented movingly. She can also critique a sermon like a theater critic:

> The other day we heard the Abbé de Montmor. I have never heard such a good sermon from such a young man; I wish you could have the same instead of your Minim. He made the sign of the cross, spoke his text, didn't scold us, didn't call us names. He bade us not to fear death since it was the only route we had for rebirth with Christ, and we agreed. We were all pleased. There is nothing in him to shock.

She takes a similar attitude to French neoclassical drama, which she knew well (she preferred Corneille to Racine), in that decorum has a high value for her. Still, her son's tangled affairs with actresses are humorous grist for the mill. She reports on religious controversies (she herself was linked to the Jansenists) and wittily highlights the gap between the reactionaries and the discoveries of the seventeenth century: "The Jesuits are more powerful and fanatical than ever. They have forbidden the Oratorian fathers to teach the philosophy of Descartes, and consequently the blood to circulate." But Madame de Sévigné also recounts matter-of-factly the torture of a woman poisoner, Brinvilliers, after she had already confessed: "This confession notwithstanding, they put her to the torture first thing in the morning both ordinary and extraordinary, but she said nothing more." Learning and taste, cruelty and indifference, exist side by side in her letters.

She can also write pithily of her relationship with her daughter in a style that both conceals and reveals her feelings; "Decorum plays no part whatever in anything I do, which is why the excessive liberty you ascribe to me wounds my heart. This heart of mine has resources that you can't understand."[11] Her loneliness here is perhaps shared by parents across time, but the reference to decorum also indicates that she and her daughter cannot agree on what is appropriate language from a seventeenth-century mother. Under the circumstances, the language of religion becomes a way of expressing her love. According to Wilder, religion plays a significant role in the letters, a part of what he calls "the notation of the heart" (*Bridge,* 18). "In some earlier letters," Wilder says of de Sévigné, "she confesses to having insufficient religious faith. . . . later she refers to the consolation she's found in attributing everything to *la volonté de Dieu.*"[12] But accepting the will of God is difficult, both for de Sévigné and for her fictional representation, the Marquesa. The Marquesa longs for the love of her daughter and yet realizes that it can never be perfect enough. Ultimately she learns from Pepita that it cannot be selfish, that love asks for nothing in return and cannot be bargained for:

> At last she cleared away the table and sitting down wrote what she called her first letter, her first stumbling misspelled letter in courage. She remembered with shame that in a previous one she had piteously asked her daughter how much she loved her, and had greedily quoted the few and hesitant endearments that Doña Clara had lately ventured to her. Doña María could not recall those pages, but she could write some new ones, free and generous. (*Bridge,* 48).

Most readers will recall 1 Corinthians 13 here, I suspect, but the portrayal of the Marquesa indicates the difficulty of love and faith. If her tragedy is partly that of any mother with a daughter who cannot appreciate her, it is also partly the tragedy of a woman of genius in a provincial town. Wilder takes the gifted de Sévigné and not only presents her perhaps obsessive devotion to her daughter, but also imagines her without the brilliant circle that can appreciate her and love her back. And indeed, the novel imagines the strain on women of vision who can dimly glimpse something better but do not know how to get there. The stoic faith in the will of God is both a religious statement and an unconscious indictment of a cruel society.

Conflicts over values, both ethical and aesthetic, occur throughout the novel. Camila and Uncle Pio recall: "We come from a world where we have known incredible standards of excellence, and we dimly remember beauties which we have not seized again; and we go back to that world" (*Bridge,* 103). In the earlier playlet "Nascuntur Poetae," Wilder suggested that this was a universal difficulty. But, in *The Bridge,* Camila's problem is specifically grounded in her being a Spanish-speaking actress:

> A certain intermittent contempt for acting made her negligent. It was due to the poverty of interest in women's roles throughout Spanish classical drama. At a time when the playwrights grouped about the courts of England and France (a little later, of Venice) were enriching the parts of women with studies in wit, charm, passion and hysteria, the dramatists of Spain kept their eyes on their heroes, on gentlemen torn between the conflicting claims of honour, or, as sinners, returning at the last moment to the cross. (*Bridge,* 103–4)

Camila is thus drawn to the false goal of respectability because the theater of her time and language does not allow her genius the room to express itself. She tells Uncle Pio, "The audiences come for prose farces. We were foolish to try and keep alive the Old Comedy" (*Bridge,* 119). Unable to be truly herself, she becomes embittered, not just as a part of the human condition but also as the product of a society existing in history.

The Abbess is similarly isolated by time and place.[13] She can imagine a world where disabled people are treated rather than confined in her hospital: "I can't help thinking that something could be done for the deaf-and-dumb. It seems to me that some patient person could . . . could study out a language for them" (*Bridge,* 146). She also suspects that the contemporary treatment of insanity is flawed: "I am old, you know, and I cannot go where these things are talked about, but I watch them sometimes and it seems to me . . . In Spain, now, are they gentle with them? It seems to me that there is a secret about it, just hidden from us, just around the corner" (*Bridge,* 147). Instead, she spends her life begging for money for her hospital, and, when Pepita is killed in the collapse of the bridge, she accepts her life stoically: "The night before she had torn an idol from her heart and the experience had left her pale but firm. She had accepted the fact that it was of no importance whether her work went on or not; it was enough to work" (*Bridge,* 141). Here, Wilder critiques the social and religious structures that allow preventable suffering. The Enlightenment will begin a process that eventually leads to some ameliorations that the Abbess foresees, but her culture is far from acknowledging any need for changing the status quo.

The Puritanism that some critics have seen in Wilder is somewhat in evidence in *The Bridge of San Luis Rey*. At least, Peru's Catholic Church is plagued with the faults that Thornton Wilder's father saw as endemic to Catholicism. His father instructs Wilder on how to experience Rome in a letter of March 26, 1921:

> May you have [your?] sense of reverence deepened in Rome—get a grip on the deep solemn relationship between God and Man. All this richness with the Catholic end properly, kindly, firmly appraised; remember that re-iterating couplet in Lowell's religious play—I read it many years ago and am hazy but this I recall: "Not he that speaketh the Name / But he that doeth the will." It should be over every Catholic church door especially where the pull is so strong to substitute devotion for humble, loyal devotion to truth and duty.[14]

The contrast being made here is between religious ritual and action, between the ceremony of the Church and the practice of virtue in and for society. More than in any other work, Wilder does subject a Catholic prelate to satire in *The Bridge*. The Archbishop of Lima is the epitome of the fat, wealthy churchman: "A curious and eager soul was imprisoned in all this lard, but by dint of never refusing himself a pheasant or a goose or his daily procession of Roman wines, he was his own bitter jailor" (*Bridge,* 109). He knows both classical literature and the Church Fathers, but spends his time reading Brantôme (memoirs of the promiscuity of the upper classes) or looking at the engravings of Aretino (Renaissance pornography). Despite his luxurious habits of body and mind, he knows the state of his archdiocese:

> The Archbishop knew that most of the priests of Peru were scoundrels. It required all his delicate Epicurean education to prevent his doing something about it; he had to repeat over to himself his favourite notions: that the injustice and unhappiness of the world is a constant; that the theory of progress is a delusion; that the poor, never having known happiness, are insensible to misfortune. (*Bridge,* 110)

Clearly as a character he is contrasted unfavorably with the Abbess. Her faith requires her to take action, while his allows him to retreat to his library and the dinner table. Witty and impious, he thinks as a Baroque churchman (or at least a Baroque churchman as conceived by Browning and appropriated by Wilder) might be expected to think. That is, his personal failings are symptomatic of a dysfunctional social and religious order.

The Archbishop's belief in an unchanging, fallen world is also contrasted with Brother Juniper: "Joy was in him; things were not going badly. He had opened several little abandoned churches and the Indians were crawling in to early Mass and groaning at the miracle as though their hearts would break" (*Bridge,* 5). Juniper, active in the community, provides consolation and reassurance that God cares for the poorest. As such, he is wholly admirable. But he becomes problematic because of his investigation into the lives of the five people killed when the bridge breaks. He happened to be looking at the bridge at the time, perhaps because "it was the memory that brushed him for a moment of the poem that bade him raise his eyes to the helpful hills" (*Bridge,* 5). The allusion here is to Psalm 121:

> If I lift my eyes to the hills,
> where shall I find help?
> My help comes only from the LORD,
> maker of heaven and earth.
> He will not let your foot stumble;
> he who guards you will not sleep.

The psalm introduces the classic problem, why and when does the Lord allow death? The skeptic's answer is that death is a merely random event. The introductory section of *The Bridge* ends with paired allusions to Shakespeare, who in different plays seems to imply different conclusions: "Some say that we shall never know, and that to the gods we are like flies that the boys kill on a summer day, and some say that on the contrary, that the very sparrows do not lose a feather that has not been brushed away by the finger of God" (*Bridge,* 9). This concept of people as flies killed by boys, meaninglessly, pointlessly, is from *King Lear* 4.1 and suggests an empty universe. The sparrow losing feathers suggests Matthew 10:29: "Are not two sparrows sold for a penny? Yet without your father's knowledge not one of them can fall to the ground." The passage from Matthew specifically concerns Jesus telling the apostles that God has even numbered the hairs on their heads; it is not a promise of safety, but of divine purpose. In *Hamlet* 5.2, Hamlet accepts the divine will; he will die when God determines that he should. Thus, Hamlet's allusion to the Gospel suggests an entirely different worldview from Lear's despair, and the contrast between the two is one of the themes of the novel.

But while the Baroque Church of the Archbishop is contemptible on some level, Brother Juniper becomes involved in the tragedy as a man of the Enlightenment, confident that he can answer a question that can only be approached on the level of faith as if it were a mathematical theorem. Brother Juniper is prepared to demonstrate, with mathematical certainty, that this was the perfect time for each of the fallen to die. When he is introduced, however, it is with an echo of the famous joke about the weather frequently attributed to Mark Twain. The bridge breaks, and the narrator tells us, "Everyone was very deeply impressed, but only one person did anything about it, and that was Brother Juniper" (*Bridge,* 5). From the tone the reader knows from the beginning that Brother Juniper is bound to fail, just as one cannot really do anything about the weather. But he thinks like an early eighteenth-century man: "it was high time for theology to take its place among the exact sciences and he had long intended putting it there" (*Bridge,* 6). This is not an anachronism. Locke, in his *Essay Concerning Human Understanding,* is convinced that from our knowledge of God and our knowledge of ourselves as rational creatures, morality is among "the sciences capable of demonstration."[15] Thus, paired with the skepticism of the Enlightenment is optimism about the reach of human intelligence. As a student, Brother Juniper is taught by a skeptical master who "whispered in the Franciscan's ear such thoughts and anecdotes as belied the notion of a guided world" (*Bridge*, 134). But he is not shaken by this: "It was by dint of hearing a great many such sneers at faith that Brother Juniper became convinced that the world's time had come for proof, tabulated proof, of the conviction that was so bright and shining within him" (*Bridge*, 134).

Since Brother Juniper knows in advance that God must be behind this, he knows how the experiment must come out. When he cannot make the numbers add up, he becomes a danger to the Church and is burned at the stake—the victim of an unresolved conflict between the Baroque and the Enlightenment based on a developing fallacy in the modern world and the older faith's inability to adapt. Blaise Pascal, like Brother Juniper, knew the mercy of God. It comes to him specifically on Monday, November 23, 1654, "from about half past ten in the evening until about half past midnight": "God of Abraham, God of Isaac, God of Jacob, not of philosophers and scholars."[16] In his *Pensées* (published posthumously in 1670), the great mathematician reflects on the barrenness of proof outside of mathematics: "How few things can be demonstrated! Proofs only convince the mind; custom provides the strongest and most firmly held proofs; it inclines the automaton, which drags the mind unconsciously with it. Who has proved that tomorrow will dawn, and that we will die? And what is more widely believed?"[17]

There is more involved here than the standard seventeenth-century objection that proof can only happen in a deductive argument and that inductive arguments cannot "prove" anything. Rather, Pascal is aware of the problems of the various kinds of intellectual proof for the existence of God. He argues: "if there is a God, he is infinitely beyond our comprehension, since, having neither parts nor limits, he bears no relation to ourselves. We are therefore incapable of knowing what he is, or if he is. That being so, who will dare to undertake a resolution of this question? It cannot be us, who bear no relationship to him." Nevertheless, "we know of his existence through faith. In glory we will know his nature."[18] Pascal insists that man is not limited to knowledge obtained by his reason, and that not all knowledge can be expressed either mathematically or through formal logic:

> We know the truth not only by means of the reason but also by means of the heart. It is through the heart we know the first principles [space, time, movement, number], and reason which has no part in this knowledge vainly tries to contest them. The Pyrrhonists who have only reason as the object of their attack are working ineffectually. We know that we are not dreaming, however powerless we are to prove it by reason. This powerlessness proves only the weakness of our reason, not the uncertainty of our entire knowledge as they claim.[19]

Elsewhere, Pascal explains that the argument from design speaks powerfully to those who, through grace of God, already believe but will not convince anyone else who does not. Argument does not lead to faith. Pascal sees that a category error is deeply embedded in the philosophical systems of the Enlightenment: people attempt to supply a mathematical formula for matters that cannot be understood mathematically and are incapable of formal demonstration. Hence, the famous affirmation, "It is the heart that feels God, not reason: that is what faith is. God is felt by the heart, not by reason. The heart has its reasons, which reason itself does not know: we know that through countless things."[20]

By the nineteenth century, Goethe, whom Wilder admired deeply, writes about the hubris of mathematics: "Mathematicians are a strange tribe; because of the great things they have achieved, they have donned the mantle of a universal guild and don't want to recognize the validity of anything except that which fits into their own ambience, and what their organ can deal with." Thus, the mathematician distorts by forcing into a mathematical mode what is essentially not a function of mathematics (and by this Goethe means both the formal mathematical proof and the assumption that all knowledge is quantitative): "Mathematicians are like a certain type of Frenchman: when you talk to them they translate it into their own language, and then it turns into something completely different."[21] The great German humanist brings up the point again in conversation with Eckermann:

> As if, forsooth! things only exist when they can be mathematically demonstrated. It would be foolish for a man not to believe in his mistress's love because she could not prove it to him mathematically. She can mathematically prove her dowry, but not her love. The mathematicians did not find out the metamorphosis of plants. I have achieved this discovery without mathematics, and the mathematicians were forced to put up with it.[22]

There are many kinds of knowledge in myth, art, religion, and even science that are fundamentally not expressible in mathematics. Pascal suggests that the Enlightenment has gone off track with its search for formal proof, and Goethe thinks that the error has reified. Brother Juniper cannot recognize that his experiment is a part of a fundamental confusion about kinds of knowledge.

Amos Wilder writes about the knowledge drawn from myth and says, "The human heart would suffocate if it were restricted to logic."[23] Moreover, the Enlightenment view of man as a rational agent acting out of self-interest is itself reductive, according to Amos Wilder. When Jesus taught, "his appeal was finally not to fear, or avidness for safety, but to the assent of the heart. This confidence of Jesus in the persuasive power of truth and in the ultimate moral discernment of common men seems to have taken precedence with him over enforcing features."[24] In the hearts of men, miracles follow love, not love from miracles. We know things that cannot be demonstrated or translated into some scientific paradigm.

A somewhat similar analysis is offered in Willa Cather's novel *Death Comes for the Archbishop* (1927) by the archbishop after he hears of the miracle of Our Lady of Guadaloupe:

> "Where there is great love there are always miracles," he said at length. "One might almost say that an apparition is human vision corrected by divine love. I do not see you as you really are, Joseph;

I see you through my affection for you. The Miracles of the Church seem to me to rest not so much upon faces or voices or healing power coming suddenly near to us from afar off, but upon our perceptions being made finer, so that for a moment our eyes can see and our ears can hear what is there about us always."[25]

The presence of Our Lady of Guadaloupe does not create love; rather, because of love, Our Lady is seen. And in *The Bridge of San Luis Rey,* Brother Juniper's love for God and his parishioners creates his faith, a faith that renders proof irrelevant.[26] He already knows God, and his knowledge is shown in his works in the village. His allegiance to Enlightenment values merely confuses the issue, but he is all the more representative of an unresolved cultural conflict.

As the novel's ending declares, the bridge between God and man and the living and the dead is love. But in my view, *The Bridge of San Luis Rey* not only is an examination of love, but is also an analysis of religion sidetracked by false questions. The Baroque Church of miracles confronts the Enlightenment and either responds with a search for the wrong kind of explanation (Brother Juniper) or retreats in fear (his burning at the stake). Just as *The Woman of Andros* portrays the spiritual crisis leading to the transformation of the classical worldview, *The Bridge of San Luis Rey* looks at Baroque Christianity in its last unsustainable days. But the Enlightenment lost something, too: the explanatory power of myth, which can be apprehended only through the human heart. The twentieth century has difficulty in finding a still vital myth and thus is in danger of losing an important class of knowledge. *The Cabala,* set in Italy after World War I, is in part an anatomy of the exhaustion of the Catholic Church (itself shaped by the Baroque and the classical heritage) and the stagnancy of European culture in general.

In *The Cabala,* the Cardinal (one of Wilder's recurring skeptics and to some extent a portrait of the Jesuit missionary Matteo Ricci, at least in regard to his career in China)[27] sits in his garden. "A pile of volumes lay on the table beside him: *Appearance and Reality,* Spengler, *The Golden Bough, Ulysses,* Proust, Freud" (*Cabala,* 106). The importance of Spengler, *The Golden Bough,* and Freud to the atheism of the modern age has already been discussed in the introduction, but the other works contribute to spiritual or creative malaise as well. Amos Wilder, writing about the French neosymbolist movement, includes Proust and Joyce as members: "This succession of writers, forced by their hostile and impervious environment to turn in upon themselves to an unprecedented degree, have sought resources for life and literature in the unconscious. . . . But the possibilities of the method have been fully exploited. Nothing important will be done in this direction that is not either completely incomprehensible or of the nature of repetition."[28] The shift to radical subjectivity in the form of minute explorations of various layers of consciousness is a major technical achievement, but Proust and Joyce have taken the form as far as it can go. *Appearance and Reality* (first edition 1893, second revised edition 1897), by Francis Herbert Bradley, argues that appearance is inconsistent, reality is truly consistent, and God is merely an appearance of absolute reality: "We may say that God is not God, till he has become all in all, and that a God which is all in all is not the God of religion. God is but an aspect, and that must mean but an appearance, of the Absolute."[29] The Cardinal pushes over his books and tells Samuele not to pick them up: "Let the animals soil them. What is the matter with this Twentieth Century of yours . . . ? You want me to compliment you because you have broken the atom and bent light? Well, I do, I do" (*Cabala,* 108). The scientific achievements of the twentieth century are significant, but the Cardinal is contemptuous of its art and philosophy.

The Cardinal's friends want him to write a book refuting modernism and arguing for the divine right of kings. Not only does the Cardinal know that this is absurdly anachronistic—"Would you be surprised if I gave up my life to reviving the brother-and-sister marriages of Egypt?"—but he also fears to write at all: "Oh, Samuele, Samuelino, how bad of you to come here this morning and awaken all the vulgar prides in an old peasant" (*Cabala,* 108). The works of the twentieth century are, in the Cardinal's view, "ordure," but he is afraid that his own might be the equivalent of Montaigne, Machiavelli, or Swift, all of whose work subvert the existing order in one way or another. The Cardinal, unbeknown to his friends, represents not a defender of the old order, but rather a cleric who has lost his faith and found nothing to replace it.

It is important not to confuse the Cardinal's views of the modern age with Wilder's. Aside from his admiration for Joyce and Proust, he esteemed Freud as a positive force. He writes to Amos on January 31, 1935, "Freud came into the world with genius and healing in his wings." He goes on to say that he particularly admires *Totem and Taboo;* "Freud is not only a clinician, he's a great metaphysician and a philosopher."[30] This appraisal comes long after the composition of *The Cabala,* but Wilder becomes critical of Freud only much later in his life. Further, the Cardinal does not represent a New England intolerance for the Roman Church. Certainly, anti-Catholicism was a part of Wilder's heritage. His father writes to Wilder on October 25, 1921, when Wilder is in Italy studying: "Poor old Italy and its civilization—what an impeachment of the Catholic system, where for centuries it had complete authority until now it is despised or [made] negligible by millions."[31] But Thornton chastises his brother Amos for his anti-Catholicism on December 13, 1920, on the occasion of finding a room in Rome for Harry Luce and Bill Whiting near the College of the Propaganda of the Faith: "little distinguished in your mind, you Calvin, from the Inquisition and other practices of the Whore of Rome, about which you have only the vaguest and most superstitious of ideas." In the same letter, Thornton rhapsodizes about the Catholic liturgy:

> . . . a liturgy built like Thebes, by poets, four-square, on the desert of man's need. You and I will never be Roman Catholic, but I tell you now, you will never be saved until you lower your impious superiority toward this magnificent and eternal institution, and finally sit down to learn from her the secret by which she held great men, a thing the modern church cannot do; and a church without its contemporary great men is merely pathetic.[32]

The great symbolic drama of the Mass and the active participation of great men within the Church is implicitly contrasted here with American Protestantism as represented by Amos. Partly this is youthful enthusiasm before the magnificent physical edifice of the Italian Church, but it is also an attempt to incorporate the historical Catholic religious impulse within Wilder's own Puritan heritage.

The irony of the novel, then, is that the Cardinal, who embodies both the endurance of the Church *in extremis* through his missionary work in China and its immense learning built up over the millennia, is himself no longer religious. In his old age he sits quietly in Italy, regarded with annoyance by the Church and with suspicion by his countrymen. His loss of faith is not only intellectual, but it also reflects the leaching away of commitment:

> He must surely have asked himself often in what year his faith and joy had fled. Some said he had become attached to a convert who had relapsed into paganism; some said that one day under torture he had renounced Christianity to save his life from the hands of brigands. Perhaps it was only that he had attempted the hardest task in the world and found it not so difficult after all. (*Cabala*, 42)

Striking here is the linkage of faith and joy: faith is shown in its works, and its consequence is joy. No longer working or joyous, the Cardinal "may well have felt the world not to be worth the thunder of admiration and applause that was so continually mounting to heaven in its praise. Perhaps one of the other stars is more worthy of one's best effort" (*Cabala*, 43). This is worse than despair: it is indifference.

Thus, the Cardinal represents a troubled and troubling figure. He is, as David Castronovo has described him, "a kind of intellectual and emotional distillation of European decline, self-absorption, and exhaustion."[33] His loss of faith is symptomatic of modern angst, but his reading of modern texts offers no alternative to the system through which he made sense out of his life and directed his works. An important figure in the Catholic Church, he is now viewed with suspicion, and, it turns out, rightly so. His friend, the deeply pious and ignorant yet immensely wealthy Mlle. de Astrée-Luce Morfontaine, is utterly unaware that he has lost his faith. The Cardinal reveals a kind of religious snobbery when he discusses her with Samuele:

She has a fair pure heart. It is sweet to be in the company of a fair pure heart, but what can one say to it?

There was St. Francis, Father . . . ?

But he had been a libertine in his youth, or thought he had.— Senta! Who can understand religion unless he has sinned? who can understand literature unless he has suffered? who can understand love unless he has loved without response? (*Cabala*, 107)

The Cardinal's position here is not particularly unusual. Those who have experienced *weltschmerz* have a stronger faith than those whose faith is never challenged. The Cardinal, however, lost his faith under some previous challenge; thus, his judgment upon Mlle. de Astrée-Luce is both uncharitable and hypocritical. His understanding of religion can only be of its emptiness in that he no longer believes that his sin can find forgiveness and his despair consolation.

And it is a sin to threaten the faith of the simple; for example, early in the novel Samuele mentions a character who has become "an *animae periculum*" (*Cabala*, 10), because he tries to engage his wife in "irreverent argument over the liquefaction of the blood of St. Janarius" (*Cabala*, 10). Mlle. de Astrée-Luce is stunned when the Cardinal turns on her and attacks her belief in the efficacy of prayer:

It was the idea of a benignant power that was behind the world that was being questioned now. For the Cardinal it was an exercise in rhetoric, sharpened by his temperamental skepticism on the one hand and by his latent resentment against Astrée-Luce on the other. It was a kind of questioning that would have no effect on sound intellectual believers. (*Cabala*, 112)

Subsequently, when the Cardinal tells her a story of a father who leaves a child alone in a swamp, Mlle. de Astrée-Luce tries to kill him. For her, "It [the story] was a taunt. It was a sort of curse. Look at the world without God, he was saying. Get used to it. If she had lost God, oh how clearly she had gained the devil." Without a God who answers prayers, comforts the afflicted, and regards the fall of a sparrow, she is only a simple woman in a cruel world. But the shot she fires at him awakens the Cardinal to the emptiness of his vocation: "It had required Astrée-Luce's shot to show him that belief had long since become for him a delectable game. One piled syllogism on syllogism, but the foundations were diaphanous" (*Cabala,* 122). Her faith was real and thus could be damaged. Finally, the Cardinal regains the virtue of humility. When he is dying on shipboard on his return to China, he convinces the sailors to bury him at sea (although he knows that they will face resentment from the Church) so that he need not lie as "a sinner of sinners, under a marble tomb with the inevitable *insignis pietate,* the inescapable *ornatissimus*" (*Cabala,* 123).

The Cardinal's life had meaning only in action, not contemplation. "Faith," says Samuele, "is fighting, and now that he was no longer fighting, he couldn't find his faith anywhere" (*Cabala,* 109). But for the members of the Cabala, including the Cardinal, there are no genuinely meaningful fights, at least in the sense of having some real effect. Samuele comes to realize this after his initial infatuation:

> I soon saw that I had arrived on the scene in the middle of the decline of their power. At first they thought they could do something about strikes, and about Fascismo, and the blasphemies in the Senate; and it was only after a great deal of money had been spent and hundreds of persons ineffectually goaded they realized the century had let loose influences they could not stem, and contented themselves with less pretentious assignments. (*Cabala,* 61)

To some extent, Samuele reflects a typical American Protestant's attitude toward the Church as a fundamentally archaic institution. The rise of Mussolini and labor conflicts are the product of a world that the Church only dimly understands.

That was certainly the view of Thornton's brother. Despite his admiration for T. S. Eliot, Amos Wilder dismisses the Catholic or Anglo-Catholic writer as fundamentally ill equipped not only to create poetry that can cope with the radically transformed modern age, but also as someone who has retreated from engagement with contemporary life:

Yet in becoming a Catholic or an Anglo-Catholic a man of today still leaves unresolved for himself and for those he would lead, the more crucial personal issues of Christianity in the modern world. . . . And nothing seems clearer from the main movement of modern life than that the great solution of contemporary ethics and religion will have to come from those churches and groups that have wrestled most fearlessly and empirically with modern thought. Our age waits for Eliots who will fight it out on the exposed and hazardous front where the Protestant tradition is today reshaping itself both in theology and life, and where it is passing beyond Protestantism into something new.[34]

Catholicism, according to Amos, is ultimately a submission to an ignorant and reactionary faith. Thornton portrays such a figure sympathetically. A scholarly member of the Cabala, M. Léry Bogard, in his youth wrote pages "faintly tinctured with venom, on Church History" (*Cabala,* 35). But his views and Samuele's are now utterly incompatible. M. Bogard has become an obedient son of the Church and suggests that his early works should be burned:

Let us read no more, my son. Let us seek out some congenial friends. Let us sit about a table (well-spread, pardi!) and talk of our church and our kind and perhaps of Virgil. My face must have shown the suffocation I experienced at this plan of life, for M. Bogard became at once more impersonal. (*Cabala,* 35)

Henceforth their conversations are polite and general. What Bogard has to teach is not what an active young American can learn. Samuele loses much by his inability to consider seriously the aging Catholic's contented vision of man in his established church, political structure, literary canon, and national cuisine, but there is also little doubt that this is a cosmology wholly inappropriate for Samuele to accept. However alluring this life might be, he cannot take it back to New England with him.

The members of the Cabala are not just Catholics losing touch with the rest of society. They are aristocrats, relics of the last age, and as such are both attractive and mysterious to Samuele. The Duchess d'Aquilanera explains to Samuele why he should try to help her son:

> We are of a very old house. Our family has been in the front of Italy, everyone in her triumph and in her trouble. You are not sympathetic to that kind of greatness in America, not? But you must have read history, no? ancient times and the middle times and the like? You must realize how important the great families are . . . have always been to . . . countries. (*Cabala,* 32)

Yet, like the rest of the Cabala, the Duchess is pathetic rather than impressive. As a woman of legal affairs she is shrewd and sharp on a petty scale, but her rank will not allow her to achieve anything more. Except when trying to promote her family's welfare, she sits in fear that someone will ignorantly try to take precedence over her. She is trapped by the fading European aristocratic order to which she belongs.

Worse, her family line is threatened with extinction. Her son Marcantonio cannot be married until he gets his libido under control, and hence the enlistment of Samuele as mentor. Regrettably, Marcantonio has sex with his sister Juliet and then commits suicide. The names themselves indicate the decline of European civilization. Shakespeare's and Dryden's Marc Antony, who gives up the world for love, is transformed into a dissipated sixteen-year-old boy, "an incredibly slight and definite little elegant" (*Cabala,* 50). Shakespeare's chaste and passionate Juliet becomes Julia, a girl who "guessed at a criminal world and presently when marriage suddenly opened up to her every freedom, she played her part in it" (*Cabala,* 53).

Samuele not only cannot help Marcantonio; he drives him to suicide. Rounding on Marcantonio, he informs him that he is a sinner in the hands of an angry God:

> My little tirade was effective beyond all expectation and for a number of reasons. In the first place, it had the energy and sincerity which the Puritan can always draw upon to censure those activities he cannot permit himself,—not a Latin demonstration of wealth and

tears, but a cold hate that staggers the Mediterranean soul. Again, all my words had already their dim counterpart in the boy's soul. It is the libertine and not the preacher who conceives most truly of the ideal purity and soundness, because he pays it out, coin by coin, regretfully, knowingly, unpreventably. (*Cabala,* 55–56)

Wilder's irony here underscores the failings of Samuele's Puritan sensibility. He hates what he cannot have, and his conviction of sin gains on Marcantonio only because the Italian understands it on a level deeper than the American ever could. Devoid of Christian charity (and classical wisdom), Samuele characterizes his diatribe as a "brief and vindictive speech" (*Cabala,* 56). Samuele's Puritanism is reminiscent of Oliver's in Santayana's novel *The Last Puritan* (1937), an "integrity of purpose and scorn of all compromises, practical or theoretical." And the consequence is an inability to entertain any sympathy for the fading systems of Europe and Catholicism. When Santayana's Oliver hears a cousin defend Catholicism, he flees as rapidly as he can from "a labyrinth of linked superstitions from which, if you were once caught in it, there might be no escape."[35] The American Puritan, whether Samuele or Oliver, combines the inflexibility of youth with intolerance for the inevitable weakness of human nature, with the result that he cannot remotely sympathize with what was valuable in the Catholic heritage and the societies formed by it.

The inability of the Old World and New to communicate, as well as the opposition between southern European sensuality and American asceticism, is also stressed in Samuele's second failure. Those who meet Alix, the Princess d'Espoli, "felt ourselves permitted to glimpse into the Seventeenth Century and to reconstruct for ourselves what the aristocratic system must have been like in its flower" (*Cabala,* 62). She, however, falls in love with Samuele's friend Blair, a heartless Harvard man "frightened by life." Not so much a scholar as he is an antiquarian, "his endless pursuit of facts (which had no fruit in published work and brought no intrinsic esthetic pleasure) was not so much the will to do something as it was the will to escape something else." For Blair, "to look into any face, however beautiful, is to see pores and the folds about the eye. Only those faces not present are beautiful" (*Cabala,* 66).

Samuele can do nothing to ameliorate Alix's despair over her doomed infatuation. Blair in his asceticism can scarcely be said to live at all.

The Alix episode reveals clearly that Wilder is critiquing more than just the Catholic Church and the fading European aristocracy in *The Cabala*. Describing the novel forty years later in a letter, he writes that the story is that of a "naive youth in the dark forest—among enigmatic divinities."[36] Blair is Adonis, more drawn to his hunt for facts than he is to the goddess of Love, Alix. Ultimately, their relationship is fruitless on every level. Symbolically, it suggests that for Americans the appeal of Europe is merely that of a beautiful but vanishing past. Blair loves the antiquities of the Roman Empire, and Samuele is drawn to Alix as an emblem of the grace and charm of the seventeenth century. Neither man sees Europe, however charming and graceful, as a viable way of living in the modern world, although Blair has really no wish to do so.

Samuele's paradoxical relationship with the Cabala is the core of the novel. Although hinted at earlier in the story, it is near the end when Mrs. Grier finally tells Samuele the mystery of the Cabala: "the gods of antiquity did not die with the arrival of Christianity." However, "when they began to lose worshippers they began to lose some of their divine attributes. They even found themselves able to die if they wanted to. But when one of them died his godhead was passed on to someone else" (*Cabala*, 127). That the Greco-Roman divinities could still exist is not in itself particularly heretical or even surprising. G. K. Chesterton in *Orthodoxy* (1908) is not troubled "to be told that the Hebrew god was one among many. I know he was, without any research to tell me so."[37] C. S. Lewis, in the *Out of the Silent Planet* trilogy, has the classical divinities as the tutelary deities of the planets named for them: Jupiter, Venus, Mercury, and so on. Hilaire Belloc, a very pious Catholic, in *The Path to Rome* (1902), visits The Hill of Venus near Viterbo and feels their presence: "There was no temple, nor no sacrifice, nor no ritual for the Divinity, save the solemn attitude of perennial silence; but under the influence which still remained and gave the place its savour, it was impossible to believe the gods were dead. . . .The mind released itself and was in touch with whatever survives of conquered but immortal spirits."[38] The ancient gods in Belloc are no longer ascendant but nevertheless immortal. Even Amos Wilder plays with the idea of the survival of the gods of antiquity in his poem "The New Aphrodite" (1928):

> Unborn! Unborn! Sister of Christ arise;
> Start from the wave of Europe's tragedies
> Or justify Iona's prophecies.
> > Columba's isle
> > Awaits thy smile.[39]

Amos's poem is inspired by a Celtic myth about the millennium and suggests a syncretism of Celtic, classical, and Christian mythology. The sister of Christ is a more perfect love, hence the title of the poem. But like Lewis and Belloc, Amos here suggests that Christianity can incorporate earlier divinities.

What *The Cabala* emphasizes is how such deities would operate in the modern day. The Cardinal, Jupiter, accomplishes great things but is not at all sure about their worth. Alix, Venus, is fated to a succession of unhappy love affairs. Miss Grier, Minerva, although wise (or perhaps because of it), cannot sleep at night but passes the hours listening to music played by her own musicians. The title of the last section of *The Cabala* sums up the status of its members: "The Dusk of the Gods"; they are for the most part men and women of diminishing vitality.

Samuele discovers eventually that he is one of the Cabala. He is the god Mercury, whose attributes are described by his predecessor in the role: "Godlike I never reflect; all my actions arrive of themselves. If I pause to think I fall into error . . . . I love discord among gods and men. I have always been happy. I am the happiest of the gods" (*Cabala,* 129). This, of course, helps to explain his utter inability to help either Marcantonio or Alix. Moreover, Samuele shares the character of the members of the Cabala. Godlike, he wants to see their inner lives and does. Like him, they are "fierce intellectual snobs" but archaic: "I fancy it's like this: you've heard of scientists off Australia coming upon regions where the animals and plants ceased to evolve long ago? They find a pocket of archaic time in the middle of a world that has progressed beyond it. Well, it must be something like that with the Cabala" (*Cabala,* 4). Samuele's snobbery is turned on his own countrymen:

Opposite them sprawled three American Italians returning to their homes in some Apennine village after twenty years of trade in fruit and jewelry on upper Broadway. They had invested their savings in the diamonds on their fingers, and their eyes were not less bright with anticipation of a family reunion. One foresaw their parents staring at them, unable to understand the change whereby their sons had lost the charm the Italian soil bestows upon the humblest of its children, noting only that they have come back with bulbous features, employing barbarous idioms and bereft forever of the witty psychological intuition of their race. (*Cabala*, 2)

This passage occurs in the third paragraph of the novel and, if one is to take it seriously, requires a great deal of faith upon the part of a reader who as yet knows nothing about its narrator. The fastidious disdain for people with bulbous features who wear too much jewelry and, worse, are engaged in trade sounds odd coming from an American commenting on his countrymen abroad.[40]

As the novel proceeds, we discover that Samuele is very young and works apparently at nothing except meeting and attempting to ingratiate himself with the Cabala. One suspects that it is he who must learn to grow beyond the faded glamour (in both senses of the term) of classical and European civilization or, at least, to incorporate it within an American framework that can encompass the breadth of the old with the passion of the new. We see Samuele at his most jejune when he calls on the dying Keats (Wilder's historical analysis does not commit him to fictional realism). Keats speaks enthusiastically of Chapman's Homer, and Samuele hurts his feelings by responding thoughtlessly that Chapman's translation is scarcely Homer at all. The revelation into the dying poet's desires is a clear contrast to Samuele's own snobbery:

He was beyond feeling indignant at abuses, beyond humor, beyond sentiment, beyond any interest in any bits of antiquarian lore. Apparently for weeks together in the wretched atmosphere of the sickroom Francis had neglected to speak highly of anything and the poet wanted before he left the strange world to hear some portion of it praised. (*Cabala*, 26)

The world must be worth something for the poet's songs about it to have any meaning. The experience of the world's value must also not be isolated; the poet must share the praise with someone else, know that there is agreement that the world has value, for death to be bearable. Mercury, we are told, "is not only the messenger of the gods, he is the conductor of the dead as well" (*Cabala*, 131). Dismissive judgment is not appropriate to that conduct.[41] Samuele, to be a poet, must learn what a poet does.

In the first paragraph of *The Cabala*, Samuele looks out of the train window at the countryside around Rome: "It was Virgil's country and there was a wind that seemed to rise from the fields and descend upon us in a long Virgilian sigh, for the land that has inspired sentiment in the poet ultimately receives its sentiment from him" (*Cabala*, 1). There is an Olympian character to this judgment, something the novel shows to be invariably suspect, but it sums up the mood of the novel as a whole: Rome can be expressed in a sigh, a statement of loss. The Samuele who summons Virgil at the end of the novel is much more willing to be instructed. Virgil says, "Nothing is eternal save Heaven. Rome existed before Rome and when Rome will be waste there will be Romes after her. Seek out some city that is young. The secret is to make a city, not rest in it" (*Cabala*, 133). In the 1930s, Wilder will turn from distant times and foreign lands and set his plays and novels mostly in America. While the classical and Catholic traditions are not forgotten in Wilder's works published during the Great Depression, he seeks to make a new city in the American landscape, and that city requires a new religious expression.

It would be a mistake to argue that the only, or even the central, theme of *The Cabala, The Bridge of San Luis Rey,* or *The Woman of Andros* was the tension between the psyche's quest for the sacred and the cultural forms of the historical period. All three works are about love. In *The Cabala* the European Venus and the American Adonis (the Princess and Blair) are profoundly ill suited, and this expression of failed human experience requires the mythical framework of classical antiquity because it recurs eternally. They are also, in a sense, Heloise and Abelard, she disappointed in her love for the scholar, he castrated by his own fear of life. In *The Bridge of San Luis Rey,* tragic love requires self-renunciation redeemed by the realization that love is its own justification and requires nothing in return. And in *The Woman of Andros,* love struggles with social constraints and death, while the Incarnation, the ultimate expression of divine love for erring humanity, awaits to give meaning to these struggles.

Nonetheless, even love is expressed, denied, or limited by the historical milieu. The love of Chrysis for Pamphilus in *The Woman of Andros* is one that dares not speak its name; she is, after all, a prostitute and he is the first son of the first citizen of the island. When La Perichole turns from Uncle Pio and the theater and seeks respectability in *The Bridge of San Luis Rey,* she is turning away from the man who truly and altruistically loves her and seeks only to develop her great gift, toward an empty social pretense of respectability that even she knows does not make her happy, although she does not know why. What the peasant girl was denied, the actress seeks, at the cost of her art. And in *The Cabala,* the princess discovers that while she can tell a Harvard man, she cannot tell him much, in particular, that she loves him.

This historical dimension of Wilder's works has been too often neglected. Even when he does turn his attention to America in the 1930s, he does so with a keen eye for social and economic realities, and his approach to religious issues is bound up with, and rooted in, time and place. After Wilder had developed his craft by talking about other places—Samuele is a kind of alter ego for Thornton Wilder—he returned ready to write about home, always affectionately, but well aware of America's problems.

Chapter Two

Coming Home to America

In *The Cabala,* the Cardinal calls Samuele the son *"di Vitman, di Poe, di Vilson* [presumably Woodrow Wilson], *di Guglielmo James,—di Emerson" (Cabala,* 106). It is difficult to see how Poe fits onto this list, but otherwise Wilder's American observer is identified with his homeland's transcendentalists, pragmatists, and liberals. While Puritan overtones are present at the end of the novel when Virgil tells Samuele to make a city, it is not the spiritual city on the hill but one grounded in the practices and ideals of American life. In fact, Wilder's first full-length work, *The Trumpet Shall Sound* (1919), is an attack on the self-righteousness of the American Puritan. When Wilder turns to America in some of the one-acts from 1931, the hugely underrated *Heaven's My Destination* (1935), and *The Merchant of Yonkers* (1938)— which, with minor revisions, became *The Matchmaker* (1954)—his focus on American culture and religion is not divorced from social and economic concerns. In fact, his work shows a people attempting to deny reality and struggling with depression both economically and morally.

When *The Trumpet Shall Sound,* about servants who rent out rooms in their absent owner's house, was produced in New York by the important director Richard Boleslawsky in 1926, the *New York Times* described it as a murky pastiche of other works about erring humanity.[1] Malcolm Goldstein dismisses the play as an obvious allegory about "God's infinite capacity for pardoning even the worst of sinners."[2] M. C. Kuner sees it as either about God's infinite mercy or as an ironic commentary about the self-righteous owner Peter Magnus, but claims that "the intention is blurred."[3] Lincoln Konkle is almost alone in taking the play seriously and treats it as an allegory of the Last Judgment. The returning landlord represents Christ judging the sinners. As Konkle notes, some readers have difficulty with this interpretation because Magnus's judgments are frankly unfair by modern standards: "it may be that the message is more disagreeable or inconsistent with post-Calvinist Christian doctrine than it is unclear."[4] Konkle regards any skepticism in the text about Magnus's role as ironic. Thus, when the detective Dexter reports his superior's comment that Magnus is attempting to play God, Konkle regards this as a cue for the audience to regard Magnus as Christ. To defend his thesis that Wilder's play is a Puritan allegory, Konkle must rely on predestination to explain Magnus's pardon of Dabney, for instance, who left a ship full of Irish Catholics to drown since they were damned anyway.

Such a reading really does divorce Wilder from his historical context. Far from being the Yale undergraduate reading Proust and Lawrence and contemptuous of Hawthorne, he becomes a seventeenth-century Puritan divine. It also divorces *The Trumpet Shall Sound* from its source, Ben Jonson's *The Alchemist* (1610), itself a satire on, among other things, Puritanism. In that play the absent owner's servant Jeremy transforms himself into Captain Face, and, with his alchemist partner Subtle and the prostitute Dol, uses the house as headquarters to fleece the fools of London. But while Subtle and Dol escape with only their hides intact, Jeremy is protected by the householder Lovewit, who profits by their labors in gaining both treasure and a young widow and forgives Jeremy all:

> That master
> That had received such happiness by a servant,
> In such a widow, and with so much wealth,
> Were very ungrateful, if he would not be
> A little indulgent to that servant's wit,
> And help his fortune, though [with] some small strain
> Of his own candour.[5]

In a comic sense, Jonson plays off the biblical parable of the talents (Matthew 25:14–30) with his servant profitably increasing his master's assets. The people cheated in Jonson's play deserve to be cheated and enrich the absent master; as such they have a great deal in common with the sinners who rent from Flora in Magnus's household in Wilder's play. But the contrast between the amiable and shrewd Lovewit and Magnus indicates the superiority of Lovewit. Magnus is described, when he is first introduced, as "a low, squat man with a bald head, heavy spectacles and sideburns. His pursy, self-important face is red with excitement" (*TSS*, 138). Somehow, one does not think that Wilder would have an audience regard Christ at the Last Judgment as low, squat, or full of self-importance.

The *Trumpet Shall Sound,* like the plays of *The Angel That Troubled the Waters,* dramatizes the difficult struggle toward faith, in this case in an America infected with equally repugnant strains of Puritanism and greed. Dabney represents the Puritan evangelical strain and his crime is the same as Conrad's Lord Jim. He is wanted for having deserted his ship, which he justifies by his knowledge of his higher calling: "Here stood I, entering upon a great life-work of evangelization, and here lay hundreds of stammering ignorant peasants, one indistinguishable from another. No, sir. The man whose mind is free from the barbaric and vengeful conception of justice, is able to see that I have offended only against a moral principle, and am answerable only to Him, from whom all moral law is an emanation" (*TSS*, 200). Very simply, Dabney sees his life as more important than the lives of the Irish peasants, who, he tells Flora earlier in the play, "be of that faith for which judgment and destruction are laid up in the book of Revelation" (*TSS*, 131). In philosophical terms and as a proposition widely accepted since the eighteenth century, the God who could regard with indifference the death of hundreds of Irish peasants is in fact a demon rather than a god. That is to say, some notion of the good must be antecedent to the idea of divine judgment, or else the concept of the good has no meaning at all; the good cannot simply be good because God says it is. Only a truly hard-line Calvinist who regarded the judgment of God as utterly inscrutable to fallen humanity could possibly regard Dabney as anything other than a cowardly hypocrite. This does not mean that he is beyond divine forgiveness, but even that can take place only through repentance or conviction of personal sin, and Dabney shows no evidence of either.

That Wilder was aware of the element of anti-Catholicism in his New England heritage cannot be contested, but he regarded it with amusement. In a letter to his sister Janet that appears to be dated March 15, '96 (which obviously cannot be correct), he recalls an incident from his childhood:

> I'll tell you in detail about my appendectomy—which is really a story about my father who was brought up in the State of Maine to regard the Roman Catholic Church as SINISTER, CORRUPT, LASCIVIOUS and so on; but who had to see me transported to St. Rafael's Hospital and visit me there, amid crucifixes, incense, rosaries and nuns! The patient as happy as a cricket, but the patient's father sweating at every pore and like to swoon![6]

Certainly, his father's view of Catholicism was not Wilder's within a couple of years of writing *The Trumpet Shall Sound*. In a letter to his brother Amos on September 7, 1917, he refers to "the Roman Catholic tendency in me that pains dear papa so"; and then, on September 13, he writes that "I've a good mind to go to Harvard, which Father would permit and to enter the Catholic Church which would unbalance him."[7] In an undated letter, Wilder tells his father that he does not wish to leave Oberlin for Yale: "Albeit if you hear well of some Catholic college I will discuss that seriously. I think that after all I am an acutely religious temperament and that beside it nothing else matters."[8] Thus when Magnus leaps to his feet to honor Dabney and says, "This misfortune of six years' ago is not for man's disposition; it has doubtless been justified a thousand times" (*TSS,* 201), the expected response, to see Dabney and Magnus as religious bigots utterly lacking in common humanity, is consistent with Wilder's religious views. And the American audiences who thronged to see Anne Nichols's *Abie's Irish Rose,* about a happy marriage between the Jew Abraham Levy and his Catholic bride Rose Mary Murphy, for a record-breaking run from 1922 to 1927, would almost certainly have regarded Magnus and Dabney with horror.

The characters that Magnus pardons are all vicious. Miss Flecker, the roomer who writes to Magnus to tell him of the abuse of his house, is motivated by simple greed. She replies to Dabney when he asks why she has not left the misused house, "I don't mind telling you. You won't like it, being a religious fanatic and all that: It's for what I can get out of it!" (*TSS*, 83). She also thinks Magnus "a great fool" (*TSS*, 140). And she is unmistakably hypocritical when Magnus makes her a gift: "I did not look for this, Mr. Magnus. I felt it was no more than justice to warn you" (*TSS*, 206). Utterly pitiless, she looks upon herself as a lady and the other tenants of the house as riffraff. But Magnus, as he did with Dabney, sees her as "justified."

Miss Flecker angrily denies any relationship to Charles Flecker Hammersley, the "Carlo" who has carried on an affair with Flora, but both have used Flora to their profit. Carlo continues to enjoy Flora even though he tells her bluntly that he will not marry her: "You're a smart girl and all that. I *do* say I never met a girl that beat you for sense. I'll say that. But you're a servant-girl, and you can barely read and write. (*Doggedly*) I'm sorry, Flora, to say it: but you're expecting too much. (*She sits down at the table, crushed. After a moment he turns to go debonairly:*) I'm sorry, Flora" (*TSS*, 128). Magnus overhears the best attempt at a marriage ceremony that Flora can obtain from Carlo and subsequently praises him for betraying his vows: "Your repudiation of this woman's degraded and superstitious travesty of the marriage sacrament was most commendable" (*TSS*, 203). In practice, however, Carlo's chief repudiation of the ceremony is his failure to come to Flora's aid when she needs it, which he has promised to do. When Magnus shakes hands with Carlo, he accepts equality with a scoundrel.

But Miss Del Valle, the prostitute dying of tuberculosis, unlike the criminally negligent sea captain, the avaricious and hypocritical informer, and the caddish seducer, is shown no mercy:

MAGNUS: Very well. Miss Del Valle, I'll ask you to leave the house in three minutes.

MISS DEL VALLE (*whispering, her hand at her throat*): I've this cough, sir. I'm like to die.

MAGNUS (*in a tremendous indignation, bringing both fists down upon the table*): Not another word! There are modest women present; there are decent women present, I say. What right have you to speak? It is you that brings empires to decay. Do you hear me? Now, leave the house. (*TSS,* 202)

Miss Del Valle then turns to Flora, who gives her a bracelet so she will not be utterly destitute. In short, Magnus's indignation is reserved for a dying woman, while the self-righteous (rather than the righteous, of whom there is none in the play) are treated with honor. Surely any audience familiar with the Bible will recall passages where Jesus speaks of forgiveness for prostitutes (Matthew 21:32) or actually forgives the prostitute who washes his feet with her tears (Luke: 7:44–50). In the dramatic context the women present are Sarah, Flora's co-conspirator (albeit a somewhat unwilling one), the odious Miss Flecker, the miser Fru Soderström, and Flora: there are only sinners in this room.

Flora, who in Konkle's view is a demonic figure, and, as he rightly points out, is more than once referred to as a "wicked girl," is the play's central character. Indeed, she too suspects that she is predestined to evil. When Carlo tells her that he will have her, she replies "(*suddenly bitter*): Yes. But I'm only half wrong. It's like things have been planned to come out this way" (*TSS,* 130). She asks him what he thinks she is: "Devil! Fool! Devil! Fool! is that what you think?" (*TSS,* 129). However, the text suggests that predestination is social rather than divine. Flora, we know, can barely read, and she comes from a poor background "back South." Carlo tells of seeing her father "copying his little figures in the customs-house. He's changed since you've gone, Flora. He misses you, likely. I talked to him a little, but he didn't know I knew you. He showed me your brothers out working in the fields. As black as niggers they are. And there were little kids all about the yard. Brothers and sisters, eh?" (*TSS,* 89–90). They are, it turns out, half brothers and sisters, so the implication is that Flora was raised in poverty and by someone other than her own mother. Nor has she received any religious instruction: "You know I've never in my life been in a church, before you took me tonight. I've tried to go a thousand times, but I've always been afraid. Sometimes I go stand in front of them. I should love to be in one when they're doing things. And when they pray they kneel down" (*TSS*, 143). It is possible for a Calvinist to regard as damned those ignorant of true religion. But it is not possible for Wilder, who has Virgil condemn Dante at the end of *The Cabala* for condemning him to the Inferno, and who says that the pagan can be saved.

From a young age, Wilder had discarded a simplistic moralism. In a letter to his father apparently from 1915, he writes of his impatience "with your solicitousness, your overemphasis of the rigid necessity of being moral and 'good'; when there's really such license allowed to personality to do honorably such unspeakably un-moral things. Now do confess that to be glad and aspiring and intimate makes 'being a Christian' and doing one's iron duty and 'weeping over the unsaved' negligible."[9] So when Magnus details Flora's crimes, we need not take them as a final statement of her moral status: "You stand accused of theft, fraud, immorality, and irreligion" (*TSS*, 205). Flora admits guilt, but in comparison with the other sinners of the house her guilt is almost virtuous. It is true that she deceives her master by filling the house with roomers, but she gives the rent to Carlo, so it is not done out of greed. And it is true that she is guilty of fornication with Carlo, but that is done out of love. Wilder, as it happens, disputed the importance of celibacy. He admonishes Amos in a letter of December 13, 1920, "I'm not at all sympathetic with your shockedness over fellow students' conduct: you haven't learned Morals, you've learned the *Code* of Morals. Politeness and Celibacy are a matter of indifference to God. Go deeper. If possible, sin yourself and discover the innocence of it."[10] Flora, neither polite nor celibate, should not be seen *a priori* as damned.

The wedding ceremony that Flora concocts when Carlo will not marry her legally, and which he and Magnus regard as sacrilegious, is in fact a statement of natural piety:

Angels and God, amen. Flora Hypatia Storey and Charles Flecker Hammersley come to you to be married in the right way, by your holy wish, amen. Angels and God, forgive us for not doing it the way most people do. You can see how it is; me, I'm only a servant-girl, after all, and can only read and write a little; and he's a sailor. Keep us happy and true, and let us know if you don't favor what we're doing. You made things like this, and how can you call it wrong when it's the natural way things fall out? Angels and God, don't make us unhappy out of it. (*TSS*, 144)

Flora tells Carlo, "It may be different words from you're used to, but underneath it's the same." She attempts marriage in the eyes of God; and in Renaissance England, for instance, these words would have constituted a legal ceremony. The middle name of Flora, Hypatia, is significant as well: Hypatia was a mathematician, astronomer, and Neoplatonic philosopher in Alexandria, murdered in 415 AD when the Romans cracked down on paganism. Both Flora and her namesake are victims of religious intolerance.

When Flora commits suicide, Magnus says about the body, "She seems to have been kneeling, poor girl—Ah, well! So pleasure will be paid" (*TSS*, 207). It is clear that she kills herself because of Carlo's desertion in her hour of need, so if she is genuinely guilty it is of the sin of idolatry and worshiping a false god. But Flora dies praying for mercy, apparently, and Magnus's trite judgment that this is the reward of fornication rings tinny in the extreme. Even he acknowledges that "there is a judgment seat to face beyond this, wiser than man's. Yes, I own it. It may even be that my verdicts will be reversed. Some of them, I say. At midnight the cry goeth forth, and we shall all be snatched up. You know the text, Dexter?" (*TSS*, 205). The reference is to Matthew 25:1–13, the parable of the bridesmaids awaiting the bridegroom, and it echoes the warning given by the undertaker at the beginning of the play: "We know not the day or the hour" (*TSS*, 16). But to my mind, the question of who needs to fear judgment in the play remains not murky but carefully unresolved.

Magnus's house recalls John 14:2: "There are many dwelling-places in my Father's house; if it were not so, I would have told you: for I am going to prepare a place for you." This is a statement of the mercy of God; Jesus teaches his disciples that because he prepares a way for them, God will take them in. But the newcomers are seen as a violation by Magnus: "Great God, that my house, the store of my pride and sorrows, where pure manners have held among generations of my fathers, should so shortly become a haven for ingratitude, dishonesty and vice!" (*TSS,* 139). However, Magnus's house has been kept empty except for servants. It is a monument to his dead, not a shelter for the living, nor can it be made allegorically the heavenly mansions of the justified. The stage directions for those whom Flora admits lead to a tableau of the living, whom Magnus would and eventually does exclude:

> *A silent and furtive crowd files gradually into the room. "The halt, the deaf, the dumb, the blind," figuratively speaking. A strange company, shabby, cautious and suppressed. Conspicuous among them is a young mother with a crying child in her arms. They settle into chairs, the faces assume a fixed expression, staring either at the ceiling or the floor, and the curtain falls.* (*TSS,* 26)

The quotation here alludes to Matthew 11:5–6, where John the Baptist sends to question Jesus about his deeds, and Jesus tells John's disciples, "the blind recover their sight, the lame walk, lepers are made clean, the deaf hear, the dead are raised to life, the poor are brought good news—and blessed are those who do not find me an obstacle to faith." The blind, lame, sick, deaf, and poor—those are the people whom Flora brings into the house. Her focus is on easing present-day suffering, not on preserving a mausoleum of the past.

Ultimately, then, *The Trumpet Shall Sound* depicts the spiritual poverty of the American Puritan tradition: self-righteous and unfeeling, it has nothing to offer those who suffer. I am not claiming that the play is entirely successful. But I would claim that it shows Wilder's concern with the weaknesses of American culture from the beginning of his career. However, those weaknesses cannot be translated without remainder into economic terms. And when he does turn to American topics from 1931 to 1938, he does not ignore the suffering caused by the Great Depression, but he also sees Americans as profoundly deracinated and undergoing alienation as a consequence.[11]

It sometimes seems as if any work on the early Wilder begins with Michael Gold's attack in *The New Republic* of October 22, 1930, but I shall also examine it because it reveals the extent to which Wilder was on a different page from so many of his contemporaries. Gold's essay was also sufficiently important to be reprinted in the anthology *Proletarian Literature* in 1935, and it inspired a war of letters in *The New Republic,* which indicates that it struck a nerve with its readers. Gold's interpretive framework is Marxist in origin, so merely turning to American subjects would not have constituted a response by Wilder. That is, any discussion of contemporary life that did not recognize that the "our genteel bourgeoisie" had drawn their income from "the billions wrung from American workers and foreign peasants and coolies"[12] was simply escapism. Even Wilder's religious impulses, according to Gold, lack "the crude self-tortures of the Holy Rollers, or the brimstone howls and fears of the Baptists, or even the mad titanic sincerities and delusions of a Tolstoy or Dostoievsky."[13] Wilder's religion, on the other hand, "is that newly fashionable literary religion that centers around Jesus Christ, the First British Gentleman. It is a pastel, pastiche, dilettante religion, without the neurotic blood and fire, a daydream of homosexual figures in graceful gowns moving archaically among the lilies. It is Anglo-Catholicism, that last refuge of the American literary snob."[14]

The tone of Gold's polemic is partially a function of the social construction of the left wing in the 1930s; Gold's aggressive machismo can be found in the members of the Group Theater as well. But ideology is also at work. Gold suggests that any approach to the religious spirit can be bounded by, at its best, neuroses (Tolstoy and Dostoyevsky), and, at its worst, by masochism and paranoia (Holy Rollers and Baptists). All other religious views, Catholic or Protestant, are simply lumped together under the dismissive heading of Anglo-Catholicism, which appeals not only to snobs but also to homosexuals. Red-blooded, heterosexual writers have long since discarded religious fiction in favor of novels that depict the oppression of the urban proletariat. This is another statement of the contemporary indifference to religion among the intelligentsia that I discussed in the introduction.

Wilder had always had reliable champions writing for popular magazines, including, from his alma mater Yale University, William Lyon Phelps and Henry Seidel Canby. And plenty of people immediately sprang to Wilder's defense, pointing out the problems, as Henry Hazlitt wrote in *The Nation,* of criticism that "hoots or hails a work of art in proportion as it seems to oppose, ignore, or support the opinions of a German economist who died in 1883."[15] But the ones who sided with Gold were the avant-garde of criticism. Granville Hicks endorsed Gold unreservedly in *The Great Tradition* (1933).[16] Margaret Marshall and Mary McCarthy attacked Phelps and Canby specifically for their praise of Wilder, a "pale" talent.[17] Edmund Wilson in an unsigned piece in *The New Republic,* while criticizing Gold for an insufficient appreciation of the writer's craft, nevertheless defended Gold's basic point:

And so in Wilder the pathos and the beauty derived from exotic lands of the imagination may be, as Michael Gold suggests, a sedative for sick Americans. The sedative and the demand for it are both products of the same situation: a people disposed to idealism, but deprived of their original ideals and now making themselves neurotic in the attempt to introduce idealism into the occupations— organizing, financing, manufacturing, advertising, salesmanship— of a precarious economic system the condition for whose success is that they must profit by swindling their customers and cutting one another's throats.[18]

Waiving Wilson's indictment of capitalism, and his nod in the direction of fashionable psychoanalysis, he is nonetheless making a claim far advanced from Gold's and one with which Wilder's works from 1931 onward show sympathy: America has lost some of its original ideals, and some of its citizens have an inadequately grounded sense of their own identity.[19]

The one-act play "Such Things Happen Only in Books" illustrates one kind of deficiency: the loss of the possible in the face of the probable. The play itself lacks complexity and even dropped out of the collection of one-acts in an edition in 1980.[20] Its central conceit is slight enough: John, a young novelist, explains to his wife that there is little connection between life and the plots of literature:

> JOHN: Plots. Plots. If I had no conscience I could choose any of these plots that are in everybody's novels and in nobody's lives. These poor battered old plots. Enoch Arden returns and looks through the window and sees his wife married to another.
> GABRIELLE: I've always loved that one.
> JOHN: The plot that murderers always steal back to the scene of their crime and gloat over the place.
> GABRIELLE: Oh, John! How wonderful. They'll come back to this house. Imagine!
> JOHN: The plot that all married women of thirty-five have lovers.
> GABRIELLE: Otherwise known as the Marseillaise.
> JOHN: They're as pathetic and futile as the type-jokes—you know: that mothers-in-law are unpleasant, that . . . that cooks feed chicken and turkey to policemen and other callers in the kitchen . . .
> GABRIELLE: Katie! Katie!—Once every twenty-one times those plots really do happen in real life, you say?
> JOHN: Once in a thousand. Books and plays are a quiet, harmless fraud about life. (*CP,* 123–24)

Gabrielle's quip about the Marseillaise implies that the theme of the adulterous wife is particularly French, and (along with Anna Karenina), Flaubert's Madame Bovary is perhaps the most famous adulterous wife in fiction. The joke is that Gabrielle, like Emma Bovary, bored with life in her country town, is having an affair. Katie, the servant and cook, does not feed the police in the kitchen but instead has burned herself while feeding her brother, an escapee from prison, at night in the kitchen right under their noses; the servant who hides her escaped brother is found, for example, in Conan Doyle's *The Hound of the Baskervilles.* And Raskolnikov does not return to gloat, but he does return to the scene of his crime in Dostoyevsky's *Crime and Punishment.* And the brother and sister who have killed their father return to look for the money hidden in the house in this play.

The reference to Tennyson's narrative poem *Enoch Arden* is the most telling indication of John's detachment from life. The title character leaves his wife and children to go to sea in order to support them. Shipwrecked on an island, he comes back years later, but his wife has married another man. He never tells her of his return, thus investing his loss with a kind of tragic dignity, but he himself has created the problem (by leaving his wife and children in the first place) in his flawed conception of masculine integrity. In "Such Things," John has separated himself from his wife in his work, and thus he has also separated himself from life. When Dr. Bumpas tells Gabrielle what Katie has done, she promises secrecy: "Oh, I never tell John anything! It would prevent his working" (*CP,* 125). The old plots are, the play suggests, true ones, and the implication is that a true plot, life, would disrupt John's concentration. His mind is too pure to be infected by the actual.

John rejects these plots on the grounds that they are improbable: they happen once in a thousand lives. However, all other criteria, such as whether the plot is exciting (*The Hound of the Baskervilles*), significant (*Enoch Arden, Crime and Punishment*), or moving (*Madame Bovary*), are of secondary importance. For John, this is a matter of conscience. He is a kind of Aristotelian, constructing his plots out of rules of probability, as opposed to a Romantic or Platonic artist given to flights of inspiration (that is, the sort of poet whom Wilder sees being born in "Nascuntur Poetae," in what Wilder calls the three-minute plays of *The Angel That Troubled the Waters*). As "Such Things" begins, he is playing solitaire and calculating how often he is blocked. At the end of one hand he tells his wife, "Well, I guess this is stuck. It really looked as though it were coming out. I can see that if I moved just one card it would open up a lot of combinations." His wife observes "(*Without malice*): But you have too much conscience" (*CP,* 123). His choice of a game played alone is indicative of his solipsism, but what is laudable in the game—abiding by the rules—is deplorable in an author. When he is blocked again at the end of the play, his wife says, "I don't see why that game shouldn't come out oftener. (*Pause*) I don't think you see all the moves." John retorts, "I certainly do see all the moves that are to be seen.—You don't expect me to look under the cards, do you?" (*CP,* 128). Of course, the true artist in nonmimetic theories of art sees beyond the merely probable to the essence of life; such an artist indeed looks under the cards. But the implication here is that a play ought to be about what is possible, not merely what is probable. And if the rules preclude this, then the rules must be discarded.

There are religious implications here. John thinks that he can reduce events to mathematical probabilities. He tabulates the results when describing a series of hands and draws a conclusion: "Listen to the scores this evening: zero, two, five, three, zero, six, and now five. The full fifty-two [cards] come out every twenty-one times. So that from now on my chances for getting it out increase seven point three two every game" (*CP,* 121). On the one hand, this is simply fallacious. The likelihood of an outcome is *a priori* exactly the same; how many hands have been successfully completed is irrelevant to whether the next hand will be. But John, while a poor mathematician, is trying to reduce life and art to probabilities, as if only that which can be quantitatively described counts as real knowledge. He says, "You see it's like fiction. You have to adjust the cards to make a plot. In life most people live along without plots. A plot breaks through about once every twenty-one times" (*CP,* 123). If he looked at what was happening around him, then not only would his confidence in probability be shaken, but he would also discover that lives have plots and are not simply incidents. That is, the individual's life is a narrative possessing design, and not just a product of a random series of events that can only be viewed as a kind of bell curve of human activity. Seeing the design is not easy, but, once seen, it is a kind of knowledge that is not quantitative in nature. And belief in design, in even the necessity of the designer, precedes evidence.

But if John's problem is a failure to grasp the facts of life that surround him, misguided as he is by a faulty confidence in the probable, then a more central problem is that Americans have trouble rooting themselves in America. "Queens of France," in the same collection of one-acts from 1931 as "Such Things Happen Only in Books," illustrates this failure. The characters not only deceive themselves but also identify with the royal family of France; the dupes reject their lives as

Americans and long for validation by a foreign aristocracy. The depth of this denial is comical. The play takes place in the most European of American cities, New Orleans, in 1869. A lawyer, M'su Cahusac, convinces several women that they are the descendants of the true heir to the French throne, who disappeared during the Revolution in 1795 at the age of ten. Thus, if he had lived, he would at the time of the play have been 84 years old. The last to enter M'su Cahusac's office is *"a woman of some hundred years of age"* (*CP,* 92); it is physically impossible for her to be the heir to the French throne, yet we are forced to conclude she believes she is nonetheless. And as usual with Wilder's works, the date of the play is significant. On September 14, 1870, Napoleon III, the last monarch of France, will fall; subsequently, to be a member of the French royal family becomes wholly irrelevant except as a courteous honorific.

The confidence game works by convincing a woman that only a few more documents will make her claim to the throne indisputable. To finance the research necessary, the "historical society" may need to sell off certain priceless royal heirlooms. The woman, wishing to save the relics of her "house," buys them herself. Finally, the last crucial document cannot be found; it is suggested that the woman's own family may have destroyed it, and she is left with a letter from the historical society confirming that nevertheless she is the rightful ruler of France. Although it is not explicitly stated, M'su Cahusac can be sure that the woman will not embarrass herself by revealing how she has been duped.

Why most of the women wish to be duped is established delicately. Marie Cressaux, we are told, has "half a dozen houses and gardens already. She persuades every one of her lovers to give her a little house and garden. She is beginning to own the whole parish of Saint-Magloire" (*CP,* 84). If she is the rightful Queen of France, she gains respectability. Mamselle Pointevin is a schoolteacher and a spinster. She tells M'su Cahusac, after he has told her that her family must have destroyed the final proof of her claim, "It was so beautiful while it lasted. It made even school teaching a pleasure, M'su" (*CP,* 91). Even Mme. Pugeot, married with children, fancies herself healthier while under the spell of greatness: "I used to do quite poorly, as you remember, but since the wonderful news I have been more than well, God be praised" (*CP,* 85). The fantasy, while expensive, is preferable to her real life. The difficulty is that it threatens Mme. Pugeot's family. Not only is she selling her family's property (a gigantic folly since she has numerous children), but she is also becoming contemptuous of her "common" husband: "He has no part in my true life. He has chosen to scoff at my birth and rank, but he will see what he will see . . . . Naturally I have not told him about the proofs that you and I have collected. I have not the heart to let him see how unimportant he will become" (*CP,* 85).

The usual thing for an American woman to attempt if she is unhappy with her life is to change it; plasticity of character and circumstance is central to the American self-conception. Birth is not fate. Marie Cressaux, for instance, has the wealth to cease being a prostitute; and, with three children, it is important for their sake that she build a new, real life. Even if Mamselle Pointevin has no alternative to her life as a schoolteacher, at the end of the con she is still a spinster schoolteacher, only now a much poorer one. All of these women hope that fate is going to rescue them from the quotidian malaise. M'su Cahusac deceives them, but they eagerly grasp the deception with both hands. The set indicates their folly: "*The office door to the street is hung with a reed curtain, through which one glimpses a public park in sunshine*" (*CP,* 80). All of these women choose to enter the shadowy office of "a dry little man" to warm themselves with dusty documents from numerous drawers, when the sunshine and park await them outdoors.

Neither John nor the women of New Orleans are willing to look at the reality around them and change it. Of course, a standard charge was that this was the fault of religion in general and Christianity in particular. Bertrand Russell is representative of this view in his 1930 essay "Has Religion Made Useful Contributions to Civilization?" The obvious answer, according to Russell, is that religion thrives on fear and hatred and stands in the way of a Golden Age made possible by developments in the social sciences and industry. Christianity, like stoicism, turns the individual inward toward "a conception of personal holiness as something quite independent of beneficent action, since holiness had to be achieved by people who were impotent in action. Social virtue came therefore to be excluded from Christian ethics. . . . The most virtuous man was the man who retired from the world."[21] Where Michael Gold sees Wilder as unwilling to address economic oppression, Russell would have presumably seen him as sidetracked by individualism and therefore unable to acknowledge that, through social engineering, the human race could be made happy. Both men would agree that the idea of free will was untenable.

There can be no doubt that neither Thornton nor Amos Wilder would concur with the conception of human nature implicit in either Gold's Marxism or Russell's Positivism, but neither of the Wilders would have accepted the premise that religion precluded action. Amos sees this error as castastrophic for organized religion:

> If there is one confusion more than any other which is responsible for the apostasy from Christianity of extensive groups and strata today, it has to do with this charge of false otherworldliness. Actually a whole group of confusions are involved: Jewish apocalyptic eschatology was a form of escapism; its messianism was a compensatory vision of a frustrated people; Jesus was a naïve dreamer conditioned by a simple society or was a deluded fanatic; his ethic was an impracticable perfectionism and the early church's version of it a slave morality which offered a sentimental and ascetic code in lieu of that *arête* or virtue from which they were disqualified by their social position.[22]

According to Amos, the historical error based on ignorance of the history of the Jewish people and the uses of language in the Bible is compounded by erroneous modern interpretations of the data: for instance, that Jesus was delusional. The idea that the early church expressed a slave morality rather than a desire for the excellence of Homeric Greece is from Nietzsche. Over the course of his career, Amos was at some pains to dispute many of these claims. Jewish eschatology was focused on the transformation of this world, and the teachings of Jesus are not at variance with that tradition.

Jesus' own conception of his role in the bringing of the apocalypse (or revelation) of God's kingdom may have changed over the course of his ministry, but it was always very much engaged in the Incarnation, the Word made Flesh:

> Jesus' proclamation of the kingdom was not a fantasy projection or the portrayal of an escapist's paradise. It was a prophetic forecast of the human destiny resting on the whole of Israel's best experience and her witness to the agelong purpose and work of God the creator. This forecast had to do with ultimates; and it rested on ultimates. It had to do with last things, and it rested on first things. But it was directed to the present moment and to the actual scene and was lived out in the concrete process of history, and it bore on that concrete process in its future aspects.[23]

In a way, the criticism that Gold launched at Thornton Wilder, that his work had nothing to say to the historical moment, is a variant of the criticism of Christianity that Amos Wilder strenuously denied. The Christian who would live a life like Jesus' must deal with historical realities of this world and participate in its transformation: this is an inevitable consequence of the doctrine of the Incarnation.

The Great Depression therefore represented a specifically religious crisis for the Wilder brothers. Even their sister Charlotte, something of a freethinker, saw the economic disaster in a religious context. In a short poem "Sanctuary" from her 1939 collection *Mortal Sequence,* "the Lord" looks at his flock:

"I see my dead, lying in the slops
     of the gutter,

I see my dead, driven from the doors
     of the shelter,

I see my dead, harried to the holes
     of the shambles,

I see my dead," saith the Lord:

"He sees his dead," say the dead,
"clinging to the ghost of his altar."[24]

Charlotte's poem does not suggest an optimistic view, but her examples of suffering are concrete rather than of internalized statements of despair. Moreover, Isabel Wilder's novel *Heart Be Still* (1934) in one section looks at the struggles of the roomers in a boardinghouse who have failed in American society. Celia, the heroine, both admires their courage and pities their isolation (it mirrors her own in this part of the novel). Maximillian Prior, for instance, a Bible teacher, had been sent to Central America before he had been sufficiently trained. Now he does his best to survive:

> Mr. Prior cooked his meals in his room. Celia looked at him and saw within that fat body and behind those puffed-out cheeks, an ill-nourished, exhausted man suffering not only economic loss but spiritual failure.
>
> As she listened to-night, she thought: They're too brave. No one should have to be so courageous. Why do they put up with it? I know I wouldn't. I'd . . . I'd die first.[25]

Celia eventually prospers in New York (although she will be laid off from her job). The consequence of this economic security (a decent apartment, responsible work, respect for Celia's competence) is an increasing emotional stability that enables her to renounce a fruitless infatuation with a cad and move on to a healthy relationship with a good man. But the economic and the spiritual are related, if not inseparable. When day-to-day existence becomes a matter of physical and emotional survival, no time exists for a spiritual connection to the numinous or even to society.

Thornton Wilder's recognition of social trauma is apparent even in the farce *The Matchmaker* (1954), or, in its earlier form, *The Merchant of Yonkers* (1938).[26] Even as farces go, it is exceptionally good-humored; most of the characters find the appropriate person to love and suffer nothing more than embarrassment for their folly. Indeed, Horace Vandergelder, the merchant, does much better than he deserves, marrying

Dolly Levi, the matchmaker herself. Harry Levin is surely correct in seeing the play as a celebration of the spirit of the gamester, or "playboy," in his taxonomy of forms of comedy.[27] Wilder himself writes, "My play is about the aspirations of the young (and not only of the young) for a fuller, freer participation in life" (*CP*, 687). While it may seem wrongheaded to ask what blocks the characters from a free participation in life on the grounds that farces do not have serious ideas, I think that the play does comment upon the economic issues of the 1930s that Wilder examines more fully in *Heaven's My Destination*.[28]

"Since farce is an intellectual exercise," Wilder claimed, "the only ornament it welcomes is the additional intellectual pleasure of lines of social comment and generalization" (*CP*, 692). Farces do not avoid serious subjects: they bracket them with swift action and comical dialogue so that the audience can contemplate them without feeling threatened.[29] Farce makes the subject bearable by providing a safe perspective from which to view it. In *The Matchmaker*, when Vandergelder is bribing a coachman to kidnap his own niece, the common-sense coachman keeps pointing out the difficulties, and Vandergelder keeps raising the ante. When he reaches fifteen dollars, the new employee Malachi interjects that "Murder begins at twenty-five" (*CP*, 334). Because of the rapidity and tone of the dialogue, the overplayed characterizations of farce, and the audience's awareness that the romantic young couple will ultimately be reunited, the scene remains funny. Humor is, of course, its own justification.[30] But that does not alter the fact that Vandergelder thinks that familial and social constraints become meaningless if enough money is applied to the problem.

Malachi is the commentator who reminds the audience of the thin line between farce and black satire. When Vandergelder loses his purse, Malachi rapidly hands it over to Cornelius (whom he does not know), not because he is opposed to theft but because he believes in indulging in only one vice at a time. Some people deserve to be robbed: "For a while, I too was engaged in the redistribution of superfluities. A man works all his life and leaves a million to the widow. She sits in hotels and eats great meals and plays cards all afternoon and evening, with ten diamonds on her fingers. Call in the robbers!" (*CP*, 342–43).

In the context of Wilder's career, this is strikingly similar to Uncle Charlie's speech to his niece Charlie in the Alfred Hitchcock film *Shadow of a Doubt* (1943), for which Wilder wrote the screenplay: "They die and leave their money to their wives. And what do *they* do? You can see them in the hotels, by the thousands, . . . eating great meals . . . playing bridge all afternoon and all night . . . diamonds sparkling all over their big chests. Vapid, useless lives. Thousands of them" (*CP,* 782). Uncle Charlie is a murderer, Malachi only a commentator, but both see money wasted in an orgy of conspicuous consumption; Michael Gold would have agreed with both of the characters. One of many Hitchcock villains more appealing than the police who hunt him, Uncle Charlie is almost sympathetic in that the widows he murders really have no value outside their mere humanity. But since *Shadow of a Doubt* represents the sudden arrival of a psychopath in Wilder's *Our Town,* and Uncle Charlie's presence becomes a threat to his niece, Hitchcock's audience is not left in a quandary of moral judgment. On the other hand, in *The Matchmaker* the audience can laugh at rich, useless women. In the Great Depression (or in World War II, for that matter) this kind of waste is particularly egregious, and thus the farce retains some satirical content. As Malachi says, "Everybody should eavesdrop once in a while, I always say. There's nothing like eavesdropping to show you that the world outside your head is different from the world inside your head" (*CP,* 333).

So it is legitimate to examine the blocking figure in *The Matchmaker,* Vandergelder, as a symptom of social dysfunction. Thus, the play essentially is about the difference between the world itself and the world inside Vandergelder's head. He is an authoritarian miser. When Ambrose, the young man in love with his niece Ermengarde, informs him that she is not only of age but that it is a free country, Vandergelder contradicts him: "there are no free countries for fools" (*CP,* 287). Ambrose relies on the law, an utter irrelevancy to Vandergelder: "The law is there to prevent crime; we men of sense are there to prevent foolishness. It's I, and not the law, that will prevent Ermengarde from marrying you, and I've taken some steps already." Because Ambrose is an artist, he lacks, for Vandergelder, any real economic function and therefore any real social value: "A living is made, Mr.

Kemper, by selling something that everybody needs at least once a year. Yes, sir! And a million is made by producing something that everybody needs every day. You artists produce something that nobody needs at any time" (*CP,* 288). Not only are artists useless, but wage slaves enjoy their servitude, in Vandergelder's view. He tells Mrs. Molloy that she is too generous to the young women in her hat shop: "You pay those girls of yours too much. You pay them as much as men. Girls like that enjoy their work. Wages, Mrs. Molloy, are paid to make people do work they don't want to do" (*CP,* 321).

Vandergelder is not merely obtuse here. For him, labor is something you get as much out of for as little as possible. In 1938, with the United States once more mired in a recession that threatened the economic progress that had been made over the course of most of the 1930s, his self-absorption makes his rapaciousness simultaneously funny and ominous, in that we know that he is the biggest of the fools in the play, no matter how much money he has in the bank, and yet he holds the power. As Malachi tells the cabman, "I can see you're in business for yourself because you talk about liking employers. No one's ever liked an employer since business began" (*CP,* 335), and Vandergelder is the most employerly of employers. This is, of course, a long way from the enraged laborers yelling "Strike" at the end of Clifford Odets's *Waiting for Lefty* (1935), but it still illustrates the difference between the world inside Vandergelder's head and the one outside of it.

Vandergelder's greed makes it all the more essential for his pride to be humbled, his will circumscribed, and his niece, employees, and money freed. Although already rich, he wants Dolly to find him a wealthy bride because "I have a large household to run" (*CP,* 302). And he makes it clear that a wife is simply another kind of laborer, although one with low-level management capabilities, and that is why he plans to marry: "I like my house run with order, comfort and economy. That's a woman's work, but even a woman can't do it well if she's merely being paid for it. In order to run a house well, a woman must have the feeling that she owns it. Marriage is a bribe to make a housekeeper think she's a householder" (*CP,* 295). Taken out of context, many of these speeches sound grimmer than they actually are in performance. Again, they are comical because we know that things will not turn out the way that Vandergelder has planned them. But, in fact, Wilder subtly reminds the audience that some women will settle for this kind of servitude because society does not allow them any other kind of life.

Mrs. Molloy, Vandergelder's intended, is a widow who wants to remarry. As someone in the clothing industry (a joke on the traditional listing of the occupation of prostitutes as "seamstresses"), she must consider her reputation: "I can no longer stand being suspected of being a wicked woman, while I have nothing to show for it" (*CP*, 310). She must remarry because only in a legal tie to a man can she have any freedom at all. And Dolly wishes to remarry because she is exhausted from living by her wits. In a soliloquy addressed to her first, dead husband, the man she loved (and who significantly was not an American), she explains why she will now marry a man she does not love:

> Ephraim, I'm marrying Horace Vandergelder for his money. I'm going to send his money out doing all the things you taught me. Oh, it won't be a marriage in the sense we had one—but I shall certainly make him happy, and Ephraim—I'm tired. I'm tired of living from hand to mouth, and I'm asking your permission. (*CP*, 363)

Her personal and social motivations are harmonious: she needs a rest, and the world needs Vandergelder's money in circulation. This is a compromise, even with her own sense of right and wrong. But self-interest and the social good here correspond.

And short of the Second Coming, life is a compromise, especially within a competitive economic system:

> Money! Money!—It's like the sun we walk under; it can kill or cure.—Mr. Vandergelder's money! Vandergelder's never tired of saying most of the people in the world are fools, and in a way he's right, isn't he? Himself, Irene, Cornelius, myself? But there comes a moment in everybody's life when he must decide whether he'll live among human beings or not—a fool among fools or a fool alone. (*CP*, 363)

Vandergelder's failings are pride and greed on the one hand, and lack of charity, in every sense, on the other. Living in isolation is one thing; forcing others to live in isolation because of an unwillingness to share one's wealth is another.

As Dolly elaborates, the world is always in peril from men such as Vandergelder, the rugged capitalist who makes his own fortune and is indifferent to the community of which he is a part:

> Yes, we're all fools and we're all in danger of destroying the world with our folly. But the surest way to keep us out of harm is to give us the four or five human pleasures that are our right in the world,— and that takes a little *money!*
>
> The difference between a little money and no money at all is enormous—and can shatter the world. And the difference between a little money and an enormous amount of money is very slight— and that, also, can shatter the world.
>
> Money, I've always felt, money—pardon my expression—is like manure; it's not worth a thing unless it's spread about encouraging young things to grow. (*CP*, 363–64)

Wilder is no radical. Money is not the root of all evil, but can in fact act as a fertilizer. Nor is the opinion that huge concentrations of wealth can threaten the world a radical position: Thomas Jefferson would have agreed.

And the choice of genre is fundamentally optimistic. In farce, Vandergelder can be brought to make Cornelius his partner, allow Ermengarde to marry, and even make himself happier than he deserves to be by marrying Dolly, who will make both him and everyone around him happy. The comic vision of *The Matchmaker* suggests that the world must be fought for; and while the fight may not be won, humanity is not defeated so long as the struggle continues to be guided by love. *Heaven's My Destination* (1935) affirms much the same theme but with a more open exposition of the spiritual malaise that underlay the country during the Great Depression.

In a letter to his niece Dixie on August 22, 1969, Wilder writes about his second lecture tour during the Depression: "what I saw 'fed' my *Heaven's My Dest.* which is in every paragraph a 'depression' novel. Then Bob Hutchins invited me—fall of 31—to teach in Chicago . . . overpaid me, I'm ashamed to say. Woeful stories of my students poverty, malnutrition, etc."[31] More than in any of his works until *The Eighth Day* more than thirty years later, Wilder accepts the conventions of the realist novel in *Heaven's My Destination* and portrays in vivid detail the financial crisis and its consequences for families at the time. For example, when George Brush, the novel's protagonist, attempts to pull his savings out of a bank because, for him, savings show fear and hence a lack of faith in God, he also refuses the interest accrued because he does not believe that "money has the right to earn money" (*Heaven's,* 12). The bank manager, Southwick, explains that George's money has made the bank profits, even though the manager knows that his bank is doomed to fail. In other words, Southwick defends the status quo right up to the moment of disaster. Unable to visualize a different order, he remains trapped by inertia.

Dick Roberts, whom George follows when he may or may not be about to commit suicide, also internalizes the economic crisis. His wife tells George, "He's real proud. He thinks so much of having a nice home in a good neighborhood. He's real proud. Sometimes it seems like he thinks the depression's his own fault. You know, he'd kill himself for the insurance" (*Heaven's,* 36). The problem here is systemic. Roberts has a loving wife and children, yet his big house is his pride; he cannot see that his faulty valuation of what matters is a central part of his problem. Yet another despairing character, Helma Solario, sardonically predicts future disasters. As she tells George when he has temporarily lost track of Roberts, "All right, Michigan, when you find this guy tell him life's a big thrill. See? Tell him to stick around; we're going to have some more world wars. He'll love it. Tell him from me the depression's only begun. Next year's going to make this year look sky high" (*Heaven's,* 58). Like Southwick and Roberts, Helma regards this as an inevitable result. Her only response is adultery and alcohol.

My point here is that the depression of *Heaven's My Destination* is related to the economic catastrophe sweeping the country, but not restricted to it. In his *Spiritual Aspects of the New Poetry,* in a chapter entitled "A World Without Roots," Amos Wilder argues that the "negation and decadence" of modern poetry, fiction, and drama are an accurate reflection of "the breaking down in modern society of what may be called the basic organic unities necessary to men's full health and sanity and to a true culture." No one cause can be assigned to the pernicious effects of this cultural fracture, but the evidence of the wreckage is threefold: "These unities are (1) that which binds man to the soil, to the life-giving breast of mother earth; (2) that which binds men to their clan or tribe or nation—that warm and close sense of belonging to a social group that sustains the individual with a sense of general security; and (3) that which binds the sexes in their normal fulfillment in the family."[32] In Thornton's novel, although George's job takes him through agricultural country, his life as a traveling salesman is spent in hotels and roominghouses, and the people he meets are primarily, in one way or another, out of touch with the earth, their social group, and their families.

The most drastic examples of this alienation are George's "friends," who live in Queenie's decaying roominghouse in Kansas City and who tolerate him because of his magnificent singing voice. Meanwhile, they live in squalor (and will not allow their rooms to be cleaned), get drunk, and visit prostitutes when they can afford it. Confronted with George's purity, they trick him into getting drunk and take him to dinner at a brothel without telling him what sort of place it is. Their ultimate wrath is inspired when George refuses to see himself as the victim of a joke: "You fellows pretend you don't know what it's all about, but you know. You're just pretending. You spend your whole life pretending it's not serious. . . . I wish I was talking to them [the prostitutes] now. . . . I'm glad I went, I thank you very much" (*Heaven's*, 86). His assertion of value accuses their nihilism and despair. And the proof that he is right—they do know that life is serious and they are wasting it—is that they beat him so savagely, he ends up in the hospital.

Herb, the "friend" who begins the savage attack on George, exemplifies the rootlessness and cynicism of modern society. Although married with a child, he "lived at Queenie's, and she lived with some friends of hers. We hadn't quarreled or anything . . . we weren't separated . . . it was just that way, and that's all. I didn't see the point of living in the same house with her" (*Heaven's*, 113). His marriage is entirely one of convenience—his own. His wife eventually leaves him, and he pays someone else to care for the child. Dying, he asks George to take his savings and look after the child and his own mother, but he insists that he does not care: "It's not even a favor I'm asking you; it's just a proposition. I'm not going to thank you, either. It's just one of those things; take it or leave it" (*Heaven's*, 113). Obviously, Herb still has some sense of parental and filial obligation, and some sense that he and George are or were members of a social group (the barbershop quartet), but he must insist, right up to the time of his death, that he does not have any connections whatsoever: "They can all go to hell, for all I care. I'm glad I'm clearing out." And George, confronted with Herb's determination to appear disinterested in his own family, essentially a negation of piety, can only mourn: "Something's the matter with the world, through and through" (*Heaven's*, 115). Mrs. McCoy, earlier in the novel, also suggests that George live in the moment. There is no purpose in reflection: "I mean, look around you. We'll be dead soon. Thinking doesn't change anything. It only makes you twice as blue" (*Heaven's*, 28). If one is sufficiently indifferent to life, one cannot work up the energy to be depressed.

The recurrent assessment of George in the novel is that he is crazy. Wilder writes in a letter in December 1966 that he is "Da Heilige Narr cum Don Quixote"—the Holy Fool.[33] Louie, an orderly in a hospital and another of the "friends" who beats up George, tells George on his sickbed, "Get to be one of the fellas. Learn to drink, like anybody else. And leave other people's lives alone. Live and let live. Everybody likes to be let alone. And run around with women. You're healthy, aintya? Enjoy life, see? You're going to be dead a long time, *believe* me" (*Heaven's*, 89). At first, this looks like an appeal to George to develop tolerance. But, for Louie, running around with women means visiting prostitutes and drinking means getting drunk. Far from being a statement of classical Epicureanism (which always lays stress on restraint and moderation), this, too, is a claim that nothing matters because there is only death at the end. This is alien to the Christian sensibility. As Paul admonished the Romans, "It follows, my friends, that our old nature has no claim on us; we are not obliged to live in that way. If you do so, you must die. But if by the spirit you put to death the base pursuits of the body, then you will live" (Romans 8:12–13). George responds to Louie, "It's the world that's crazy. Everybody's crazy except me; that's what's the matter. The whole world's nuts" (*Heaven's,* 89). George stands as a challenge to those who think that life, indeed, history, is a meaningless succession of events. As such he is holy.[34] After visiting the dying Herb and contemplating what life would be like for himself if he lost his faith, he says, "The world isn't worth living for its own sake" (*Heaven's,* 116). Or, to put it in the terms of the Russian Orthodox existentialist Nicolai Berdyaev in *The Meaning of History* (1936), it is not possible to have a philosophy of history unless one thinks that tangible reality and the sequence of events in one's life take their meaning from a higher reality: "Thus the real philosophy of history is that of the triumph of authentic life over death; it is the communion of man with another everlastingly broader and richer reality than that in which he is empirically immersed."[35] In the purely material modern world of 1930s America, Louie, Herb, Mrs. McCoy, and the other characters in the novel cannot escape depression because their lives, without purpose or community, are death in life.

Initial reviews of the novel had significant problems with George. John Chamberlain, writing in the *New York Times,* claims that Wilder's attitude toward George is "ambiguous": "One gathers that Wilder likes George Brush, and would like to approve of him. Yet the palpable idiocies which Brush believes cannot be part of Wilder's own mental equipment."[36] The author himself writes to William Frazier on July 5, 1935, that George's "instinctive goodness and his instinctive view of what is essential in living is far superior to the groups among which he moves. But I hold that he has been badly educated—badly educated even in religion. The fundamentalist tradition in American Protestantism has made into fixed hard unimaginative laws the substance of the Gospel" (*SL,* 296).

In the early pages of the novel, George seems perfectly happy. When a fellow hotel guest criticizes him in the first chapter for writing biblical texts on the blotter at the public writing desk, George tells him, "Mr. Blodgett, I've found a good thing and I want to tell every-body about it" (*Heaven's,* 7). Other than in his peripatetic lifestyle, he also does not seem much like a picaresque hero: neither a con man nor a thief, he is exceptionally good at his job and embarrassed by the raises he keeps receiving. In most towns he visits, he volunteers to sing for the church and is so good at it that he is offered a contract to sing for the radio in Chicago. And although he is sensitive, it is not the sensitivity of an intellectual. Told that *King Lear* is the greatest work in English literature, he attempts to memorize it in small sections every morning while he is shaving, even though "Brush had read the play ten times without discovering a trace of talent in it" (*Heaven's,* 71). Physically, he is an imposing figure, more manly than Michael Gold. When a passenger in the smoking car on the train throws George's briefcase out the window because George approaches him about sal-vation, George smiles stiffly and says, "Brother . . . it's lucky for you I'm a pacifist. I could knock you against the roof of this car. I could swing you around here by one leg. Brother, I'm the strongest man that was ever tested in our gym back home" (*Heaven's,* 11).[37]

However, George Brush is a lost soul, and a part of him knows it. Even his parents are alienated from him. He tells an orphan girl, Jes-sie, whom he meets in a summer camp, "you know, I feel like an or-phan, too, almost. I love'm, of course, but always there is a kind of wall between them and me. You see, they didn't want me to go to col-lege" (*Heaven's,* 48). And Shiloh Baptist College ("a very good school," he tells people at every opportunity) was itself a shattering experience. One of his most admired professors, his teacher in Religion 6A, "got really mad" at him:

> "You've got a closed mind, Brush, an obstinate closed mind. It's not worth wasting time on you," he said. "I wash my hands of you," he said; "*you'll never get anywhere!*" Imagine someone saying that! "Now get away," he said. "Get away from me. Don't trouble me any more." You know that was awful to me. Sometimes it comes back to me still, like it was the moment he said it, and the sweat—I mean the perspiration—comes out on my forehead. I don't want to live if I've got a closed mind and can't get anywhere—anywhere in *think-ing,* I mean. (*Heaven's,* 49–50)

And George has begun to absorb some of the despair that surrounds him: "I live traveling around on trains all the time and I meet a lot of people, but almost everybody I meet depresses me terribly. Why, just this afternoon and evening in this camp I've met the most depressing people and it was beginning to have a bad effect on me" (*Heaven's*, 47). A salesman, he has lost his connection to the land and to the seasonal cycle of his parent's farm. His friends are not really his friends. On poor terms with his parents and unable to find the farm girl whom he regards as his wife, he has no family: "And maybe that means I can't settle down and found an American Home. Sometimes I think I may get so discouraged that I may fall sick—or worse. Because that's all sickness is—discouragement. That's one of my theories, too. I have a theory that all sickness comes from having lost hope about something" (*Heaven's*, 27).[38] All George has is his religious faith, and that is inadequate: he is horrified when he discovers that the nice orphan girl is studying biology at Oberlin and believes in evolution.

But while George suffers from alienation in Depression-era America, he is nevertheless striving toward sainthood, although he is in the early stages. He is not, as it happens, narrowminded, despite the accusation by his college professor. While he is appalled at the idea of evolution, he has no problem with the geologic conception of time; he explains the Ice Age and the formation of the Midwest to a disbelieving Lottie, who patently does not believe him when he says it occurred 800,000 years ago (*Heaven's*, 167). Wilder also incorporates in the character ideas from Nietzsche. In a letter to Glenway Westcott, Wilder mentions one of Nietzsche's theses about Christianity: "Nietzsche said Jesus was unkind and unfeeling—imagine that in the theological seminaries—in the Sermon on the Mount. If you offer the other cheek to the person who has smitten you, you 'humiliate' in his humanity [*sic*]—you should slap him slightly."[39] Thus, George explains to Burkin why he slaps the thief Hawkins: "If you do pure good to a man that's harmed you, that shames him too much. No man is so bad that you ought to shame him that way" (*Heaven's*, 154). Even if only in pamphlet form, George reads about the ideas of Tolstoy and Gandhi in an attempt to make sense out of the world. George is a fool, but he is a conscientious one.

In some ways, George is already saintly. When he pulls his money from the bank (causing the bank run), he tells Southwick, the manager, that he must do so because it conflicts with his vow of voluntary poverty: "When my paycheck comes every month . . . I immediately give away all money that's left over from the month before, but I always knew that at bottom that wasn't honest. Honest, with myself, I mean, because all this time I had five hundred dollars hidden away in this bank here" (*Heaven's,* 13). But prudence of the sort that keeps money in reserve is not a virtue, because Jesus has said, "So do not be anxious about tomorrow; tomorrow will look after itself" (Matthew 6:34). Moreover, although he probably does not know it, George is acting with saintly precedent. Thus, Ignatius of Loyola is troubled by the same problem:

> He had six or seven ducats which they had given him for the passage from Venice to Jerusalem; he had accepted them, being somewhat overcome by fears they had aroused that he would not be able to go in any other way. But two days after leaving Rome he began to realize that this was a lack of faith on his part, and it bothered him a good deal that he had accepted the ducats, so he decided it would be good to get rid of them. He finally decided to give them freely to those whom he encountered, who usually were poor. He did so, and when he arrived at Venice, he had no more than a few *quattrini* which he needed that night.[40]

Faith means that if you truly trust in God, there is, as George tells the bank manager, "no worst coming to worst for a good man" (*Heaven's,* 14). But it takes courage to act on one's faith. Perhaps not incidentally, both Saint Ignatius and George are locked up by the authorities. And in the America of the Great Depression, refusing to save money against the morrow can only be either a saintly act of faith or utter folly.

Besides calling George a Holy Fool, Wilder paired him with Don Quixote, as noted earlier. Wilder regarded Cervantes as one of the five greatest writers who ever lived.[41] In his lecture notes, Wilder describes the spirit of *Don Quixote:* "It is the insult [to] reason on the grounds that there is A HIGHER STANDARD required of MAN than a reasonably framed CODE. The CODE of MANKIND should not be based on Reason and Good JUDGEMENT: It should be based on VIRTUE and LOVE and virtue and love are not fundamentally by REASON."[42] Anyone who believes this will look mentally deranged to the rest of the world. Some episodes in *Heaven's My Destination* even allude to specific episodes in *Don Quixote*. Quixote releases prisoners condemned to be galley slaves in chapter 22 of Part One. However, they all richly deserve this punishment, and they stone him as soon as they get the chance. Subsequently a priest tells Quixote of the crimes the prisoners have committed and says of the rescuer, whom he knows to be Quixote, "there can be no doubt that he was out of his mind, or as great a villain as they." But Quixote is unabashed in his explanation to his squire, Sancho Panza, who had chimed in on the side of the priest:

> "Imbecile," said Don Quixote, "it is not the responsibility or concern of a knight errant to determine if the afflicted, the fettered, and the oppressed whom he meets along the road are in that condition and suffering that anguish because of misdeeds or kind acts. His only obligation is to help them because they are in need, turning his eyes to their suffering and not their wickedness."[43]

On a pragmatic level the priest is correct: the fact that the rescued prisoners have gone on to commit more crimes shows that Quixote acted irresponsibly and imprudently. But Quixote's response shows that the priest's judgment is morally and spiritually inferior, in that helping those who are suffering is the right thing to do whatever the consequences. This is the greatness of the novel; Quixote's idealism transcends his folly, and the reader longs for a world where he would be right.

In George's case he steers a thief to money hidden by an old woman, gives the thief some of his own, and lets him go free. When George attempts to explain himself and tells her that he will fully repay her, the old woman both pities George and doubts his reason:

> "Mrs. Efrim, don't be mad at me. I had to act that way to live up to my ideals."

"You're crazy."

"No, I'm not."

"You are. You're crazy. Whoever heard of anybody going out of their way to give money to a burglar. Yes, and letting him go free, too. No, I won't take your money. Look at all that's been took from you already. Now go away before the police come and arrest you." (*Heaven's,* 128)

George and Quixote risk everything to exemplify a life of virtue and love. Miguel de Unamuno called Don Quixote the only possible model for modern man, and the same quality that he attributes to the knight also applies to George: "The greatest height of heroism to which an individual, like a people, can attain is to know how to face ridicule; better still, to know how to make oneself ridiculous and not to shrink from the ridicule."[44]

Don Quixote and George are protected by human decency when they least expect it. Pedro Alonso, a farmer, carries the beaten knight on his donkey, and when they reach his village, he waits until it is dark "so that no one would see what a poor knight the beaten gentleman was."[45] In *Heaven's My Destination,* Judge Carberry arranges a just outcome for George's trial (in spite of the law) and tells him gently as he sets him free, "Go slow; go slow. See what I mean? I don't like to think of you getting into any unnecessary trouble. . . . The human race is pretty stupid, . . . Doesn't do any good to insult'm. Go gradual. See what I mean?" (*Heaven's,* 151).

I discussed in the introduction Burkin's attack on religious belief by way of anthropology and psychology. George's response is fundamentally Quixotic: "All you've done is *think* about it as though it were . . . as though it were a *fish* a long ways off. Even your doubts aren't the right doubts to have" (*Heaven's,* 164). Again, Unamuno's views are relevant. The Spanish existentialist sees reason itself, at least as practiced in the modern age, as tending toward death:

A terrible thing is intelligence. It tends to death as memory tends to stability. The living, the absolutely unstable, the absolutely individual, is, strictly, unintelligible. . . . Identity, which is death, is the goal of the intellect. The mind seeks what is dead, for what is living escapes it; it seeks to congeal the flowing stream in blocks of ice; it seeks to arrest it. In order to analyze a body it is necessary to extenuate or destroy it. In order to understand anything it is necessary to kill it, to lay it out rigid in the mind. Science is a cemetery of dead ideas, even though life may issue from them. Worms also feed upon corpses.[46]

The analytical must freeze what it considers and thus kills it. That is, when we analyze speech or love, for instance, we abstract from its living existence a skeleton whose structure we can diagram. We look at causes, effects, and model the relation between the two, trying to eliminate what is inessential. The diagram, however, is not speech or love, both of which can only be experienced as contingent events in time and space. Speech and love are events in existence: they do not have an essence, at least as humans experience them. Equally religion is something we live, not an object to be looked at, like a dead fish.

Kierkegaard has asserted in his diary that "it is not the reasons that motivate belief in the Son of God, but the other way round, belief in the Son of God constitutes the evidence." Reasons belong to a lower realm of consciousness, whereas it is "choice" that constitutes the true evidence of belief: "one can only defend one's conviction ethically, personally, that is, through the sacrifices one is willing to make for it and by the dauntlessness with which one maintains it."[47] Through living one finds conviction, where abstract, objective reason provides no reason for anything at all.

And Wilder's George seeks to live, to found an American family, to connect. When he does find Roberta, the farmer's daughter whom he impregnated, he does marry her. She agrees only so that her father will forgive her, and the marriage fails. One cannot become a complete human being by being the punch line of a traveling salesman-and-the-farmer's-daughter joke.[48] The problem for George is not that he is a Puritan, but that he is only a Puritan, which has limited his ability to see the world accurately and consequently to reform it. Amos Wilder explains that while we like Don Quixote and George, we are also frustrated by their limits:

Our sympathies, indeed are with Don Quixote as against his mock-
ers, and in this case with George Brush as against the crass Babbitry
of his mission field in Main Street. But one wishes that all this har-
diness could be sagaciously applied. It is not that we underestimate
the effectiveness of dreams or the power of martyrdom, but we note
that such things count only when there is a real nexus between
dreams and reality, and a real collision between faith and fact.[49]

Again, it is apparent that in Amos Wilder's conception of Christian
witness, one must engage the world; until a person can do that, can
see the world as it is, then the dreams of improvement are incomplete.
George must grow in vision. Ill and dying in a hospital, George recov-
ers only when he receives a spoon belonging to the recently dead Father Pasziewski, a character whom we never meet but who also struggles with his faith. Hermann Stresau is on the right track with his
description of the conclusion of the novel, although he misses the
comic tone: "The novel ends in a pessimism that now seems hopeless—
unless the existence of the fool in Christ proves to be indispensable
to human society, which, alongside or beyond or in the midst of its
worldly needs, also has its spiritual needs."[50] Pessimism may be appropriate since neither the world nor George seems any more equipped
to deal with the depression of modern life, and yet George is essential
to modern life—the man who insists on meaning and purpose and
without whom the universe becomes empty.

The novel does suggest a synthesis that will allow George to grow
toward wisdom. Among his weaknesses is the tendency of his ideals
not only to exclude pleasures such as alcohol and tobacco but also to
bar him from that fuller life of the mind that he seeks, and which in
the novel is embodied in a woman. The orphan Jessie who attends
Oberlin and studies biology, the "gray-eyed girl who immediately
makes a great impression on him" (*Heaven's,* 43), has agreed to write
to him. Gray eyes are, of course, a traditional attribute of Athena, the
goddess of wisdom.[51] And, at the end of the novel, George has grown
enough to move beyond his dogmatic rejection of evolution and to
arrange for college for a waitress whom he finds reading Darwin's *The
Voyage of the Beagle.*[52] The question is left open: Will George eventually reconnect with Jessie? While she has the attributes of Athena, her

name also indicates a Jewish-Christian promise: "Then a branch will grow from the stock of Jesse, / And a shoot will spring from his roots. / On him the spirit of the LORD will rest: / a spirit of wisdom and understanding, / a spirit of counsel and power, / a spirit of knowledge and fear of the LORD; / and in the fear of the LORD will be his delight" (Isaiah 11:1–2). The classical and the Puritan, the spirit of wisdom and the fear of the Lord, must find a synthesis in George for him to transform the world in which he lives. But he never settles all his doubts, nor does he find a place where he can put down roots. This is not a catastrophe; he is, after all, only twenty-four at the end of the novel. But as an American *picaro* he deserves a place in our literature next to Saul Bellow's Augie March, another restless seeker after some better life, another avatar of the American Adam.

Whether deliberately or not, Wilder had responded to Gold in *Heaven's My Destination,* and not just by writing a novel set in contemporary America. Gold had also accused him of having the "smug" style of the "lesser latins." In *Heaven's My Destination,* Wilder tells a tale that is as valid as any urban, industrial story, one of a pilgrim's progress throughout the southern reaches of the Midwest. George's peregrinations are marked in this catalogue:

> On being discharged from the hospital Brush set out again on that long swing of the pendulum between Kansas City and Abilene, Texas, that was his work. At Abilene he waited his turn in the halls of Simmons University, McMurray College, and Abilene Christian College. He visited Austin College at Sherman, Baylor College at Belton, and Baylor University at Waco. He visited Daniel Baker College and Howard Payne College at Brownwood; he visited the Texas Teacher's College at Denton, Rice Institute at Houston, Southwestern University at Georgetown, and Trinity University at Waxahachie. He looked in at Delhart and Amarillo. He went down to San Antonio to see Our Lady of the Lake and to Austin to place an algebra at St. Edward's University. Returning through Oklahoma, he visited the state university at Norman, the Baptist University at Shawnee, the college at Chickasha, the Agricultural and Mechanical College at Stillwater. He digressed in Louisiana and called at Pine-

ville and Ruston; He spent a solitary Christmas in Baton Rouge. Arkansas tempted him to Arkadelphia and Clarksville and Onachita. (*Heaven's*, 90–91)

This is positively Whitmanesque, an inclusive statement of America. It includes secular, Protestant, and Catholic schools, and conjures up a vision of a country still educating itself about its place in the cosmos. And George is a part of that ongoing process, selling the textbooks that will help Americans transform themselves. William James describes the quandary of the saint in the world, and in doing so he might well be talking about George: "The world is not yet with them, so they often seem in the midst of the world's affairs to be preposterous. Yet they are impregnators of the world, vivifiers and animaters of potentialities of goodness which but for them would be forever dormant."[53] George is a model of evolving goodness, but one rooted in the social realities of his time, as is Dolly Levi and the characters of some of the one-act plays from 1931; and the works in which they appear are close to the conventions of realist drama and theater. In the other one-acts as well as in *Our Town* and sections of *The Skin of Our Teeth*, Wilder seeks to describe the virtues of piety and to find the universal in the American experience.

Chapter Three

Piety, the Individual, and the Community

I have argued in the introduction that the religious elements in Wilder's works must be understood in the context of an artistic and intellectual community that at least in part regarded religion as a dead issue. In the first chapter I suggested that Wilder's first three novels examine religious systems under stress at times of transitions between historical epochs. In the second chapter I attempted to document Wilder's concerns with contemporary American culture and his critique of its culture, social, material, and spiritual failings. In this chapter I shall sketch out Wilder's portrait of American malaise in "The Long Christmas Dinner" and "Pullman Car Hiawatha" and the alternative of piety that he presents in "The Happy Journey to Trenton and Camden" and *Our Town*. The dramatic experimentation of these works is a function of the modern temper, in that for the twentieth-century individual to see his world through art, he must eschew traditional presentations.

In a thoughtful article from 1939, Dayton Kohler says about *Our Town* that Wilder "attaches an almost mystical significance to the ritual of daily living, believing that man's common habits of action and belief represent the long line of tradition in civilized life." While I disagree with much in Kohler's article, including his view that Wilder is indifferent to the issues of contemporary American life and as a humanist is concerned only with timeless human values, I do think that his perception that Wilder addresses "natural pieties" that give "dignity and purpose to man's world" is essential to understanding the masterpieces of the one-act plays of 1931 and *Our Town*.[1] Wilder seeks to find a way to present the common actions of daily life, from cooking and stringing beans to marriage and childbirth, so that the audience can see them anew and, in doing so, value them as they ought.

This new vision and reevaluation are necessary because Americans had lost their way. The deracinated George Brush of *Heaven's My Destination* (1935) and the comically manipulative Dolly Levi of *The Merchant of Yonkers* (1938) and *The Matchmaker* represent more than just an economically troubled nation dropping "natural tears"; they embody the American Adam and Eve for whom, in Milton's "Paradise Lost," "The World was all before them, where to choose / Thir place of rest, and Providence thir guide" (Book XII). Amos Wilder, drawing on the work of R. W. B. Lewis, would later argue that the American Adam was central to modern American literature, and he cites as an important example Robert Penn Warren's *Brother to Dragons:*

> Here a drastic revision of the American Dream is suggested. For in the person of Thomas Jefferson, the excessive confidence of the Founding Fathers in the goodness of man and in democratic institutions meets with a stunning shock. In American literature today as inspired by the modern crisis, the greatest interest attaches to how this shock is met by a disabused and fallen Adam.[2]

Warren's poem is about the savage murder of a slave by a nephew of Thomas Jefferson; Jefferson himself despairingly considers whether human nature can ever be worthy of democratic ideals. Wilder's vision of American life, however, is never that bleak. In the comic works such as *Heaven's My Destination* or *The Matchmaker,* the plot suggests a malleable universe where happy outcomes are still possible. Shocked and fallen they may be, but George and Dolly can at least continue to struggle with an America that does not live up to their expectations. They are the battered but undefeated Adam and Eve.

But the limited time that people have to find their place in the world, the contingency of existence, are the themes of the more experimental plays. The larger issue in American literature, according to Amos Wilder in his reading of Lewis, is of "an Adam who is painfully initiated into the meaning of good and evil, and who has to come to terms not only with nature but with history, not only with space but with time."[3] In "Pullman Car Hiawatha" and "The Long Christmas Dinner," characters wander from home and may not find their way back. Adam has been expelled from Paradise and has nothing to take its place. Moreover, these characters, as well as those in *Our Town*, live as if they had all the time in the world and consequently have less of it than if they were aware of its passing. In a sense, Thornton Wilder in these plays is stressing that one must live always with a sense of death to experience life properly.

"The Long Christmas Dinner" begins while the Bayards' house and the nation are still new. "My dear Lucia, I can remember when there were still Indians on this very ground, and I wasn't a young girl either. I can remember when we had to cross the Mississippi on a new-made raft. I can remember when St. Louis and Kansas City were full of Indians," Mother Bayard recalls (*CP,* 62). But memories lapse. A couple of minutes of stage time and several decades later, Lucia repeats the story to her children, Charles and Genevieve, who regard this account with disbelief: "She couldn't have, Mother. That can't be true" (*CP,* 68). Lucia assures them that it is, but for the Bayards the past exists only in the rituals of the Christmas dinner, such as comments on the sermon and the neighbors' illnesses and the toast, "a glass of wine with you, sir." In very little stage time, Roderick has trouble remembering how old the house is, and Mother Bayard tells him, "Five years. It's five years, children. You should keep a diary" (*CP,* 63). But no one does anything of the sort. A recurring response to any question about the past is, "It's all down in a book somewhere upstairs" (*CP,* 62), but no such book exists. As Genevieve becomes an old maid, she assumes the role of keeper of the family's history. Charles, unconscious of previous iterations, repeats the line about the book upstairs, and Genevieve tells him sharply, "Nonsense. There are no such books. I collect my notes off gravestones, and you have to scrape a good deal of moss—let me tell you—to find one great-grandparent" (*CP,* 73). Under the moss the stone will eventually crumble, even if anyone remains to scrape off the moss. "Time certainly goes very fast in a great new country like this," observes Charles, while proffering the cranberry sauce, unaware of the full weight of his statement.

This sublime indifference to the passage of time is not entirely negative. An observation about the beauty of the winter recurs: "It's glorious. Every least twig is wrapped around with ice. You almost never see that" (*CP,* 67). Of course, each generation sees that, but it remains beautiful because each generation reacts as if the world were new. When a son is born, fathers across generations warn the nurse, "Don't drop him, Nurse. Brandon and I need him in the firm" (*CP,* 65). This hope is fulfilled in one generation and disappointed in another, but each generation makes this demand on time because they have forgotten the possibility of disappointment. As an early reviewer, Robert P. Tristram Coffin, pointed out, "It is as if one had accelerated a motion picture, and saw all the more clearly how flowers come up, unfold, blossom, and wither in an exquisite rhythm. This modern thing is as right as the four seasons that pass in a moment in 'Gawain and the Green Knight.'"[4] Equally, in "The Long Christmas Dinner," the demands on time made by grief, as when a baby dies, can only be endured because we know it will diminish: "Only time, only the passing of time can help in these things" (*CP,* 69). The Major who suffers from sciatica "says it'll all be the same in a hundred years" (*CP,* 64), which makes him, as another character says, "a great philosopher."

But stoic indifference to mutability does not eliminate any particular grief, nor should it. When her mother Lucia dies, Genevieve, in a line that anticipates *Our Town,* mourns that "I never told her how wonderful she was. We all treated her as though she were just a friend in the house. I'd thought she'd be here forever" (*CP,* 71). And callousness toward future loss is stunningly illustrated in one of American drama's finest *coups de théâtre:* Charles says complacently, "Perhaps an occasional war isn't so bad after all. It clears up a lot of poisons that collect in nations. It's like a boil" (*CP,* 73). Seconds later, his son Sam enters, wearing his uniform, chats very briefly, and walks through the portal indicating death. Whenever I have seen the play, there has been an audible gasp somewhere in the audience while Charles and Lucia sit at the table with lowered eyes. Charles's casual acceptance of war is related to an unconscious certainty that war cannot touch him. The death of his son shows that he is mistaken.

The play's dramatization of an American family over ninety years illustrates the lost Eden of Americans who refuse to settle down and plant roots. The house and town, once so new, become a burden, especially as the family gains position and respectability. In the third generation, Roderick becomes a rebel: "Great God, you gotta get drunk in this town to forget how dull it is. Time passes so slowly here that it stands still, that's what's the trouble" (*CP,* 75). For restless American youth, reverence for their home and family is impossible. Impiously, Roderick tells his father, "I have better things to do than to go into your old factory. I'm going somewhere where time passes, my God!" (*CP,* 75–76). His departure begins the general exodus: Charles and Genevieve die, Roderick's sister Lucia marries and moves away, Leonora leaves to be near her daughter, and the play's last moments are of the unmarried cousin Ermengarde alone in the house until her death. By the third generation the family has started over again from scratch, and an empty house surrounded by factories is all that remains of their attempt to build a lasting presence.

For the first generation the house is something to celebrate. Fifty years later the family is rich, and the new wife Leonora calls it "so ugly"; Genevieve, again trying to maintain a link to the past, pleads with her brother not to alter the house, but he insists that they must "remove the cupola and build a new wing towards the tennis courts" (*CP,* 72). On the one hand, this indicates that the family and its dwelling are alive and changing. On the other, it suggests an indifference to the architectural integrity of the house and a tendency to yield to fashion. When Genevieve surrenders to despair, the past is ultimately lost entirely:

> I can't stand it. I can't stand it any more. I'm going abroad. It's not only the soot that comes through the very walls of this house; it's the *thoughts,* it's the thought of what has been and what might have been here. And the feeling about this house of the years *grinding away.* My mother died yesterday—not twenty-five years ago. Oh, I'm going to live and die abroad! Yes, I'm going to be the American old maid living and dying in a pension in Munich or Florence. (*CP,* 77)

It is striking that Genevieve, the family historian, the character most aware of the passage of time, finds the past a burden rather than a source of comfort. She will attempt to escape time just as the rest of her family escapes place, and no one will remember the hopeful beginning of the house.

In an essay on Thoreau, initially given as a lecture while Thornton Wilder was Charles Eliot Norton Professor of Poetry at Harvard in 1950–1951, Wilder describes two types of American loneliness, the sentimental and the proud:

> Both proceed from the fact that the religious ideas current in America are still inadequate to explain the American to himself. The sentimental loneliness arises from the sense that he is a victim, that he was slighted when Fortune distributed her gifts (though it is notably prevalent among those who seem to "have everything"); the proud loneliness arises from the sense of boundlessness which we described as related to the American geography and is found among those who make boundless moral demands on themselves and others.[5]

If Roderick represents the sentimental loneliness, born to wealth and position and bored to death with both, then Genevieve represents the proud American loneliness. According to Wilder, the European receives support "from all those elements we call environment—place, tradition, customs: 'I am I because my neighbors know me.'"[6] This is a source of comfort and reassurance for the European.[7] It is not, however, for the American, who frequently lacks a settled place, enduring traditions, and long-standing customs. Genevieve cannot maintain a historical and geographical continuity despite her best efforts and dies alone far from home, while the house she sought to save is empty, and no historical record exists of the efforts of her family.

In "Pullman Car Hiawatha," only the dead and mad can actually see the world. The mad woman tells the angels: "everyone is so childish, so absurd. They have no logic. The people are all so mad. . . . These people are like children; they have never suffered" (*CP,* 105). Her madness, an altered vision caused by some undisclosed suffering, allows her more clarity than the other characters. She alone can see the Stage Manager, and only she and the dead Harriet can see the angels. Cryptically, knowledge is not enough. When she asks for something to do, the angels suggest that it is not her time. She accepts the providential order ("Well, you know best"), but her presence in the play emphasizes the blindness of the other characters.

Other characters are more or less lost. This can be represented by as little as a desensitization to the world. Thus, the doctor in Lower Three berth "*reads aloud to himself from a medical journal the most hair-raising material, every now and then punctuating his reading with an interrogative 'So?'*" (*CP,* 95). This is not a moral failing, per se. When he is summoned to the dying Harriet, he goes without hesitation. But his knowledge inures him to the effect of suffering on the body: it is simply a phenomenon stripped of human consequences. Other characters are types of the lost and confused Americans so common in Wilder's works in the 1930s. Lower Nine anguishes over his errors:

> That was the craziest thing I ever did. It's set me back three whole years. I could have saved up thirty thousand dollars by now, if I'd only stayed over here. What business had I got to fool with contracts with the goddam Soviets. Hell, I thought it would be interesting. Interesting, what-the-hell! It's set me back three whole years. I don't even know if the company will take me back. I'm green, that's all. I just don't grow up. (*CP,* 96)

The financial loss is serious (the play appears in 1931, after all); and while he contemplates that loss, he is oblivious to the world as it passes. Rootless and aimless, his experience of his own life is essentially limited. His friend in Lower Seven struggles to determine his relationship with a woman, Lillian: "Lillian, if you don't turn out to be what I think you are, I don't know what I'll do.—I guess it's bad politics to let a woman know that you're going all the way to California to see her. I'll think up a song-and-dance about a business trip or something" (*CP,* 95). He understands love as politics, and as such he seeks advantage through tactical ploys. He remains unaware that his own inability to be honest requires that Lillian also conceal her feelings.

Travelling on a railcar through the night—an obvious metaphor
for a journey through life cut off from home—all of the characters in
the berths are, in one way or another, cocooned from reality. The
dead Harriet sees at the end how she has wasted her existence, even as
she is summoned from the world by the angels: "I haven't done anything. I haven't done anything with my life. Worse than that: I was
angry and sullen. I never realized anything. I don't dare go a step in
such a place." She asks to suffer to redeem herself: "But no one else
could be punished for me. I'm willing to face it all myself. I don't ask
anyone to be punished for me" (*CP,* 105). This is American self-
reliance at its best and worst; she wants responsibility for her life, even
though it is now over. At the same time there, she is apparently unaware that Christ has already suffered to redeem her. She sees the
world only in the present and only determined by her actions. She
represents the loneliness of the American divorced from her spiritual
heritage. Convinced by the angels that she can join them, she says,
"I'm just a stupid and you know it. I'm just another American"
(*CP,* 106).

Life teems around the train's passengers. A field in Ohio catalogues its contents: "In this field there are 51 gophers, 206 field mice,
6 snakes and millions of bugs, insects, ants, and spiders. All in their
winter sleep" (*CP,* 100). History surrounds them as well. The ghost of
a German railway worker misquotes the Gettysburg Address, a mis-
quotation reiterated by the Stage Manager: "'Three score and seven
years ago our fathers brought forth upon this continent a new nation
dedicated' and so on" (*CP,* 101). Of course, the German workman's
father did not literally do anything of the sort, and, in any case, both
he and the Stage Manager have the historical address wrong. Historical accuracy, however, is irrelevant. What matters is that the German workman, by dying while working on the railroad, has become
a part of America; his recollection, repeated by the Stage Manager,
emblematizes the organic nature of culture; it is something that lives
in memory, inaccuracies and all, and is dynamic rather than static.

And above the Pullman car hangs a Platonic realm, reminiscent of
some of the plays in *The Angel That Troubled the Waters,* where "the
minutes are gossips; the hours are philosophers; the years are theolo-
gians. The hours are philosophers with the exception of Twelve

O'clock, who is also a theologian." The brief measurement of time is concerned with ephemera, the longer period with knowledge, and the longest period of all with final things. Ten O'clock, Plato, contemplates the aesthetic: "Are you not rather convinced that he who sees Beauty as only it can be seen will be specially favored?" Eleven O'clock, Epictetus, the Stoic philosopher, is concerned with ethics as determined by our role in the cosmos: "If then I were a nightingale, I would do the nightingale's part. If I were a swan, I would do a swan's. But now I am a rational creature. . . ." Happiness and virtue are dependent on seeing the right order of things and acting in accordance with that order; thus, to be happy, man must act as a rational creature, which is also to be virtuous. Twelve O'clock, Saint Augustine, talks with his mother: "And we began to say: If to any the tumult of the flesh were hushed. . . ." (*CP*, 102). On one level, this simply refers to the idea that we must transcend the sinful flesh to draw closer to God. But more, it reminds the audience that it was the faith of Augustine's mother that drew him to Christianity, away from lust for women and fame. The saint was not alone in his search for salvation. All of these philosophical and theological resources surround the train's passengers, who wait to be called on.

The trouble is that they are not called on. It is instructive to compare this with the Renaissance conception of the cosmic concord above the discord of human life. Lorenzo says to Jessica in Shakespeare's *The Merchant of Venice:*

> Look how the floor of heaven
> Is thick inlaid with patens of bright gold.
> There's not the smallest orb which thou behold'st
> But in his motion like an angel sings,
> Still quiring to the young-ey'd cherubims;
> Such harmony is in immortal souls,
> But whilst this muddy vesture of decay
> Doth grossly close it in, we cannot hear it. (5.1.58–65)

As part of the fallen world, Lorenzo and Jessica cannot hear the music of the spheres; but secure in his faith and love, Lorenzo nonetheless knows it is there, at least while in Belmont. But the Americans of

"Pullman Car Hiawatha" are much closer to the citizens of Venice, struggling with personal blindness. While the Hours pass in a kind of cosmic choir, the passengers on the railcar remain locked in solipsistic thought.

How can the playwright get the audience to see that they are not alone and not without a place in a purposive universe? This generates Wilder's brilliantly imaginative dramatic form.[8] The initial reviews of the collection *The Long Christmas Dinner* can perhaps best be summed up by Fred Eastman's complaint that except for the title play, they "are weak in such essential dramatic elements as character, emotion, conflict, choice, theme and climax"—in short, the elements of the conventional realistic drama of the period.[9] I have argued elsewhere that Wilder saw the realist theater as losing the possible in the probable; theatricality was necessary for an audience to see truths beyond the "truth of the unique occasion" embodied in the realist theater.[10] Wilder needs to shake the audience's categories of theatrical experience to allow them to see the individual as a part of a larger continuum, while at the same time retaining the value of the individual experience. The relationship between the individual and the cosmos is dynamic, but the isolated American sees only his or her frame of reference, one inadequate for a fuller existence.

In "Pullman Car Hiawatha," Harriet does come to see the cosmic in the specific as she leaves:

> Goodbye, 1312 Ridgewood Avenue, Oaksbury, Illinois. I hope I remember all its steps and doors and wallpapers forever. Goodbye, Emerson Grammar School, on the corner of Forbush Avenue and Wherry Street. Goodbye, Miss Walker and Miss Cramer who taught me English and Miss Matthewson who taught me biology. Goodbye, First Congregational Church on the corner of Meyerson Avenue and 6th Street and Dr. McReady and Mrs. McReady and Julia. Goodbye, Papa and Mama. (*CP,* 106)

Only in death can Harriet come to love specific places and people: her school, her church, her minister, her friend, and her parents. Finally, in loss she actually sees them in memory; this eschatological vision ties her entire experience together. In her final speech, "I see now. I see now. I understand everything now" (*CP,* 107).

In Dostoyevsky's *The Possessed* (1871–1872), Shatov turns on his liberal friends and denounces them for their cool disengagement from Russia and its people in favor of French ideas: "And a man who has no country has no God either. Rest assured that those who cease to understand the people of their own country and lose contact with them also lose the faith of their forefathers and become godless or indifferent."[11] A loss of piety, or loyalty to those things to which one should be loyal, such as one's country, people, and the god or gods of that place, leads, in Dostoyevsky's view, to nihilism.[12] But one need not accept Dostoyevsky's contempt for Western liberalism, capitalism, or Catholicism to see that he is making a compelling claim about modern malaise; the intellectual who has turned his back on his homeland loses more than just a sanctuary. George Santayana, after a lengthy discussion of the piety of Aeneas, argues that for man as a creature rooted in space and time, piety "resides, so to speak, at his centre of gravity": "It exercises there the eminently sane function of calling him home. It saves speculative and emotional life from hurtful extravagance by keeping it traditional and social." Patriotism is a form of piety, which, while not excluding a cosmopolitan acceptance of other cultures, helps "to give the will definition." And for Santayana, the man who lacks piety wanders aimlessly through a purposeless existence:

> But happiness and utility are possible nowhere to a man who represents nothing and who looks out on the world without a plot of his own to stand on, either on earth or in heaven. He wanders from place to place, a voluntary exile, always querulous, always uneasy, always alone. His very criticisms express no ideal. His experience is without sweetness, without cumulative fruits, and his children, if he has them, are without morality. For reason and happiness are like other flowers—they wither when plucked.[13]

Here, piety has a religious function, although it is in no way connected to the supernatural. The deracinated American is fundamentally out of sympathy with the world. The characters in "The Long

Christmas Dinner" and "Pullman Car Hiawatha" lack a local allegiance and therefore they cannot harmonize their aspirations with society and the natural order.

In "The Happy Journey to Trenton and Camden," piety is celebrated. Ma repeatedly asserts excellence in unlikely objects or people. Her husband Elmer is "just the best driver in the world" (*CP,* 130). Her mass-produced car is nevertheless "the best little Chevrolet in the world" (*CP,* 132). As for her place of origin, "I'm glad I was born in New Jersey. I've always said it was the best state in the Union" (*CP,* 137). Unconcerned about her limited frame of reference, she has, for instance, never been to Ohio. This happy assurance extends to people. To her children's annoyance, she announces loudly to the neighbors where they can find the key to the back door. At a gas station she asks the attendant about the YMCA where her husband and son will be staying. He turns out to be Catholic (apparent from his membership in the Knights of Columbus), but he played basketball there and "it looked all right to me" (*CP,* 137). Immediately a bond is established: "The world's full of nice people.—That's what I call a nice young man" (*CP,* 137). When Elmer informs their young son Arthur that there are a hundred and twenty-six million Americans, Ma squeezes Arthur's shoulder while she tells him, "And they all like to drive out in the evening with their children beside'm" (*CP,* 139). Of course, this is false, but for Ma, something like it ought to be true, and Ma will insist on the possibility in order that her children can have an ideal of the family in which to believe.

A director seeking evidence for an ironic production of the play will find ample material. When the family stops on the road to allow a funeral to pass, Ma remembers a family loss: "Well, we haven't forgotten the one [funeral] that we went on, have we? We haven't forgotten our good Harold. He gave his life for his country, we mustn't forget that" (*CP,* 133). By 1931 many people would have regarded this view of the First World War as naïve. And when she turns on her son shortly thereafter, the moment is clearly comic. Arthur has said "*sullenly,*" "Ma's always talking about God. I guess she got a letter from him this morning" (*CP,* 135). Ma tells her husband to stop the car; she will not ride in it with the irreverent Arthur. Even when persuaded to allow Arthur to stay on for the trip, she says, "Where'd we all be if I started talking about God like that, I'd like to know! We'd be in the speak-easies and night-clubs and places like that, that's where we'd be" (*CP,* 135–36). The play even begins on a comic note. When Arthur cannot find his hat, Ma scolds him, "Well, you don't leave Newark without that hat, make up your mind to that. I don't go on no journeys with a hoodlum" (*CP,* 130). Arthur, who is shooting marbles during this scene, scarcely seems like gangster material.

But an ironic reading of the play misses utterly the point of Ma's determination to stand for decent behavior. Her daughter asks her to make a wish on a star and keep it secret:

> MA (*with almost grim humor*): No, I can make my wishes without waiting for no star. And I can tell my wishes right out loud too. Do you want to hear them?
>
> CAROLINE (*resignedly*): No, ma, we know'm already. We've heard'm. (*She hangs her head on her left shoulder and says with unmalicious mimicry:*) You want me to be a good girl and you want Arthur to be honest-in-word-and-deed. (*CP,* 140).

Ma herself has no subterfuge or subtlety. She is honest in word and deed and a good woman.

In a charming scene, Arthur wonders why the family cannot have the spaghetti he sees advertised on a billboard, and Ma doubts that he would eat it. Caroline takes Arthur's side:

> CAROLINE (*with gesture*): Yum-yum. It looks wonderful up there. Ma, make some when we get home?
>
> MA (*dryly*): "The management is always happy to receive suggestions. We aim to please."
>
> *The whole family finds this exquisitely funny. The children scream with laughter. Even* ELMER *smiles.* MA *remains modest.*
>
> ELMER: Well, I guess no one's complaining, Kate. Everybody knows you're a good cook.
>
> MA: I don't know whether I'm a good cook or not, but I know I've had practice. At least I've cooked three meals a day for twenty-five years.

ARTHUR: Aw, ma, you went out to eat once in a while.

MA: Yes. That made it a leap year.

This joke is no less successful than its predecessor. (*CP,* 134)

Very simply, Ma has earned her right to dictate behavior to her children; her hard work and devotion cement the family bond. When they finally do arrive at Beulah's house, the oldest daughter of the family and the purpose of the trip, Caroline, impressed by Beulah's neighborhood, asks if Beulah is richer than they are. Ma instructs her in propriety: "Mind yourself, missy. I don't want to hear anybody talking about rich or not rich when I'm around. If people aren't nice I don't care how rich they are. I live in the best street in the world because my husband and children live there" (*CP,* 141). To a cynical intellectual, this is painfully corny. To Ma, it is a simple statement of fact. Where she lives must be the best street in the world, because all that matters to her can be found there.

The actual reason for the trip is covered only in the last few minutes of the play. Beulah has lost a baby in childbirth and is still recovering. The family has come to comfort her:

BEULAH (*puts her head on her mother's shoulder and weeps*): It was awful, mama. It was awful. She didn't even live a few minutes, mama. It was awful.

MA (*looking far away*): God thought best, dear. God thought best. We don't understand why. We just go on, honey, doin' our business. (*CP,* 142)

Ma's answer, faith and endurance, would be empty coming from almost anyone else. But coming from her mother, Beulah can accept comfort, because her mother's life, a living example of piety, shows Beulah that she can go on in the face of loss, just as Ma went on after the death of Harold. She is, as Beulah says, "the best ma we could ever have" (*CP,* 143). Because her world has order and purpose, Ma can accept pain even if she cannot understand it, and her family can accept it because she does.

There is no contradiction between Wilder's use of avant-garde staging and an affirmation of conventional values. Modernism could combine experimentation in form or subject with sincere defenses of traditional *mores*. For instance, Gertrude Stein, Wilder's close friend from 1935 onward, in her novel *Q.E.D.* (written in 1903 but published posthumously), both portrays a lesbian lifestyle and allows one of the three women involved to offer a ringing peroration in favor of middle-class morality. Adele (the character most like Stein herself) tells Helen and Mabel:

> You have a foolish notion that to be middle-class is to be vulgar, that to cherish the ideals of respectability and decency is to be commonplace and that to be the mother of children is to be low. You tell me that I am not middle class and that I can believe in none of these things because I am not vulgar, commonplace and low, but it is just there where you make your mistake. You don't realize the important fact that virtue and vice have it in common that they are vulgar when not passionately given.[14]

Adele denies that an expansion of experience must mean a rejection of those things previously valued. "Passion" transforms any affirmation, whether in love or in ethics. In fact, the unfamiliar context of an affirmation of middle-class values from an early twentieth-century lesbian jolts the reader into reconsidering those values. In "The Happy Journey," Wilder's use of a virtually bare stage is meant to make strange the familiar so that the audience can see it anew and hence value it. Because Ma is presented on a stage furnished with just a few chairs, she cannot be dismissed as merely a conventional, poorly educated woman who relies upon platitudes to move ignorantly through her life, as she would inevitably appear to be if there were realistic sets. Instead, she is Everymother, defined by her love and service to her family.

The need to make the world strange so it can again be seen and the familiar once again cherished is similar to what G. K. Chesterton sees as a central task for twentieth-century Christianity, in a passage that foreshadows Wilder's masterpiece, *Our Town*. Chesterton imagines himself "writing a romance about an English yachtsman who slightly miscalculated his course and discovered England under the impression it was a new island in the South Seas." The yachtsman would, in a sense, rediscover England in all its terror and homelike security: "How can we contrive to be at once astonished at the world and yet at home in it? How can this queer cosmic town, with its many-legged citizens, with its monstrous and ancient lamps, how can this world give us at once the fascination of a strange town and the comfort and honour of being our own town?"[15] Whether or not Wilder actually took the title of his play from this passage in Chesterton, all the central themes of *Our Town* are embodied in Chesterton's fable. Unless we can somehow make the world strange again, we cannot see it. Wilder explained his concept with reference to William James, who "used to warn his students against being impressed by the 'abject truth.' [In realism] every detail is true and yet the whole finally tumbles to the ground—true but without significance."[16] If we could see our own town, we would see both its awe-inspiring and comforting qualities, whereas too many details render the action too familiar and hence without significance. In *Our Town,* Emily looks at the moon and views it as both "terrible" and "wonderful"; since she is standing at the top of a ladder, the audience imagines the moon and sees her emotional response in a way absent from the realist theater.[17]

In the Introduction to *Three Plays* (1957), Thornton Wilder writes that *Our Town* "is an attempt to find a value above all price for the smallest events in our daily life" (*CP,* 686). What is not often stressed is Wilder's awareness that contingency is the defining characteristic of life, or of the success of *Our Town* for that matter. In an interview in 1974 he mentions the flop of *Our Town* in Boston and points out it went to New York because it was a cheap play to move: "Who knows? If the play had had scenery, they might not have moved it and it would have been a total flop."[18] Any regular reader of a newspaper in February 1938, when the play premiered, would have known that recession threatened the progress made by the United States in recovering from the Great Depression, and that rapidly deteriorating international relations in Europe and Asia might well eventually involve this nation.[19] And all this was merely the background to the cosmic insecurity of modernity. In an interview in 1939, after Wilder himself had played the Stage Manager on New England's "Codfish Circuit," he said, "The twentieth-century mind recognizes that mankind is not the center of the universe and at the same time is frightened by the sense of the countless repetitions of all human vicissitudes."[20] The smallest events of our daily life are defined in relation to the vastness of time and the innumerable recurrence of loss.

Grover's Corners has its own social fault lines. The Baptist Church is "down in the holla" and the Catholic Church and Polish Town are on the other side of the tracks. And "Some people," such as Simon Stimson, "ain't made for small-town life" (*CP,* 170). He is not treated unkindly by the townspeople, but there appears to be nothing they can do to help him. But social and personal problems are incidental to the central problems of mortality and impermanence. Dr. and Mrs. Gibbs are introduced with a description of their deaths. Their lives, as we see them on stage, are rendered vivid by knowing that they are already dead. That is, we see them from the perspective of the omniscient Stage Manager, whose vision of the world is nearly divine; as God sees all of history simultaneously, so does the Stage Manager see both the present and the future at once, and the audience joins in this perspective.

This use of multiple perspectives is clearest in the treatment of Joe Crowell. He enters, age eleven, delivering papers, and chats with Dr. Gibbs about his trick knee and about his teacher, who is leaving the profession to get married. With youthful certainty he says about the teacher, "Well, of course, it's none of my business—but I think if a person starts out to be a teacher, she ought to stay one" (*CP,* 152). At eleven, choices are, or ought to be, irrevocable. He is oblivious to the limited control that anyone has over his or her own life, as we are told by the Stage Manager as soon as Joe leaves the stage: "Joe was awful bright—graduated from high school here, head of his class. So he got a scholarship to Massachusetts Tech. Graduated head of his class there, too. It was all wrote up in the Boston paper at the time. Goin' to be a great engineer, Joe was. But the war broke out and he died in France.—All that education for nothing" (*OT,* 153). Even Mary McCarthy, no fan of Wilder's before and after *Our Town,* sees the transformative effect of his technique on the audience in a review of the initial production: "The boy's morning round, for the spectator, is transfigured into an absorbing ritual; the unconsciousness of the character has heightened the consciousness of the audience."[21] Joe matters more, not less, because the audience sees his life as finite. The ultimate waste of war has, in a sense, rendered his education nothing in that it did not serve Joe's goal of being an engineer. All plans of men end alike in the grave. But in a larger sense, his honors degree from MIT means something as a part of his experience, not as a step to something greater.

The play stresses the fact that not only do individuals die, but also that entire cultures disappear. The former inhabitants of the area, the Cotahatchee tribes, of whom there was "no evidence before the tenth century of this era . . . hm . . . now entirely disappeared . . . possible traces in three families" (*CP*, 159), have been supplanted by the European settlers. The Stage Manager reminds us:

> Y'know—Babylon once had two million people in it, and all we know about 'em is the names of the kings and some copies of wheat contracts . . . and contracts for the sale of slaves. Yet, every night all those families sat down to supper and the father came from his work, and the smoke went up the chimney,—same as here. And even in Greece and Rome, all we know about the *real* life of the people is what we can piece together out of the joking poems and the comedies they wrote for the theatre back then. (*CP*, 166).

On the one hand this suggests that the past does not matter since we know little about Greece and Rome and less about Babylon. The names of kings and caesars have nothing to do with us, and the real life of the period can be only dimly perceived through popular art in the age of the Greeks and Romans and not at all in the case of Babylon. Nor is the past something to be reverenced uncritically: slavery is a legacy that a painful civil war abolished, at least in the United States of Grover's Corners. Thus, when the Stage Manager decides to include a copy of the play in a cornerstone so that "people a thousand years from now'll know a few simple facts about us," the real question is, Why would those people of the future care? The Stage Manager's apostrophe to this unseen future audience only rephrases the question: "So—people a thousand years from now—this is the way we were in the provinces north of New York at the beginning of the twentieth century.—This is the way we were: in our growing up and in our marrying and in our living and in our dying" (*CP,* 166). Wilder's choice of the word "provinces" emphasizes the unimportance of Grover's Corners, while his fixing the time of the play at "the beginning of the twentieth century" reminds us that this is not an epitome of some significant cultural epoch. It is, as Mr. Webb says, a "very ordinary town, if you ask me. Little better behaved than most. Probably a lot duller" (*CP,* 161). Nevertheless the play is a statement of piety and therefore itself is an answer to the question that the Stage Manager's statement raises.

The people of Grover's Corners know that it is a quiet backwater, and sometimes they long for a vision of the larger world. Mrs. Gibbs tells Mrs. Webb (who has just admitted she was taken to see the Atlantic Ocean only because she kept dropping hints) about the possibility of selling her grandmother's highboy and says that "it seems to me that once in your life before you die you ought to see a country where they don't talk in English and don't even want to" (*CP,* 158). Emily tells her mother, "I'm going to make speeches all my life" (*CP,* 164). George plans to go away to college. Always, however, something holds them back. Dr. Gibbs declines any trips because "it might make him discontented with Grover's Corners to go traipsin' about Europe; better let well enough alone" (*CP,* 158). The money from the sale of the highboy is ultimately left to Emily and George and is spent on a watering trough for the livestock. The marriage of George and Emily also ends their ambitions: he never goes to college, she will not make speeches.

The constraints that ensue because of individual choices are presented alongside constraints that appear to be a matter of personal choice but are inescapable, imposed by society. As the Stage Manager says, "Most everybody in the world climbs into their graves married" (*CP,* 174). I suspect that there is a play on words here: marriage is itself a kind of death. The wives exist in a state of gender slavery: "I don't have to point out to the women in my audience that those ladies they see before them, both of those ladies cooked three meals a day—one of 'em for twenty years, the other for forty—and no summer vacation. They brought up two children apiece, washed, cleaned the house,— and *never a nervous breakdown*" (*CP,* 175). Of course, the women act out of love, but that does not alter the fact that marriage is always a dicey proposition: Emily dies in childbirth. Both Emily and George at the very moment of their wedding realize that they are now moving into an adulthood for which they may not be ready, and they long to back out. The weight of social pressure, represented by Mrs. Gibbs and Mr. Webb, brings them to the altar nevertheless. Mr. Webb tells George on the morning of the wedding, "It's the womenfolk who've built up weddings, my boy. For a while now the women have it all their own. A man looks pretty small at a wedding, George. All those good women standing shoulder to shoulder making sure the knot's tied in a mighty public way" (*CP,* 181). The women require a public promise of fidelity in order for their children to grow up in a stable household. But "there's something downright cruel about sending our girls out into marriage this way," Mrs. Webb says, probably alluding to Emily's ignorance of marital sexuality, yet she realizes that the problems of marriage are fundamental: "The whole world's wrong, that's what's the matter" (*CP,* 190).

Marriage as merely a step on the inevitable progression to death is reiterated by the Stage Manager after the wedding: "The cottage, the go-cart, the Sunday-afternoon drives in the Ford, the first rheumatism, the grandchildren, the second rheumatism, the deathbed, the reading of the will,—" (*CP,* 193). We have earlier heard in his sermon that he retains a faith in the process and understands why some churches call it a sacrament: "We all know that nature's interested in quantity; but I think she's interested in quality, too,—that's why I'm in the ministry" (*CP,* 189). Donald Haberman instructively compares this idea to George Bernard Shaw's belief in "an upwardly spiraling activity in the universe" and locates the idea in Goethe as well.[22] In other words, evolution is not the random process that Darwin (and modern biologists) envision; instead, it has a direction and a purpose. As such, evolution has a religious significance, which I shall discuss more fully in chapter 5. But in *Our Town,* the Stage Manager continues, "Once in a thousand times it's interesting," implying that most marriages have no effect on this evolutionary process and are merely the couplings of habit. As an act of faith, however, he continues to marry couples, in the hopes that one of these ceremonies will be the one in the thousand that matters.

There are mitigating factors in this prosaic existence for everyone in the town, even moments of impermanent although recurring beauty: "The morning star always gets wonderful bright the minute before it has to go,—doesn't it?" (*CP,* 149). The villagers "like the sun comin' up over the mountain in the morning, and we all notice a good deal about the birds. We pay a lot of attention to them" (*CP,* 163). The trouble is, as Emily realizes after her death when she returns to her birthday, the time "goes so fast" (*CP,* 207). And it is difficult to grasp the present in the moment. Emily says early in the play to George about homework, "I don't mind it really. It passes the time" (*CP,* 163). And when describing Grover's Corners, Professor Willard asks the Stage Manager if he should mention its meteorological history and is told, "Afraid we won't have time for that, Professor" (*CP,* 159). Ordinary individuals fail to see that because time is limited, it is precious. "The saints and poets, maybe" realize life while they live it, but even they do so only "some" (*CP,* 207). Ultimately, beauty is not enough to make life endurable in the face of the passing of time. As music master of his church, Simon Stimson perhaps relies on it more than any of the other characters, but the choir cannot live up to his expectations, and he is the one who commits suicide.

Brooks Atkinson quoted Santayana when reviewing *Our Town:* "The art of life is to keep step with the celestial orchestra that beats the measure of our career and gives the cue for our exits and entrances." Atkinson then correctly points out the large scale of the play: "What matters most is not the isolated experience of the day but the whole pattern of life from the ancient past into the depths of the future."[23] I would somewhat disagree with this evaluation: the isolated experience matters every bit as much as the whole pattern of life. The famous address on an envelope that extends from "Jane Crofut; The Crofut Farm" to "the Universe; the Mind of God" (*CP,* 173) suggests a movement from the individual to the eternal, but, Rebecca informs us, "the postman brought it just the same"; the reason for the letter and its destination is the individual. But Atkinson's allusion to Santa-yana is appropriate. The individual seeks to find his place in the music of the spheres, and that congruence with a universal pattern is an act of piety. It ultimately does not matter whether or not the people of a thousand years from now find the lives of people in the provinces north of New York in the early twentieth century of interest. The Stage Manager regards their living and dying as important and thus includes the script of the play in the cornerstone, just as Aeneas car-ries his household gods from fallen Troy to Italy.

There are examples of irreverence and false piety in the play, for instance, among visitors to the cemetery:

> Summer people walk around there laughing at the funny words on the tombstones . . . it don't do any harm. And genealogists come up from Boston—get paid by city people for looking up their ancestors. They want to make sure they're Daughters of the American Revo-lution and of the *Mayflower* . . . . Well, I guess that don't do any harm, either. Wherever you come near the human race, there's lay-ers and layers of nonsense. . . . (*CP,* 196)

However, the city people who seek to affirm their own value by find-ing important ancestors miss the point. That is, one venerates and emulates the soldiers of the Revolution for seeking independence, not for validating one's own importance. The audience is reminded of true piety: "Over there are some Civil War veterans. Iron flags on their graves . . . New Hampshire boys . . . had a notion that the Union ought to be kept together, though they'd never seen more than fifty miles of it themselves. All they knew was the name, friends—the United States of America. The United States of America. And they went and died about it" (*CP,* 196). Just as Ma in *The Happy Journey* knows that New Jersey is the best state although she has seen little of the rest of the country, the Civil War–era soldiers know that the United States must remain indivisible although they literally know only their own neighborhoods. Loyalty to something larger than one-self commands respect.

Professor Willard tells the audience, "Grover's Corners lies on the old Pleistocene granite of the Appalachian range. I may say it's some of the oldest land in the world. We're very proud of that" (*CP,* 159). Exactly why does not need to be stated: It is theirs. After Mr. Webb admits to the audience that it is a dull town, he adds, "But our young people here seem to like it well enough. Ninety per cent of 'em graduating from high school settle down right here to live—even when they've been away to college" (*CP,* 161). Their loyalty to their surroundings and to each other ensures that the inhabitants need not wander in search of some deeper meaning, as do George Brush in *Heaven's My Destination* and the latter generations in "The Long Christmas Dinner." In *Our Town,* choral music even emphasizes the bonds of community. The hymn heard in the background a number of times in the play is "Blessed Be the Tie That Binds."

This is not to say that most people are conscious of the tie. Simon Stimson has a part of the truth when he criticizes the ignorance of the community in Act Three: "That's what it was to be alive. To move about in a cloud of ignorance; to go up and down trampling on the feelings of others" (*CP,* 207). And Emily pleads with her mother to look at her when she returns for her thirteenth birthday: "Mama, just for a moment now we're all together. Mama, just for a moment we're happy. *Let's look at one another*" (*OT,* 206). Years later, Wilder writes to Amy Wertheimer comparing the play to Sartre's *No Exit,* and he claims, "the last act of my play suggests that life—viewed directly—is damned near hell" (*SL,* 608). But he also writes to Heinrich Walter that "Emily's farewell to the world is from Achilles' praise of the things he valued in life: his 'fresh rainment' becomes 'new-ironed dresses'; his wine—naturally—becomes coffee" (*SL,* 477). I am not sure to what speech Wilder is referring here.[24] But no one as familiar with the classics as Wilder could forget Achilles' speech after Odysseus claims that Achilles even in death must have great authority: "O shining Odysseus, never try to console me for dying. / I would rather follow the plow as thrall to another / man, one with no land allotted to him and not much to live on, / than be a king over all the perished dead."[25]

Our Town celebrates community and that can be created anywhere. A similar theme is developed in *The Skin of Our Teeth,* a transitional piece between the works of the 1930s and Wilder's more
existential postwar plays and novels. Amid the hyperbole of Joseph
Campbell and Henry Morton Robinson's claim that Wilder had pla-
giarized Joyce's *Finnegans Wake* in *The Skin of Our Teeth,* there is one
perspicuous observation. Both Earwicker and Antrobus represent
"Adam All-Father of the World."[26] The problem that Robinson and
Campbell fail to recognize is that Adam as symbolic representation is
by no means an innovation of Joyce. As we have seen, the American
Adam is a common type both in American literature and in the work
of Thornton Wilder. George Antrobus, the father of Cain and Abel,
is from Excelsior, New Jersey. He is simultaneously, as Sabina says, "a
giant," when they think a stranger is breaking into the house, and
"your father," as Mrs. Antrobus says to their daughter Gladys and son
Henry when they realize that he has made it home from work despite
the approaching glaciers (*CP,* 227). Even as humanity is threatened by
an Ice Age, he lives in "a commodious seven-room house, conveniently situated near a public school, a Methodist church, and a fire-
house; it is right handy to an A&P" (*CP,* 214). He is a mythical patri-
arch, but he is also a comic husband from New Jersey.

George's accomplishments are profound: the invention of the
wheel as well as the alphabet. When he works out that "Ten tens make
a hundred semi-colon consequences far-reaching," even the people at
the telegraph office are impressed: "like the head man at our office
said: a few more discoveries like that and we'll be worth freezing" (*CP,*
223). He is also unstable in the extreme, jealous even of his own son
and reluctant to see his accomplishments surpassed. After he brings
home the wheel, Henry notes that it could be improved by putting a
chair on it. George says, "(*Broodingly.*) Ye-e-s, any booby can fool
with it now,—but I thought of it first" (*CP,* 229). When Henry hits
another boy with a rock, George despairs that they are merely beasts
without purpose or direction: "There is no mind. We'll not try to
live" (*CP,* 236). Always he is aware of original sin, and the weight of it
nearly crushes him when Henry attempts another murder: "All of us,
we're covered in blood" (*CP,* 237). Mrs. Antrobus is appalled when

she sees Gladys wearing makeup: "Don't you know your father'd go crazy if he saw that paint on your face? Don't you know your father thinks you're perfect? Don't you know he couldn't live if he didn't think you were perfect?" (*CP*, 226). When he becomes the President of the Mammals in a brief interlude of fair weather, he changes the rules by which the animals live: "The watchword of the closing year was: Work. I give you the watchword for the future: Enjoy Yourselves" (*CP*, 242). And he is perpetually drawn to the beautiful Sabina and away from his wife. "It's girls like I who inspire the multiplication table" (*CP*, 220), observes Sabina smugly. Father, protector, and creator, he is also lecher, threat, and profitless dreamer.

The family is ultimately the basis for his ability to go on and the reason why George always rejects Sabina/Lily for Mrs. Antrobus, who endures and preserves the household: "Reading and writing and counting on your fingers is all very well in their way,—but I keep the home going" (*CP*, 220). Mrs. Antrobus is a much more elemental figure than Ma in "The Happy Journey to Trenton and Camden," or Mrs. Gibbs or Mrs. Webb in *Our Town*: "Mrs. Antrobus is as fine a woman as you could hope to see. She lives only for her children; and if it would be any benefit to her children she'd see the rest of us stretched out dead at her feet without turning a hair,—that's the truth. If you want to know anything more about Mrs. Antrobus, just go and look at a tigress, and look hard" (*CP*, 216). This instinct to protect her family and preserve her home is both positive and negative. On the one hand, it allows her to go on in the face of the same kind of human despair that her husband feels at times because of his children. When Henry has attacked another child and Gladys wears makeup and cannot "act like a lady," Mrs. Antrobus reacts "*in real, though temporary, repudiation and despair.*) Get away from me, both of you! I wish I'd never seen sight or sound of you. Let the cold come! I can't stand it. I don't want to go on" (*CP*, 226). But she pulls herself together, sends Gladys to the kitchen to scrub her face, and, hearing a noise outside, organizes the defense of the house. Her animalistic compulsion to protect her offspring drives her onward in the face of difficulties that would stop her husband. At the same time, when George telegraphs her that it is all right to "burn everything except Shakespeare," she reacts contemptuously, "Men!—He knows I'd burn ten Shakespeares to prevent a child of mine from having one cold in the head" (*CP,* 222). Her narrow loyalties to home and family protect them against seemingly insuperable odds in the face of hardship: "I could live for seventy years in a cellar and make soup out of grass and bark, without ever doubting that this world has work to do and will do it" (*CP,* 275). And she will try to see to it, as Ma does, that her children behave as they ought, even though she will fail: "Too many people have suffered and died for my children for us to start reneging now. So we'll start putting this house to rights" (*CP,* 274). When George tells the conventioneers in Act Two to enjoy themselves, Mrs. Antrobus asks for allegiance: "My watchword for the year is: Save the Family. It's held together for over five thousand years: Save it!" (*CP,* 244).

She reminds her husband that marriage is a promise: "And when our children were growing up, it wasn't a house that protected them; and it wasn't our love, that protected them—it was that promise" (*CP,* 259–60). In the absence of fidelity, itself a subset of piety, Gladys in particular is at risk of turning into a Sabina. But the relationship between the three leading characters is dynamic. George is the creative force. Lily/Sabina is his inspiration, the *anima* that draws him to create; but she is sterile (she has no children) and thus unable to inspire him to preserve his creations. Mrs. Antrobus produces the children that give George's creations a purpose in that they represent a future, but she herself cannot inspire him to create. All three are necessary for survival, which is why Mrs. Antrobus allows Sabina a place in her home. Whether the children are worth preserving is not a question that the characters allow themselves to ask often. Henry, according to Sabina, "is a real, clean-cut American boy. He'll graduate from High School one of these days, if they make the alphabet any easier"; and Gladys will "make some good man a good wife some day, if he'll just come down off the movie screen and ask her" (*CP,* 216). Their apparent limitations are, unsurprisingly, also a consequence of man's fallen nature: Henry is homicidal and Gladys, prone to sluttish behavior and dress from the beginning of the play, is a mother with no apparent husband at the end. It is the home of the human race with all its faults. George saw three things together when he was in the war,

as he tells his wife: "The voice of the people in their confusion and
their need. And the thought of you the children and this house . . .
And . . . Maggie! I didn't dare ask you: my books! They haven't been
lost, have they?" (*CP,* 282). Obligation to the greater good is linked
with love of family and home. The moral imperative comes from
piety.

And the tools that piety can draw on are the accumulated wisdom
of the species. This is not a matter of simple cause and effect. In Act
One, Homer speaks in Greek and Moses in Hebrew, doubtless understood by only a few people in the audience. But from "Centaurs" in
The Angel That Troubled the Waters to "Pullman Car Hiawatha," Wilder
repeatedly returned to an idea expressed by Ivy in *The Skin of Our
Teeth.* Her father, a Baptist minister, explicates the third act in a voice
that is authorial: "just like the hours and stars go by over our heads at
night, in the same way the ideas and the thoughts of the great men
are in the air around us all the time and they're working on us, even
when we don't know it" (*CP,* 267).[27] The voices, in this play, of Spinoza, Plato, Aristotle, and the Bible are a part of the culture, shaping
the people of the culture, unless, like Henry, they deny it entirely.
George, for instance, tells Henry, "How can you make a world for
people to live in, unless you've first put order in yourself?" (*CP,* 277).
This question comes before the procession of the Hours, when Hes-
ter, as Ten O'clock, intones as Plato: "Then tell me, O Critias, how
will a man choose the ruler that shall rule over him? Will he not
choose a man who has first established order in himself, knowing that
any decision that has its spring from anger or pride or vanity can be
multiplied a thousandfold in its effects upon the citizens?" (*CP,* 282).
George repeats to Henry the age-old admonition of self-control, and
then the audience hears one of its sources. Strikingly, the idea of this
quotation must certainly be found in Plato, but Wilder could not find
a suitable one, so he made this one up.[28] But like the error in the allusion to the Gettysburg Address in "Pullman Car Hiawatha," this creative interaction with our cultural heritage shows the vitality of the
culture; culture is not a prison but a home.

George ultimately represents American optimism. He tells Maggie when he returns from the war,

I know that every good and excellent thing in the world stands moment by moment on the razor-edge of danger and must be fought for—whether it's a field, or a house, or a country. All I ask is the chance to build new worlds and God has always given us that. And has given us (*Opening the book*) voices to guide us; and the memory of our mistakes to warn us. Maggie, you and I will remember in peacetime all the resolves that were so clear to us in the days of war. We've come a long ways. We've learned. We're learning. And the steps of our journey are marked for us here. (*CP,* 282)

Here, George is not only the American Adam: he is the pious Aeneas. He fights for his land, his home, and his country, and he would rebuild home and country even if he had been defeated. His claim that mankind learns from its mistakes, despite all the evidence to the contrary, is an act of faith, and a brave one in 1942. Wilder, in a letter to Gertrude Stein, although not surprised by the American response to World War II, nevertheless still marvels at it: "The basic American swinging into view. The industrial organization of the factories—vast without gigantism; work, work, work, yet with the composure of a man picking his teeth with a grass-stem; the miraculous conducted as though it were the matter-of-course. Old America."[29] Personally, as a man in his forties, Wilder pulled every string to get an active role in the war effort and ended up in Intelligence for the Army Air Corps. After service in North Africa and Italy he finished the war as a lieutenant colonel. In *The Skin of Our Teeth,* he exhorted his countrymen to fight for their homes, their country, and the values of their civilization, and then he proceeded to do so himself. At the time, the outcome was not clear, but the obligation was apparent to the piety of Wilder and of millions of Americans, and the communal focus of the nation was the embodiment of its piety.

Chapter Four

The Appetite for Destruction and the Obstacles to Growth

In chapters 2 and 3, I argued that two elements coexist in Wilder's works of the 1930s: a critique of the American economic order in the wake of the Great Depression (in *Heaven's My Destination, The Matchmaker,* and some of the one-act plays of 1931); and a defense of piety in the face of the social strain of the Depression and the looming disaster of World War II (most notably in *Our Town*). In these last two chapters I shall argue that in a similar fashion, two themes that, if not contradictory, are at least in an uneasy tension coexist in many of Wilder's postwar works: a modernist, quasi-existentialist skepticism; and faith in (or at least hope for) spiritual evolution. In the wake of the war, Wilder's works reveal a more direct awareness of man's innate tendency toward destruction, the problems that come with the development of the human organism, a twentieth-century sense of the negative effects of society as well as religion on constraining human freedom, and, finally, the isolating and immobilizing effects of "sin" when an individual imprisons him or herself in the world. In the last chapter I shall also show that simultaneously these works express optimism about the ongoing evolution of humanity in the context of an expression of pluralism.

Clearly, in *The Skin of Our Teeth* the optimistic elements are predominate. The Antrobuses live to fight another day: "Their heads are full of plans and they're as confident as the first day they began" (*CP,*

284), says Sabina at the end of the play. But, at the time of the play's première in November 1942, the tide of the war might have been turning, but that would not have been apparent to many members of the theater audience. The Germans still controlled most of continental Europe and still had armies deep in Russia. Alone in Europe, the British were hanging on but were in no condition to mount any offensive against Nazi Germany. The Japanese occupied large sections of Asia and the South Pacific. An American might feel reasonably secure behind the barriers of the Atlantic and the Pacific, but a totalitarian dark age engulfing the rest of the globe was a distinct possibility. The extent of the Holocaust was not recognized yet, but that something appalling was happening to Europe's Jews was known by 1942. Perhaps no one could express so powerfully as Elie Wiesel the apocalypse of the concentration camps when he described the experience of his first night in camp and the burning of children: "Never shall I forget those moments which murdered my God and my soul and turned my dreams to dust. Never shall I forget these things, even if I am condemned to live as long as God Himself. Never."[1] *The Skin of Our Teeth* is a statement of faith in mankind's ability to endure, but the war challenged that faith in many ways.

Under the circumstances it is not surprising that amid *The Skin of Our Teeth*'s comedy and patriotism, there are moments of dark ambivalence. The play dramatizes the difficulties of making sense out of experience at *any* place or time. Sabina illustrates this point when she discusses the Antrobuses' children: "Each new child that's born to the Antrobuses seems to them to be sufficient reason for the whole universe's being set in motion; and each new child that dies seems to them to have been spared a whole world of sorrow, and what the end of it will be is still very much an open question" (*CP*, 216). Both claims are true: each child is, to a loving parent, reason enough for the world's existence, and each child, by his or her death, is spared a world of suffering. Whether that is comforting is another question, particularly to an audience whose sons would soon be in uniform.

Comfort might, for instance, be sought in philosophy. In Act Three, Bailey as Nine O'clock recites from Spinoza as he crosses the stage: "After experience had taught me that the common occurrences of daily life are vain and futile; and I saw that all the objects of my desire and fear were in themselves nothing good nor bad save insofar as the mind was affected by them; I at length determined to search out whether there was something truly good and communicable" (*CP,* 283). This passage, from the beginning of Spinoza's *Ethics,* introduces his pantheism; the good that man can achieve is "the knowledge of the union existing between the mind and the whole of Nature."[2] That which appears evil is a misperception of the mind. I suspect that few parents can maintain this perception after the death of a child. In *The Skin of Our Teeth,* Mrs. Antrobus shields Henry from a hostile world, but when Moses asks about her two sons, she walks away in an echo of David's grief for Absalom in 2 Samuel 18:33: "Abel, Abel, my son, my son, Abel, my son, Abel, Abel, my son" (*CP,* 235). Mrs. Antrobus endures but her sorrow is ineradicable. However inspiring the thoughts of Spinoza may be, they have little efficacy in assuaging real mourning.[3]

People in society represent a perhaps insolvable problem as well. Sabina has spent the war as a camp follower. How she survived is indicated when she discovers George Antrobus, Gladys, and a baby alive still: "How've you girls been?—*Don't* try and kiss me. I never want to kiss another human being as long as I live" (*CP,* 270). When she later wishes to save her beef cubes to go to the movies rather than contributing them to common stock, she breaks down to George Antrobus: "You're a very nice man, Mr. Antrobus, but you'd have got on better in the world if you'd realized that dog-eat-dog was the rule in the beginning and always will be. And most of all now. (*In tears.*) Oh, the world's an awful place, and you know it is. I used to think something could be done about it; but I know better now. I hate it. I hate it" (*CP,* 281). She then gives the cubes to Mr. Antrobus. Her thesis of a world eternally consumed by selfishness is contradicted by her own action. But the fantasy novels of Ayn Rand, with their perpetual motion machines and magical metals, will come along in a decade or so to insist that not only is Sabina right, but that it is also a fine thing that selfishness should rule. Even George feels the loss of idealism: "When you're at war you think about a better life; when you're at peace you think about a more comfortable one. I've lost it. I feel sick and tired" (*CP,* 280). Sabina tells Mrs. Antrobus, "Everybody's at their best in wartime" (*CP,* 272). This is a startlingly prescient remark considering that Wilder had not yet served in the army.[4] The redemptive and revelatory transformations of war are potentially fruitless, consumed by the desire for comfort. Heroism is replaced, if not by hedonism, with a return to the cocoon of the bourgeois family.

Henry represents evil itself, and he, too, is not transformed by the war. The stage directions in Act Three for the confrontation between Henry and his father read: "*Henry is played, not as a misunderstood or misguided young man, but as a representation of strong unreconciled evil*" (*CP,* 276). Wilder attempts to locate this evil in an Oedipal conflict: "I've spent seven years trying to find him [George]; the others I killed were just substitutes" (*CP,* 273) Indeed, in a move reminiscent of Pirandello, the character takes over the actor, who tries to fight the actor playing George and then fictionalizes a repressive father to account for his actions. This is not terribly interesting, and, in fact, Wilder's work as a whole shows that he has a problem understanding or conceptualizing evil.[5]

But the other source of Henry's destructive energy is double-edged. He says when he returns, "The first thing to do is to burn up those old books; it's the ideas he [George] gets out of those old books that . . . that makes the whole world so you can't live in it" (*CP,* 273). This is a truly radical agenda. If one could erase existing habits of thought and culture as represented by the books, then perhaps one could start over and create a new and better world. Of course, as Edmund Burke pointed out, this is the force that created the French Revolution and the Terror. This desire for the clean slate ignores both the complexity of society and the unintended consequences of any radical change, but also that society is an organic entity that exists over time, and that therefore the social contract extends from generation to generation: "It is a partnership in all science; a partnership in all arts; a partnership in every virtue, and in all perfection. As the ends of such a partnership cannot be obtained in many generations, it becomes a partnership not only between those who are living, but between those who are living, those who are dead, and those who are to be born."[6] Henry is not interested in partnerships: "Nobody can say *must* to me. All my life everybody's been crossing me,—everybody, everything, all of you. I'm going to be free, even if I have to kill half the world for it" (*CP*, 278). Burke would regard this association between freedom and terror as the inevitable consequence of revolutionary movements where the sympathies and loyalties of mankind—ties that are outside the purely rational—are disregarded. Interestingly, as a young man, Wilder, too, had no use for Burke, although Burke is a writer whose importance becomes more apparent as a reader ages.[7]

Henry speaks with the arrogance of youth. In the fragmentary work "Youth," written years later as a part of the uncompleted cycle *The Seven Ages of Man*, Wilder castigates this youthful intolerance. The character Gulliver discovers an island where the inhabitants are willingly poisoned at the age of twenty-nine: a rigid class structure has developed, men have multiple wives, the arts are nonexistent, and men spend most of their time in kite-flying competitions. "The child-hood of the race . . . You have slipped five—ten thousand years," says a shaken Gulliver and passes judgment: "Humanity is the last thing that will be learned by man; it will not be learned from the young" (*CP*, 634, 629).[8] Like *The Skin of Our Teeth*, however, "Youth" is more complex than Gulliver's summary judgment would indicate. The alternative view to Burke's conservatism, such as that espoused by Mark Twain, for example, in *A Connecticut Yankee in King Arthur's Court*, is implicit in the play as well. Twain's Connecticut Yankee, after seeing a group of peasants forced to labor on their lord's land, praises "the ever-memorable and blessed Revolution, which swept a thousand years of such villainy away in one swift tidal wave of blood—one; a settlement of that hoary debt in the proportion of half a drop of blood for each hogshead of it that had been pressed by slow tortures out of that people in the weary stretch of ten centuries of wrong and shame and misery the like of which was not to be mated but in hell."[9] Twain, doubtless thinking consciously of Burke, weighs, on the one hand, the relative crimes of church and aristocracy over centuries, and, on the other, those of the French Revolution and thus regards the eradication of the existing, evil order as fully justified.

The Duke of Cornwall, leader of the young men in the fragment "Youth," responds with scorn to Gulliver's claims that he has visited twenty countries that take pride in their names:

Among those twenty countries was there *one* that was not governed by old men—governed, misgoverned, burdened, oppressed by old men? By the pride and avarice, and the lust for power of old men? One which did not constantly war at the instigation of old men like *yourself,* to enlarge its boundaries; to enslave others; to enrich itself? We know of the War of the Roses. Or by the religious bigotry of old men—we know of the St. Bartholomew Massacre, [the] murder of Charles, king and martyr. And when these prides of yours have obtained their lands, whose bodies are those lying upon the field of battle?—they are the bodies of men under thirty. (*CP,* 626)

The legacy of a culture includes its crimes as well as its achievements, and the Duke is arguably correct that old men make wars and young men fight and die in them.

The speeches of the Duke against the government of old men resonate with intellectual forces unleashed by the Enlightenment in the eighteenth century (and hence the time frame of "Youth"), but in the second half of the twentieth century they find a ready echo.[10] The transitional figure in this case is probably Freud. As early as 1928 Wilder revealed the influence of Freud on his ideas in a conversation with André Maurois. He tells Maurois that all men are unhappy: "They are solitary, they are consumed with desires which they dare not satisfy; and they wouldn't be happy if they did satisfy them, because they are too civilized."[11] Freud theorizes in *Civilization and Its Discontents* that the conflict between the biological, creative impulse and an innate drive for destruction is "the meaning of the evolution of civilization": "It must present the struggle between Eros and Death, between the instinct of life and the instinct of destruction, as it works itself out in the human species."[12] The schematized conflict in these plays between the Duke and Gulliver or Henry and his father is between the id (the Duke and Henry) and the super ego (Gulliver and George) and ultimately one that Freud thinks cannot be resolved. Culture makes life secure and therefore more comfortable, but the restraint of desire by culture, even when internalized, creates frustration, a psychological malaise.

A desire to sweep away existing cultures and start anew is not un-reasonable even if it may be unwise. However much one may love Shakespeare and admire the complexity of his plays, as does George Antrobus in *The Skin of Our Teeth,* it is hard to ignore the fact that Shakespeare is anti-Semitic, believes in the natural subordination of women, and thinks that the social hierarchy is divinely ordained. Loyalty to such ideas is pernicious. And, after all, the old ideas proved inadequate to prevent World War II; and some of them, anti-Semitism and other ideologies of racial superiority—phenomena by no means restricted to the Germans—helped to fuel the carnage. While George simply regards his books as the essential foundation of civilization, there is something to be said for Henry's view that they are also the repository of ideas that pollute any new enterprise. The revolutionary impulse to start with a clean slate may dissolve the loyalties that hold society together, but some of those bonds desperately need to be dissolved.

Further, a part of what Henry wants, George desires as well. Henry snarls, "I'm not going to be a part of any peacetime of yours. I'm going a long way from here and make my own world that's fit for a man to live in. Where a man can be free, and have a chance, and do what he wants to do in his own way." His father sees Henry's claim to an exclusive right to this freedom as the problem: "You and I want the same thing; but until you think of it as something that everyone has a right to, you are my deadly enemy and I will destroy you" (*CP,* 277). The unstated question is, Can everybody be free? The answer is probably no. Not only are we entangled in the norms of society, but we are also insensibly guided by family and culture.

In the previous chapter I argued that loyalty to family and culture is presented in Wilder's plays as essential to spiritual and emotional health. By no means is this an inevitable view. The unfinished cycle of *The Seven Ages of Man* is largely concerned with human development and the difficulties involved with it; the cycle elaborates upon the pessimistic elements of *The Skin of Our Teeth.* Some of them are intrinsic to the species: like any animal, we are chiefly concerned with ourselves and the object of forces, some instinctual, of which we are unaware or, at best, of which we are only dimly cognizant. At the same time, society, as it attempts to control the potentially destructive nature of our impulses, also retards our development.

In "Infancy," the adults have varying levels of comprehension of the two children's actual "thoughts." Millie thinks that Tommy is a "dear little animal," although she does read the expert Dr. Kennick, who says babies are exhausted because "they're learning all the time"; "the reason why we aren't geniuses is that we weren't brought up right: we were stopped" (*CP,* 588–89).[13] The Keystone cop Avonzino inverts the hopeful Dr. Kennick: "He gotta the right idea, Miss Wilchick, I see one thousand babies a day. And what I say is: stop 'em" (*CP,* 589). It is not the case that Avonzino does not know what babies are thinking. Tommy's first speech makes his attitude clear: "I wanta make a house. I wanta make a baby" (*CP,* 586). Food and sex "and going to his potty" (*CP,* 592), are what interest the children. Avonzino's job is impulse control. The play begins with him contemplating the list of suspects: "'Suspect—old gentleman, silk hat, pinches nurses.' (*Reflects*) Pinch babies, okay; pinch nurses, nuisance." His job has made him worldlywise: "Nuisances in bushes: young gents and young girls taking liberties. (*Hotly*) Why can't they do their nuisances at home?" (*CP,* 584–85). People must learn self-control for society to function: the "thou shalt not" directive must be internalized to make civil order possible. So when Avonzino looks at Tommy, he sees a bundle of impulses that have not yet been corralled. The consequence for Tommy and everyone else is frustration of our own biological imperatives and the obstruction of the pleasure principle.

Piaget and Freud lurk somewhere behind the play, but the play is also a comic look at how adults fail to satisfy a child's ravenous desire for information. Moe's father calls him "stupid": "Maybe I am stupid.—But that's because MY MOUTH HURTS ALL THE TIME and they don't give me enough to eat and I'm hungry all the time and that's the end of it, that's the end of it" (*CP,* 593). Sometimes, the father is affectionate, but Moe can see through that: "Sometimes he holds out his hands and says: 'How's the little fella? How's the little champ?' And I give him a look. I wasn't born yesterday. He hasn't got anything to sell me" (*CP,* 594). The Oedipal conflict is rooted in the father's inconsistent treatment of his son, rather than in a conflict over the mother: "I hate him. But I watch him and I learn. *You see:* And when I get to walk I'm going to do something so that he won't *be* any more" (*CP,* 594). Moe decides to die, turning purple and creating chaos, and then decides not to. Avonzino regards the whole event sourly: "Boker baby's a great actor. Dies every performance. Thousands cheer" (*CP,* 597). But the play illustrates the enormous gap between adults and infants, and the folly of the adults is dramatically linked to their inability to understand and hence develop the infants. Since neither the infants nor the adults can gain perspective on the psychomachia that the infants are internalizing, misunderstandings are inevitable. Because the play is comic and there will always be new babies with whom to try again, this result is not tragic—but it does illustrate why any kind of intellectual progress is hard. Babies are biological organisms, and, at least here, they have no memory of some Neoplatonic prior existence.

"Childhood" is about imaginative play, the games used by children to contemplate different ways of being in society, to understand their relationship with their parents, and to come to terms with danger and even death. The young mother knows what the games are, and it bothers her: "No one told me when I was a bride that children are half crazy. I only hear fragments of the games, naturally, but do you realize that they like nothing better than to imagine us—away?" (*CP,* 602). For Billie and Dodie (ages eight and ten), the games are cathartic, allowing them to talk about their mysterious and alien father:

> BILLIE (*Excitedly*): All the *time!* He'd swear swearwords.
> CAROLINE: Well, maybe a little.
> DODIE: He *did.* I used to want to *die.*
> CAROLINE: Well, nobody's perfeck. (*Slower*) He was all right, sometimes.
> DODIE: He used to laugh too loud in front of people. And he didn't give Mama enough money to buy clothes. She had to go to town in rags, in terrible old rags. (*CP,* 605)

Themselves doubtless taught not to swear and to be quiet, the younger children find their father an embarrassment; and from an inability to "read" the exaggerated conversations of adults, they also see him as an abusive miser mistreating their mother. Caroline, a little older, sees him as merely dull: "Papa was a very fine man, and he *tried*. Only . . . only (*Reluctantly*) he didn't ever say anything very interesting" (*CP*, 605). From an adolescent's perspective, this is true. Since the father's life is about going to work, his fantasies are about winning the golf championship at his club: realistic, possible, but less significant than the children's fantasy about surviving the death of their parents. At the same time, the mother who has taught them manners also "didn't understand children." Dodie sums up every child's objections to the imposition of limits by first objecting to their mother going to visit their sick grandmother "for years" and then adding the positive result of the visit: "Well, when she was away she didn't have to say Don't—Don't— Don't all the time, all day and night. Don't—Don't—Don't." And, of course, the children see their mother most when they are most miserable. "She liked us best when we were sick and when I broke my arm" (*CP*, 606), says Caroline.

But the narratives also allow them slowly to develop an understanding of their parents' roles in their own lives. In the fantasy, the father is the bus driver who tells the children how little he is paid; he also protects them from danger. Their mother is a grieving passenger. But if the game allows them to explore the adult perspective, it does not negate the fact that that perspective is unsatisfactory. Caroline is more willing to extend the game than her brother and sister: "It's too soon to go back to where I come from, where everybody says silly things they don't mean one bit, and where nobody treats you like a real person" (*CP*, 613). The machinery of society is oiled by polite nothings, and adolescents are fortunately not treated as "real" persons, that is, as adults. But the play suggests that there is a kind of honesty about family relations in children's games that adults need to recognize. Caroline tells the bus driver/father figure: "Well . . . you see . . . you're just people in our game. You're not *really* alive. That's why we could talk to you. (*A quick glance at her father, then she looks down again*) Besides, we've found that it's best not to make friends with grownups, because . . . in the end . . . they don't act fair to you" (*CP*, 615). The difficulties of communication between parents and children are partially inherent in the inequality of ages. But if parents could only enter more fully into their children's games, that communication gap could be narrowed. In any case, the subtly didactic component of the play is a lesson about the salutary nature of childhood creativity. The latent romanticism of the work, however, suggests that this creativity of youth is inevitably crushed.[14]

The plays of *The Seven Ages of Man* cycle, despite their exploration of how children's desires are repressed, are comic: indeed, as I will argue in the next chapter, "The Rivers Under the Earth" is hopeful in that some of the chthonic forces inspire positive outcomes. But in general the experience of World War II, Wilder's interest in existentialism, and the restlessness of a modernist intellect contribute to a more pessimistic sense of man's place in society in Wilder's postwar works. Amos Wilder was aware of this element in his brother's oeuvre. In his book *New Testament Faith for Today* (1955), Amos explains that preaching the Gospel in the modern age must take into account not only skepticism but active hostility:

> The climate of modern culture has brought forth not only alienated and secularized strata but also definitely anti-Christian movements. The latter often hold that religion is an escape mechanism or opiate, or at least that it is commonly so perverted. They can crassly explain away even its supreme manifestations by some social or psychological theory. The God-idea and the Christ-concept are explained as naïve projections. Immortality is viewed as a compensatory dream. All such religious beliefs with their institutions and rites are viewed as enervating and stultifying.[15]

Whether from a Marxist, sociological, or psychological perspective, religion turns out not only to be an expression of delusion and wishful thinking, but also to be actively harmful to social and economic progress. While the religious dreamer imagines some pie-in-the-sky that will rectify injustice and redeem the righteous who have endured an unhappy and unfulfilled existence, the world continues to be unjust and people continue to behave in the same ways that guarantee their unhappiness.[16]

Strikingly, Amos Wilder quotes his brother, without naming him, from a "recent novel" about Rome (*The Ides of March*) that suggests "the plausibility of this opinion":

> Most of all, however, these observances attack and undermine the very spirit of life within the minds of men. They afford to our Romans, from the street sweepers to the consuls, a vague sense of confidence where no confidence is and at the same time a pervasive fear, a fear which neither arouses to action nor calls forth ingenuity, but which paralyzes. They remove from men's shoulders the unremitting obligation to create, moment by moment, their own Rome. They come to us sanctioned by the usage of our ancestors and breathing the security of our childhood; they flatter passivity and console inadequacy . . . what can I do against the apathy that is glad to wrap itself under the cloak of piety? (*Ides,* 6)

Religion breeds false confidence, feeds fear, and creates apathy.

I should stress that neither Wilder brother regarded a critical, even a mocking, attitude toward Christianity as harmful in and of itself. Were it not for devilish doubt, man would sink into lethargy.[17] Thus, the role of the skeptic contributes to creation, another version of the fortunate Fall. Amos Wilder praises modern literature as a kind of "lay order" of the church: "The unbelief of today is more affirmative than the shallow skepticism of yesterday. The poignant atheism of today is more pregnant than the dogmatic rationalism of yesterday. The perfect statement of the modern tragic mood is found in the words from the Gospel: 'I believe; help thou mine unbelief.'"[18] From Melville to Faulkner, Amos Wilder sees American writers on a spiritual journey but unsatisfied by the existing paths. This is a positive development both for them and for the Christian church. When the spirit ceases to engage actively in religion, its petrifaction is the death of faith.

Thornton Wilder participated in the intellectual restlessness of modern literature to a greater extent than is usually recognized. His ideas on religion were always too complex to be pigeonholed. For instance, in an undated letter to Amos (probably from the mid-1930s), he declines a request to help some of Amos's friends:

No, I couldn't write a preface on immortality for the Bradley's. I'm not even interested in immortality and regard the preoccupation with it as one of the factors that has obscured the true premises of the religion. It's a matter that [we] will be informed about later and is at present none of our business. As Stein says: it's bound up with that insistence on identity, that greed about one's self, and the Human Mind at its best knows no identity. Excuse my tone.[19]

Gertrude Stein here is used as an explanation, not as a source; the idea that individuals treasure identity and are terrified of losing it had already been dramatized in "And the Sea Shall Give Up Its Dead" in *The Angel That Troubled the Waters* before Wilder ever met Stein. His view seems to be that the individual is trapped by identity (just as authors are trapped by concern for the audience), while pure action and thought achieve freedom from narrow self-interest.

This is not a novel concept: Shaftesbury and Kant in the eighteenth century had argued that ethics must be separated from self-interest, and the aestheticists of the nineteenth century, such as Pater and Wilde, separated the artistic object from any criteria other than the purely aesthetic; the object creates intensified experience, and that is its justification. The individual should not expect the reward of immortality for faith anymore than one does the ethical thing because one expects a reward, or produces a superior aesthetic object because it will gain the approval of the audience. The "mind" ought not to be reduced to either the cause-and-effect relationship of action and reward or tied to a concept of essential identity. In religion, one apprehends, serves, or worships the divine because it is divine, not because one hopes to preserve one's identity eternally. Right now, our business lies in this world. The next one is not only something we know nothing of, but it is also a distraction, in this view. God is also a kind of audience and therefore also a distraction

Caesar in Wilder's *The Ides of March* knows that decisions based on what others will think can only influence him negatively: "I must arrive at my decisions as though they were not subject to the comments of other men, as though no one were watching" (*Ides,* 35). The problem goes beyond faulty judgment to a loss of awareness in concern for others' ideas: "It is in this sense that responsibility is liberty; the more decisions you are forced to make alone, the more you are aware of your freedom to choose. I hold that we cannot be said to be aware of our minds save under responsibility and that no greater danger could befall mine than that it should reflect an effort to incur the approval of any man, be it Brutus or Cato" (*Ides,* 34). The audience robs one of choice because it restricts choices. And the idea of choosing based on whether or not one could conceivably be rewarded in another world also robs one of responsibility and hence liberty.

The catchall term for a philosophy of freedom by which the isolated individual through choice creates not only himself but also the world as experienced is "existentialism." The difficulties of the term are inherent in the fact that Christians such as Kierkegaard, Dostoyevsky, Berdyaev, and Unamuno can be lumped together with atheists such as Nietzsche, Sartre, and Camus under this heading. Nor is it clear that existentialism is that original a position. In a letter dated March 7, from sometime in the 1940s, Amos writes to Thornton claiming, in essence, that what was true in existentialism was not original, and what was original was not true:

> Their sense of the depth of life and the unpredictable or even "irrational" act or word of God is invaluable—but the values in that can be retained by a sufficient reemphasis of what is already in the greatest Pauline-Calvinist tradition. We must not ignore or despise the concrete-historical existence—the revelation of God in the vicissitudes of a people's history—the incarnation in a historical context—the empirical conditioning of all unreligious realities. In other words—save the bigness and austerity of the existentialist but not divorce it from real life. Otherwise we get a new kind of Gnosticism.[20]

Existentialism had become significant in theology as a response to the crisis caused by German criticism of the Bible in the nineteenth century. Amos Wilder particularly identifies it with Rudolf Bultmann and those influenced by him as a "neo-Kantian existentialist focus on the basic human category of the *conatus,* the will, choice, decision, obedience, [which] took priority over the faculties of knowing and affect (feeling and imagination)."[21] The helpful part of existentialism was, surprisingly, its emphasis on absurdity and anguish. The incommensurability of the divine with human understanding could deepen faith, while anguish at one's aloneness in freedom could call one to God. Nevertheless, Amos Wilder insists that the will detached from historical necessity is equally unhelpful. In an essay entitled "Christian Social Action and Existentialism," he argues that "revelation fully involves the believer as well as God and that our knowledge of God is conditioned not only by our emptiness or need but also by our 'nature' and even our capacities. If God's revelation is rightly identified with history—though not only with history—we must understand history in a fuller sense than an existential order of interpersonal decisions, as if creation could be bracketed out."[22] Thus, Amos sees the limitation of the existentialist as a denial of the real world of which we are a part with inborn gifts and external influences.

The influence of existentialism on Thornton Wilder can be overstated as well. In an undated letter with a Harvard letterhead and thus probably from the 1950s, Thornton responds to a query from Amos on behalf of Helmut Papajewski about Thornton's familiarity with Sartre, Kierkegaard, Unamuno, Ortega, and Heidegger with undisguised irritation: "Let there be no mistake about it: I have had no training in philosophy, could not—except at the table talk level—expound what existentialism is."[23] On the other hand, Wilder had become friendly with Sartre and even translated his play *Mort sans sépulture;* it was produced in Greenwich Village in 1948 as *The Victors.* In a letter to Joseph W. Still dated "March 6 or 7 '46," he summarizes Sartre and Sartre's version of existentialism: "There is no God; there is the concession of the absurdity of man's reason in a universe which can never be explained by reason; yet there is freedom of will defended for the first time on non-religious grounds."[24] Certainly, Sartre emphasizes the absurd position of man in the indifferent and unknowable universe in ways that seem reminiscent of Wilder's Caesar: "All these trivial passive expectations of the real, all these commonplace everyday values, derive their meaning from an original projection of myself which is my choice of myself in the world." To live a passionate and authentic life, one must reject the ordinary and the passive for the heightened experience of anguish: "In anguish I apprehend myself at once as totally free and as not being able to derive the meaning of the world except as coming from myself."[25]

And in his creative works, most particularly in *Les Mouches (The Flies)*, first published in France in 1943 and in the United States in 1947, Sartre dramatizes religion as a prison of collective guilt. Zeus is "god of flies and death."[26] Orestes repudiates him: "Suddenly, out of the blue, freedom crashed down on me and swept me off my feet. Nature sprang back, my youth went with the wind, and I knew myself alone in the midst of this well-meaning little universe of yours. I was like a man who's lost his shadow. And there was nothing left in heaven, no right or wrong, nor anyone to give me orders." In this realization, Orestes discerns the tragic kinship he has with Zeus: "You are God and I am free; each of us is alone, and our anguish is akin."[27] What the play suggests is that even if there is a realm of the divine, it is not significant to human action or ethical judgment. Robert G. Olson explains that, for Sartre, "emphasis should be placed upon the fact that even if God did exist and even if man could know God, nothing would be changed. Since man is free, he must choose his own values and take upon himself the responsibility for his choice. He cannot shift this responsibility to God."[28] Religion, then, is an excuse for evasion, and Wilder's postwar work relentlessly attacks evasion.

In 1948, Wilder writes to Glenway Westcott on April 7 thanking him for his kind words about the *The Ides of March* and mentioning that the critics had not understood it: "It's been called frigid,—when it's all from and about the passions; it's been called calculated,—when it's recklessly spontaneous; it's been called hard,—when it's almost pathologically tremulous."[29] He had written to Amos more dryly on February 2 about *The Ides of March:* "That's my 'war-adjustment' book,—getting something out of my system, just as Heaven's my D—n was getting some aspects of Papa out of my system. The public pays for the therapy."[30] Wilder had never been conventionally pious: the war forced a further meditation on doubts held prior to his service. In a remarkable letter from the following year (August 28, 1949), Wilder criticizes the "Hebraic-Christian" approach to religion: "What a lot of cruel dark *nein-sagende* Palestinian provincial things it stifled the world with, and what a lot of narrow all-too-human pseudo-supernatural hocus-pocus it collected."[31] Amos Wilder would probably not have been bothered by the reference to the supernatural; liberal Protestantism had conceded most miracles in previous ages. And, of course, Amos as a biblical scholar had insisted that understanding the context of the Gospels was essential to their interpretation. But then Thornton goes much further, quoting Goethe speaking to Lavater with obvious approval: "Not even a clear and distinct voice from Heaven could convince me that water burns and fire quenches, that a woman can conceive without a man or that a dead man can rise and live again. On the contrary, I consider this a great blasphemy against the greatness of God and his revelations in Nature."[32] It is difficult to assess the significance of this letter. Wilder probably had not been a Christian in the sense of regarding Jesus as his personal savior for a long time, but he would continue to use the symbols of Christianity in his works. He claims in a letter (dated 1949) from the same folder in the Yale Collection that reading Goethe is "putting me *off* Kierkegaard," but Kierkegaard remained frequent reading, and it is difficult to read *The Alcestiad* or the later novel *The Eighth Day* without thinking of Kierkegaard's Knight of Faith. And Thornton Wilder was an artist and therefore capable of holding contradictory ideas in his head without cracking up, in F. Scott Fitzgerald's famous phrase.

In an earlier letter to Amos (February 1, 1945), Thornton illustrates his eclecticism:

> Hitler's death to me means reading all Casanova's memoirs . . . all Nietzsche, and the files of the *Journal of Religion* with excursions into the realms it points to. What splendid work you're doing by serenely accepting Catholic and Hebrew essays as being self-evidently *about the same thing.* How good for us; how good for them; how good for the Protestant Church.[33]

The scandalous autobiography of a libertine and the works of Nietzsche can coexist equably on Wilder's reading list with his brother's ecumenical work. Intellectual and religious pluralism were always congenial to Wilder. The war may have somewhat darkened his view of the cosmos, but it did not eliminate his remarkable tolerance for a wide range of ideas.

Still, Caesar certainly represents a challenge to conventional religious belief and would have been at home discussing existentialism in a Paris café in 1948. For instance, Caesar holds that concepts of divine order and providence may hinder man's acceptance of his freedom and responsibility in the world. He points out to his friend Turrinus the confusion surrounding providence even among believers: "I am amazed at the pious who insult their God by failing to see that as this world is run there is a field of circumstance that is not commensurate with God's providence and that God must have so intended it" (*Ides,* 16). Wilder probably regarded this as a perfectly unremarkable position to hold. In an undated postcard to his friend Joseph Still (from shortly after the end of the war), he explains this in response to Still's perplexity about the compatibility of divine omniscience and omnipotence and man's free will: "God's omniscience doesn't inhibit man's action; his omnipotence has been intentionally limited by himself in the gift to men of free will. That's dogma and must be accepted by every Catholic. Atheists can believe in free will, too. The imagination."[34] As for the claim about free will for atheists, the imagination during an aesthetic experience, according to Kant, "recognizes an expression of itself in the formally satisfying object—something it might itself have made, or would have made, out of freedom, though in harmony with the lawfulness (but not any particular law) of understanding."[35] On either material or theological grounds, there are no logical problems with man's free will; and if man has free will, then God's providence is not universal. Certainly, C. S. Lewis, in radio broadcasts during the war, regards this as one of the core precepts of Christianity: "Confronted with a cancer or a slum the Pantheist can say, 'If you could only see it from the divine point of view, you would realize that this is also God.' The Christian replies, 'Don't talk damned nonsense.'"[36] God created the world, but the world has gone wrong, and He calls on man to see it put right again.

But I believe that Caesar is saying more than that God's providence is logically limited. It is "impious" to attribute all suffering to God, and only the unthinking can accept the claim that what appears

to be evil is only superficially so, and thus ultimately God's will. Caesar is writing about providence to his friend Turrinus, who had been
captured and tortured by the Belgians: "They had cut off an arm and
a leg, perhaps more, put out his eyes, cropped his ears, and were about
to burst his eardrums" (*Ides,* 25). If the suffering of Turrinus is a part
of God's providence, then it is difficult to distinguish God from a
demon. Moreover, *The Ides of March* is dedicated to two friends of
Wilder's, Lauro de Bosis and Edward Sheldon. The latter is probably
the inspiration for Turrinus. A successful playwright, Sheldon was
stricken with virulent arthritis and then blindness and spent many
years bedridden: "By 1930 Sheldon's body had become fixed in a rig-
idly supine position; he was sightless, unable to move his head or hold
a pencil."[37] Despite these infirmities he was a source of wisdom and
practical advice for playwrights and others on the New York theater
scene for many years.[38]

The story of Lauro de Bosis is both sad and heroic. A friend of
Wilder's dating back to his days at the American Academy in Rome,
he translated *The Bridge of San Luis Rey* into Italian as well as Sir James
Frazer's *The Golden Bough.*[39] Appalled at the fascist regime of Mussolini, he organized chain letters of resistance (which Wilder imitates
in "The Broadsides of the Conspiracy" in Book Four of *The Ides of
March*) and put up manifestos about how to resist the regime. Finally,
he learned how to fly and flew over Rome dropping leaflets implor-
ing the king of Italy to resist Mussolini; he and his plane disappeared
on October 3, 1931. Mussolini, of course, unaffected by de Bosis'
protests, continued in power. Between the deaths of Sheldon and de
Bosis and his own wartime experiences, Wilder brought to *The Ides of
March* an emotion, if not utterly different from his works of the 1930s,
at least more fraught with an awareness of destruction.[40] He writes to
his aunt Charlotte on April 5, 1945: "Some of my colleagues are cynical when I talk of how wonderful the day of peace will be; I'm not; it's
wonderful enough to know that conscious death dealing has come to
an end."[41] A consequence of the emotions occasioned by war and the
suffering and loss of friends is a recurrent sense that the problem of
evil is unresolvable. Why and how does one live when one suspects
that there is no ultimate resolution?

Caesar has no difficulty in seeing some religious practices as purely superstitious. The first two pages of the novel emphasize his use of religion for political advantage. Annoyed by endless reports about the condition of the entrails of sacrifices, sent to him because he is "supreme Pontiff," Caesar issues orders to his "ecclesiastical secretary":

> Item I. Inform the Master of the College that it is not necessary to send me ten to fifteen of these reports a day. A single summary report of the previous day's observation is sufficient.
> Item II. Select from the reports of the last four days three signally favorable and three unfavorable auspices. I may require them in the Senate today. (*Ides,* 4)

He mirrors the use of "magic" that Frazer attributed to the intelligent rascals of history, such as Caesar, in *The Golden Bough.* But Wilder writes to Amos in 1946 affirming that he was trying to avoid the Caesars of numerous other authors: "I of course try to keep my eyes fixed only on the basic documents, so that my inevitably 'wrong' interpretation will at least be all mine, spontaneously mine."[42] But this was a hopeless endeavor, as Wilder surely knew, and nowhere more than in Caesar's refusal to be bound by convention, religious or otherwise.[43]

According to Frazer, since the smartest men knew that their claims of magical powers were false, they were in the best position to gain influence and actually advance society because they labored under no illusions. After describing the professional sorcerer of early societies as a "a man of the coolest head and sharpest wit," Frazer dismisses the sincere magician as an "honest fool" and argues that no state is less likely to move forward than a primitive democracy: "In the field of politics the wily intriguer, the ruthless victor, may end by being a wise and magnanimous ruler, blessed in his lifetime, lamented at his death, admired and applauded by posterity. Such men, to take two of the most conspicuous instances, were Julius Caesar and Augustus."[44] Whether Wilder recalled this passage in Frazer cannot be determined, but his Caesar is much closer to Frazer's than it is to, for instance, Shakespeare's.

Precisely because Wilder's Caesar is free from religious belief in the sense of a belief that the supernatural impinges on the world, he is able to employ religion for the benefit of the state by cherry picking omens to pass legislation. In fact, Wilder's Caesar considers publishing an edict announcing that none of the gods ever existed, again for the good of the state (*Ides,* 37). One need not think of scorn for religion as a particularly modern idea. Lucretius, whom Caesar refers to in connection with the erotic (*Ides,* 39), argues that there is no reason to suppose that divine beings would be interested in creating humans or anything else, and that "the universe was certainly not created for us by divine power: it is so full of imperfections."[45] Thus, although Wilder writes a novel deliberately full of anachronisms, his presentation of Caesar as a man indifferent to conventional religious belief is perfectly congruent with the historical figure.

But Wilder's modernist Caesar remains troubled by religion itself because it must flow from the human mind; its presence is an attempt to dodge freedom. This happens to the matrons of Rome in the Rites of the Good Goddess: "These women are employing but a small part of their strength, because they are ignorant that that strength is their own. They regard themselves as helpless, as victims of malevolent forces and as beneficiaries of this Goddess whom they must implore and propitiate" (*Ides,* 155). Presumably, Caesar allows the profanation of the Rites to free the women from dependence on anything other than their own creative capacity. Further complicating Caesar's desire to bring the true freedom of choice and responsibility to Rome is the fact that people have begun to worship him, from Cleopatra down to the plebians. To release Rome from this delusion, he allows his own assassination (of which he has been warned repeatedly). He writes to Turrinus, "it is by taking a leap into the unknown that we know we are free" (*Ides,* 238).

Like Wilder's first three novels, *The Ides of March* takes place at a time of historical change: the death of the Republic and the birth of the Empire. This has loose analogies to the aftermath of World War II, when the old European order was assuredly destroyed, and the United States was facing a world in desperate need of rebuilding with no blueprint from which to work. The novel does not end hopefully.

The assassins know so little of their own characters that they cannot recreate the Republic. Still, Caesar's last gift is the choice of action: "Where there is an unknowable there is a promise" (*Ides,* 239).

Wilder would write in his journal in 1955, "I must emerge from this dibble-dabble in religious subject-matter; I must shake my whole self and learn what I do and do not believe, or else eschew such themes altogether. I am ashamed of this lukewarm imitative dilettante religiosity."[46] His last two novels, *The Eighth Day* (1967) and *Theophilus North* (1973), are uncompromising in their examination and rejection of much of conventional piety in the United States. That is, Wilder does not finally eschew religious themes but subjects them to a searching critique.

In *The Eighth Day,* Wilder begins in Coaltown, a place that "receives little direct sunlight. Many of the citizens seldom see a sunrise or a sunset or more than a fragment of a constellation" (*ED,* 18). This darkness is spiritual as well as intellectual and physical. Religion there is an example of Weber's claims about Protestantism and capitalism: "The Christian religion, as delivered in Coaltown, established a bracing relation between God's favor and money. Penury was not only a social misfortune; it was a visible sign of a fall from grace. God had promised that the just would never suffer want. The indigent were in an unhappy relation to both the earthly and heavenly order" (*ED,* 47). The tormented patricide George writes to his sister about his tragic predestination: "It's the way God made the world. He can't stop it now or change it. Some people are damned before they are born. You won't like that, but I know. God doesn't hate the damned. He needs them. They pay for the rest" (*ED,* 337). Thus, George sees himself as a tragic scapegoat taking on the sins of the community. At the same time it enables him to escape responsibility for the murder that he commits: the Protestant heritage allows him the satisfaction of thinking that he was always going to do it.

In this novel even what once in Wilder's work represented gold has been transmuted to dross. There is an echo of "The Happy Journey to Trenton and Camden": "Up to the time of the First World War . . . every man, woman, and child believed that he or she lived in the best town in the best state in the best country in the world. This conviction filled them with a certain strength" (*ED*, 15). But clearly in this novel Coaltown is an ignorant and unhealthy place because "nothing escaped the eyes of Coaltown except the truth" (*ED*, 363). Loyalty to it is a mistake, and all the principal characters have to leave the town in order to grow: John as an escaped convict, but Roger, Lily, Constance, and George to exercise their abilities. Misery is also the lot of the miners in the Andes and the riffraff of New Orleans. In other words, the problem is not just here at home: the outside world itself is struggling with suffering.

A part of the difficulty in America, at least in Wilder's view, is a large-scale social reorganization from patriarchy to matriarchy, of which the characters are unaware and which forces social distortion: "we may assume that when a patriarchal order is at its height—or a matriarchal order, also—it has a certain grandeur." But just as the divine right of kings has faded, so has the father as unquestioned head of his family, although not without consequences: "It is when the patriarchal order is undergoing transition—the pendulum swings in eternal oscillation between the male and female poles—that havoc descends upon the state and on the family" (*ED*, 286). Breckenridge perpetuates on George the errors that his own father made in raising him, denigrating him whenever he fails to be a "man." Eustacia attempts to help them both as much as she can, but while she and her daughter Félicité can maintain their good spirits through humor and withdrawal, respectively, neither Breckenridge nor George has the resources to adapt to or even understand the shifting structure of society. Religion comes to Breckenridge only before he dies, and George has only his instinctive fatalism. They are would-be patriarchs in a society moving away from the divine right of white men to rule. While Lily can tell Roger with complete self-assurance that "marriage is a worn-out old custom like owning slaves or adoring royal families" and move untroubled from lover to lover, she quite rightly says, "I pity the man who'd be married to me" (*ED*, 237). She has accepted and is even instigating social change, while most men have not. What is necessary is a new set of myths allowing Americans, like the children in "Childhood," to explore imaginatively the new roles available, and American life has not developed those yet.

The shift in organizing social principle from matriarchy to patriarchy can be compared to plate tectonics, a force that people must adapt to or be crushed by in an earthquake. More immediate is a religious establishment that colludes with an oppressive economic order. T. G. Speidel is the muckraking journalist of the novel, and he reveals the systemic corruption that allows Coaltown: "The most sacred thing in the world is property." In a line that could come straight out of Upton Sinclair's *The Profits of Religion,* he tells Roger, "There's no marriage tighter than that between the banker and the bishop. The poor should rest content in the situation in which God has seen fit to place them. It's God's will that they work a lifetime over a sewing machine or in a mine" (*ED,* 210). (This is not the entire truth; the archbishop of Chicago turns out to be both pious and wise.) But, consequently, the narrator hails Speidel as a child of Apollo: "The children of the Sun reflect the characteristics of Apollo leading the muses in his train, healing, cleansing with light, dispelling mists, prophesying: Thomas Garrison Speidel" (*ED,* 214). Honest scorn remains admirable, and Roger needs to learn from it, because nothing can arise from unthinking ignorance.

And below and behind wrenching social change and the decay of established religion lies the dream of the void. María Icaza tells John his dream: "And there is this nothing—*nada, nada, nada*—but this *nada* laughs, like teeth striking together" (*ED,* 121). For John, "a man of faith," this is the worst of all possible visions: that there is no point to his love or his work. The narrator tells us, however, that "many men and women can live out their lives without any resort to superstition, magic, prayer, or fetish. They remember no anniversaries, salute no flags, and bind themselves by no oaths. They submit themselves totally to blind circumstance, who takes away without thought what it gave without plan" (*ED,* 150). Dr. Gillies, whose son had died in a sledding accident while at college, believes that "the coming century would be too direful to contemplate—that is to say, like all other centuries," and "he had no faith in progress, in the future of mankind" (*ED,* 23). As a physician he sees the material basis for human behavior, and from his late-night reading of history he believes: "There are no Golden Ages and no Dark Ages. There is the ocean like monotony of the generations of men under the alternations of fair and foul weather" (*ED*, 24). These are perfectly plausible visions, all not merely without God but also without any religious content whatsoever. Despair, indifference, and stoic resignation are all perfectly normal reactions to the data of life. While such a view is present in Wilder's prewar works (particularly in *Heaven's My Destination*), in *The Eighth Day*, Dr. Gillies is presented as an admirable character and a fair judge of men and manners, which was not true of, for instance, Burkin in the earlier novel.

And the title character in Wilder's last novel is a kind of skeptic. According to Tappan Wilder's afterword in the 2003 edition of *Theophilus North,* the German translation of the novel has, at Thornton Wilder's suggestion, the subtitle "A Saint Despite Himself" (*TN*, 378). The idea of sainthood in this context bears close examination, even though Theophilus' first ambition was to be a saint, albeit he records it "with shame" (*TN*, 2). His name may mean "lover of God," but it is not a conventional love, because, as he tells the reader on the second page, "Unfortunately I had ceased to believe in the existence of God in 1914 (my seventeenth year)" (*TN*, 2). Further, he says, "I didn't believe in any sense in the universe" (*TN*, 37). He recalls "haranguing a fellow-master at the school" about his romantic vision of the sea: "The sea is neither cruel nor kind. It is as mindless as the sky" (*TN*, 13). Interestingly, he reads, "with mounting dissatisfaction, William James's *Varieties of Religious Experience*" (*TN*, 148). The dissatisfaction is unexplained, but James takes religious experience as a fact rather than an illusion (unlike Freud writing later), and this suggests that Ted (as he prefers to be called) finds James's catalogues of religious experiences unconvincing. Certainly, the book, which is written not firsthand by Ted but as an act of memory many years later by Ted as an older man, shows traces of the twentieth century and the important acquaintances whom he shares with Thornton Wilder. Sartre's *No Exit* is quoted on the hellish claustrophobia of society: "As an author of a later day has said, 'Hell is *they*'" (*TN*, 254). And Freud discusses Oliver Goldsmith's *She Stoops to Conquer* with Ted.

It is clear that Ted thinks that there are significant weaknesses in the Anglo-Saxon Protestant culture itself. He discusses with Mino the famous passage in Dante about Count Ungolino, who eats his son, and then tells Mino that the nineteenth-century American scholar Charles Eliot Norton as well as Longfellow and Thomas Carlyle's brother all mistranslate the passage: "They've wanted the sweetness without the iron—without the famous Italian *terribilità*. Evasion, shrinking from the whole of life" (*TN*, 226). This did not keep them or their descendants from telling others how they should behave, a part of his heritage abjured by Ted: "My father and my ancestors went about grandly telling others where their duty lay. I hope that will never be said of me" (*TN*, 318). Instead, he seeks, as an anthropologist and an archeologist (two of his nine ambitions), to understand the world around him and to help others do so as well.

In all of these works, many characters lack an adequate religious myth to explain their place in being, and some are lost because of it. Nevertheless, Wilder affirms human freedom and responsibility even for the lost. In *The Ides of March,* Clodia, who, like Caesar, regards the universe as absurd, repeatedly claims that she is free. She writes to Catullus, "I shall live as I choose" (*Ides,* 69). She explains to Cassia, whose husband is a friend of Catullus, why she treats Catullus so badly: "I will not permit any man, any man, to think he has any rights over me whatever. I am a completely free woman. Catullus insists he has a claim on me. I had to show him quickly that I did not recognize any such claim" (*Ides,* 42–43). Her "freedom," however, is illusory in that she refuses to accept responsibility for her life. In the very next document, she states that Caesar has a responsibility to her because of "that monstrous thing that life did to me" (*Ides,* 45). Although it is never made clear exactly what was done to her, she remains trapped in a version of nihilism, as Caesar writes to Turrinus: she "has lost intelligible meaning to herself and lives only to impress the chaos of her soul on all that surround her" (*Ides,* 32). Both Caesar and Clodia see the universe as empty, but Caesar also sees an opportunity: "How terrifying and glorious the role of man if, indeed, without guidance and without consolation he must create from his own vitals the meaning for his existence and write the rules whereby he lives" (*Ides,* 37). The indifference of the universe does not eliminate "meaning" because "meaning" is something that man creates. Significance comes from choice, choice entails responsibility, and any attempt to shift this responsibility to another, whether an audience, a person, or God, is an attempt to deny one's freedom. Clodia's is a false freedom where, in Sartre's terms, she "apprehend[s] our particular possible by avoiding considering all other possibles, which we make the possibles of an un-differentiated other."[47] Trapped in a fictionalized essential self, Clodia is completely imprisoned in her anger and egotism.

Thus, self-imprisonment, such as Clodia's, is not to be pitied, but rather condemned as sin. In *The Seven Deadly Sins,* Wilder dramatizes some of the ways people imprison themselves and readmits a spiritual dimension by calling it sin. In "Cement Hands (Avarice)," Roger Os-terman's family can give away millions to charity but cannot leave a tip for a waiter if it means "putting their hands in their pockets" (*CP,* 572). A part of this is "irrational fear," which the family friend of Roger's fiancée explains through a parable of a shepherd who repeat-edly finds gold pieces under a tree. Since the shepherd knows he has done nothing to earn the money, he is forced to ask, "*Where do they come from? And why* are they given to *him?* Are they, maybe . . . super-natural?" The shepherd becomes used to having the money so he must propitiate the gods by giving some of it away, while at the same time he is haunted by the fear that the coins will not keep coming. Diana sees the problem: "Frightened, because . . . if the gold pieces stopped coming, he'd not only be poor . . . he'd be much more than poor . . . He'd be exposed. He'd be the man who was formerly fortunate, formerly—what did you say—intelligent, formerly virtuous and—" (*CP,* 581). Blake draws the conclusion: "So he was in the terrible situ-ation of having to GIVE all the time and of having to SAVE all the time" (*CP,* 582). The rich are different from us not because, as Hem-ingway said, they have more money, but because they know they are not more able and consequently their wealth becomes a psychological burden.

A privileged life has been given to a pleasant but otherwise ordi-nary young man with no particular intelligence or courage, and no accomplishments independent of the generosity made possible by his family's wealth. Roger says, "I'd like to give [away] everything I've got. I don't care how I live; but I don't like to be forced to give any-thing. It's not my fault that I have money" (*CP,* 580). But the conse-quences of his avarice are "an incorrect relation to . . . . To material things—and to circumstance, to life—to everything" (*CP,* 574). Blake has seen Roger's father force his mother to ask for every dime: "He would give her hundreds of thousands in her hands but she *must ask for it.* He wants that picture: that everything comes from him" (*CP,* 573). This is dehumanizing and alien to love, which gives freely, and Roger dimly recognizes it. He knows that the elderly beneficiaries of his family's charities want money: "You see, in a sense, they have everything: shelter, clothes, food, companionship. We've scarcely found one who wishes to leave the institution. But they all want the one thing for which there is no provision" (*CP,* 577). Money allows choice to the person who possesses it, and Roger and his family need control. Even discussing money distresses him intensely: "I don't think you realize, Diana, that my life is enough of a hell as it is: the only way I can cope with it is to *never* talk about it" (*CP,* 583). Whether sin or psychological trauma, Roger can never find either absolution or therapeutic recognition because his avarice cannot be discussed. Diana is herself presented with a stark choice:

> DIANA: No. I'm not an angel. I'm a very *human* being. I'll need to be fed. And clothed. And—
> ROGER: (*Bewitched; kissing her gravely*): I'll see you have everything.
> DIANA: I can look forward to everything!
> ROGER: Yes.
> DIANA: Like those old ladies in the poorhouse, I can look forward to—
> ROGER: *My* giving you everything. (*CP,* 583)

Roger can give Diana everything except money, because money confers the freedom of choice. The problem with avarice is not just that it isolates the miser; it also threatens the freedom of others. The play ends grimly, as Diana returns to tip the waiter adequately; the audience supposes that she will marry Roger after all. She is unable to confront him directly, and Blake's efforts to force Roger to some awareness of his incorrect relation to life has failed.

In "Shakespeare and the Bible (Wrath)," two of the three central characters are attempting to conceal their past. Mrs. Mowbrey once ran a brothel. She is called upon by Lubbock, a former patron of her brothel and a lawyer with a shady past, which she has unearthed. He is now engaged to her niece Katy:

> You took your time finding yourself, didn't you? All that unpleasantness down in Philadelphia. What happened exactly? Well, we won't go into it. Then you gave yourself a good shaking. You pulled yourself together. Law school—very good. People are still wondering where you got all that spending money. It wasn't horse racing. It wasn't cards. No one could figure it out. Apparently it was something you were doing up in Harlem.—Certainly your parents couldn't afford to give you anything. In fact, you were very generous to them. You bought them a house on Staten Island. (*CP,* 535)

The audience never discovers how Lubbock made his money; that past is opaque. Even his parents have been tucked away (the play is set in 1898 when Staten Island was still a rural retreat). He is thus well matched with Mrs. Mowbrey. He admires the portraits of her ancestors, and she "(*says dryly, without a smile*) It's not hard to find family portraits, Mr. Lubbock. There are places on Twelfth Street, simply full of them. Bishops and generals—whatever you want" (*CP,* 535).

The only weakness in Lubbock's façade is his betrothed. Katy knows only what she reads "in Shakespeare and the Bible. That's all I have to go by, John. Nobody else helps. You don't help me" (*CP,* 548). Yet she immediately sees that Mrs. Mowbrey is a "dreadful person," and when Lubbock insists that her failings are in the past, Katy says, "It's there—*now*" (*CP,* 545). Aware intuitively that both Mrs. Mowbrey and Lubbock are deceiving her, she breaks the engagement. And Katy is incapable of wrath, unlike her namesake in *The Taming of the Shrew,* whom she admires; and when Mrs. Mowbrey asks her if she has a temper, she responds that she wishes she did: "When things seem all wrong to me, I do something worse than have a temper. I turn all cold and stormy inside. It's as though something were dead in me" (*CP,* 543). Lubbock, on the other hand, has a violent temper and once wrecked the bar at Mrs. Mowbrey's brothel, an event she still regards as mysterious: "I can understand your losing your temper at *people,* Mr. Lubbock—we all do; but I can't understand your losing your temper at *things*" (*CP,* 551). Lubbock insists that he just lost his temper; and then, he opts to stay and eat and drink with Mrs. Mowbrey, thus effectively becoming her lawyer; his self-interest is more powerful than his love for Katy.

In this most cryptic of Wilder's one-act plays, wrath serves as an escape valve that allows one to take out on inanimate objects one's own pain. Lubbock apparently made his money by dishonest means but profits by it anyway. He chooses only what is to his advantage and relegates his failings to the past, a place far away, which allows him to conveniently forgive himself and Mrs. Mowbrey. Without this escape valve, Katy has only honesty: she cannot lose herself in wrath. But she knows ultimately who she is, while Mrs. Mowbrey and Lubbock construct façades around themselves. Wrath is a symptom of the isolation and loss of identity that follows from sin. They have affluence and have or will gain the world, but at the cost of their souls.

In "Bernice (Pride)," the choice of sin involves the refusal to accept a flawed identity. "Mr. Burgess" is in fact Walbeck, a convicted swindler. "Bernice" had been Sarah Temple, a murderer in Kansas City. But Bernice has rejected her past: "Ten years ago I made my life over. I changed my name and I changed everything about my life" (*CP,* 501). On one level this seems admirable. Bernice thinks that she has done so for her family. She says about her children, "Their mother's dead, of course. But I guess somebody's reminding them every day that their mother was a murderer.—That's bad enough, but it's not as bad as knowing their mother's alive.—Have you noticed that we gradually forgive them that's dead?" Walbeck then asks her if he should "kill off George Walbeck," and Bernice tells him, "Not so much for your sake as for other people's sake. It's not good for other people to have to do with persons who are in disgrace; it brings out the worst in them" (*CP,* 503). Ostensibly, then, this self-imposed isolation is an act of generosity, a determination not to lead others into the temptation of treating her with contempt for her "disgrace."

Thomas Merton, in a work originally published in 1961 and roughly contemporaneous with Wilder's plays in *The Seven Deadly Sins,* is instructive on sin in general and pride in particular: "For pride is a stubborn insistence on being what we are not and never were intended to be. Pride is a deep insatiable need for unreality, an exor-bitant demand that others believe the lie we have made ourselves be-lieve about ourselves."[48] The original crimes of Bernice and Walbeck are compounded by the lies they have created about who they are. The immediate choice before Walbeck is that his daughter Lavinia has written, possibly seeking to live with him, and is coming to see him. He burns the letter. When he asks what Bernice would do if her own daughter contacted her, she resists giving advice, admitting her own doubts about her flight into a new and false self: "How do I know if I did right? . . . If my daughter was with me, we'd talk . . . I got so many things I've *learned* that I could tell to a girl like that" (*CP,* 306). But to be loved, one must accept love, and pride will not allow that. Walbeck wants to leave it up to Lavinia, but Bernice tells him that young people cannot make choices because they "don't know what they're choosing":

> These are just fancies. We're a stone around their necks now! If we were with them we'd be a bigger stone. Sometimes I think death come into the world so we wouldn't *be* a stone around young peo-ple's necks. Besides you and I—we're alone. We did what we did be-cause we were that kind of person—the kind that chooses to think they're smarter and better than other people . . . And people that think that end up alone. (*CP,* 506)

The striking fact of Bernice's self-recognition is that she has not hu-mility enough to accept her sin and hence chooses isolation. Walbeck decides not to see his daughter and wonders what to tell her. Bernice makes the final judgment on both Walbeck and herself: "You go up-stairs and hide yourself. You're almost dead. You're dyin'" (*CP,* 506). We have been told that the wages of sin are death, but here the choice is an existential one. Unable to see how to free herself because of her pride, Bernice (and Walbeck) accept a living death in false identities in isolation from the world. Clodia in *The Ides of March* has done something similar.

Sin need not reach the level of pride to be rooted in self-deception. Throughout *Theophilus North,* Ted meets and frees people trapped by their fears or cultural taboos. His friend Rip, a war hero, has married a woman who, like Dickens's Mrs. Jellyby in *Bleak House* (for whom the sufferings of Africa alone are significant while her husband and children are neglected), embodies false valuation, forcing a miserly existence on her husband and children while throwing money at organizations for the prevention of cruelty to animals: "Oh it makes me boil—" fumes Ted's wise-woman friend Mrs. Cranston, "to think of that wonderful husband of hers and her children living on corned beef and kale soup while she spends thousands on dogs and cats" (*TN,* 126). Whatever one thinks about feathers on hats (a particular obsession of Rip's wife), it is still wrong to regard their ban as more important than one's family. Ted recurs to the theme that Wilder had also covered in "Cement Hands" when describing the rich: "They are haunted by the dread that what destiny, chance, or God has given them, destiny, chance, or God may as mysteriously withdraw. They are burdened by the problem of their merits" (*TN,* 357). Fear motivates Rip's wife's actions, not love of animals. Ted must show her how she is regarded by others in order for her to allow Rip freedom—and in doing so she may free herself.

I have argued in this chapter that Wilder portrays man as a biological organism as well as a product of society and institutional religion, who consequently faces enormous obstacles to freedom, but ultimately through sin he imprisons and kills the self. Still, by his insistence on freedom, he reintroduces a religious element to his works and the possibility of reformation. As I shall show in chapter 5, the sense of wonder and faith in spiritual evolution remain as the residue of religious belief in Wilder's postwar oeuvre.

Chapter Five

Mystery, Pluralism, and Evolution

Alongside the tendency to skepticism and, for want of a better term, existentialism in Wilder's postwar works, as well as the obstacles to human development in the psyche, society, and religion, there remains a religious tendency, as indicated by a recurring sense of mystery in the face of the universe. Nevertheless, while religious ideas appear frequently in these plays and novels, they reject a static omnipotent and omniscient divinity. Further, the works are expansive and tolerant of diverse traditions. Ultimately, Wilder's focus is on this world, and faith is placed in the possibility of spiritual evolution for the race, whereby even suffering serves as a developmental force.

In *The Ides of March,* what is striking is how much religious speculation Caesar indulges in. He lives as if life had meaning beyond what the individual creates for himself, and he wonders, "I cannot deny that at times I am aware that my life and my services to Rome seem to have been shaped by a power beyond myself." (*Ides,* 39). Thus, Caesar has not settled even for himself whether the universe is empty or whether the universe has design. He writes to Turrinus that he is increasingly occupied by the question, "Is there a Mind in or above the universe which is watching us?" (*Ides,* 217). Caesar does not abolish worship of the gods because he is not entirely sure that they do not exist. He also sees that the divine may be present in the erotic, great poetry, and he experiences something like union with God during his epileptic fits. In a sense, the novel presents Caesar as not choosing between theism and atheism, not holding an either/or position, but as maintaining a both/and view. In fact, he explicitly claims that both "the dream of the void" and the sacred vision "cannot be dismissed as illusions." The former "is at once laughter and menace. It turns into ridicule all delights and sears and shrivels all endeavor." But, "This dream is the counterpart of that other vision which comes to me in the paroxysm of my illness. Then I seem to grasp the fair harmony of the world."[1] The two visions are utterly contradictory. One reveals the universe as derisively mocking human hubris, a vision of irony and the death of meaning. The other presents the creation as musical composition, the dance of the spheres. "Both states arise from vapors in the body, yet of both of them the mind says: henceforth this I know" (*Ides,* 231).

From Caesar's inability to find a synthesis of these competing visions comes the technical tour de force of the novel's form. In a brilliant article about Wittgenstein, Joyce, and modernity, Thomas Singer argues that the experimental form of modern art is an attempt to point to that about which positivism cannot speak: "Significant language forms 'the walls of our cage,' and it is absolutely hopeless to say something significant about the ethical which lies outside. Outside is the world of art, of religious experience, of the mystical." Explicating Wittgenstein, Singer adds, "'Absolutely hopeless it may be, but the tendency is still significant; it still points to something; and that something is 'the most important point.'"[2] That which cannot be logically demonstrated can be, perhaps, embodied or, at least, suggested. Joyce's experimental form points to that which is beyond logical positivism. So, too, in Wilder's most formally daring novel, the reader circles Caesar from multiple perspectives, never finding an unchallengeable explanation of motives; and much remains mysterious but nevertheless important. The first book of *The Ides of March* (which concerns events from September 1, 45 BC to the morning of October 1) leads up to Clodia's dinner party for Caesar and Catullus and ends with an account of it told after the passage of fifteen years. The second book begins on August 17 and ends on October 27; Clodia's dinner party turns out to be a relatively minor event in the context of Cleopatra's visit to Rome, Caesar's ill-fated love for her, and the death of Catullus as a consequence of his unhappy love for Clodia. The third book widens the picture still further, from August 9 to December 13, and its subject is the conspiracy of Clodia and her brother to profane the mysteries of the Good Goddess, which Caesar allows to occur, despite the fact that he has been warned by Cleopatra. Finally, all of these story lines are set against the backdrop of what is historically the most important event: the assassination of Caesar, as told in the novel's last document written by Suetonius many years later. This book takes place between August 8 and the Ides of March (March 15), 44 BC, and, in Wilder's conception, Caesar clearly knows who the conspirators are and what they have planned, and he deliberately allows his own assassination to take place.[3]

I would not deny that part of the novel's form can be accounted for by Wilder's military experience in Army Intelligence. Many of the characters are either engaged in conspiracies or gathering information about conspirators. Moreover, the experimental character of the novel, with its variety of texts—graffiti, reports, letters, journals, poems—and disruptions of a linear narrative sequence, is consistent with the modernism that Wilder had championed in his prewar drama: to see Caesar anew against the background of the Caesars of Suetonius, Plutarch, Shakespeare, and George Bernard Shaw, he must be made strange, through the multiple perspectives.

But beyond these factors, the changes in perspective force the reader to reevaluate the adequacy of interpretation. Thus, the infidelity of Cleopatra and disloyalty of Marc Antony in the second book "struck to the heart" of Caesar, according to Cytheris (*Ides,* 141). Apparently the infatuated dictator sees the youthful queen with the athletic and much younger Antony and realizes the hopeless discrepancy between their ages. What the reader cannot know is how much of her memory is her emotional projection. But the reader does know that Cytheris loses Antony in the same affair, and she claims that only an actor could tell that Caesar is stricken by the event. The reader is left to wonder precisely how seriously is Caesar troubled by what, after all, is a common enough story about an older man recognizing his folly. And we subsequently discover that he leaves the party to sit by the bed of the dying Catullus.

That both events affect Caesar deeply is clear; which is more important is held in suspension. From Cleopatra's point of view, the vigil alongside Catullus is inexplicable. She asks her Secretary of State for clarification: "Are you convinced that you have explored all the significance of the Dictator's disappearance during my reception on the 27th? His attendance at the sickbed of a scurrilous versifier does not appear to afford a sufficient explanation" (*Ides*, 188). Cleopatra does not understand poetry; and, dominated by self-interest herself, she cannot understand how Caesar would mourn for a poet who had attacked him in his verses. My point here is that Wilder does not present an either/or choice between the two events to account for Caesar's depression. Both deal with the death of love and, consequently, of a kind of hope. Caesar remains, even to himself and to the other characters in the novel and to the reader, mysterious, a being rather than an essence. He cannot be reduced to the signification of words.

This kind of literary cubism parallels Caesar's awareness of the limitations of reason. As he watches over the dying Catullus, he writes to Turrinus about the meeting of Catullus and Clodia:

> Oh, there are laws operating in this world whose import we can scarcely guess. How often have we seen a lofty greatness set off a train of evil, and virtue engendered by wickedness. Clodia is no ordinary woman and colliding with her Catullus has struck off poems which are not ordinary. At the closer range we say *good* and *evil*, but what the world profits by is intensity. There is a law hidden in this, but we are not present long enough to glimpse more than two links in the chain. There lies the regret at the brevity of life. (*Ides*, 185)

This passage recalls other reflections on the inadequacy of human categories of knowledge, starting with Hamlet's remark that "There are more things in heaven and earth, Horatio, / Than are dreamt of in your philosophy" (*Hamlet*, 1.5.166–67). But the more immediate comparison would be with T. S. Eliot's "Gerontion": "Unnatural vices / Are fathered by our heroism. Virtues / Are forced upon us by our impudent crimes."[4] The mysteries of causality, particularly in the moral sphere, are too deep for a brief life to sound: the destructive Clodia has ultimately inspired great poetry. Presumably, then, it is foolish to think that human consciousness can fathom the divine, and equally foolish to dismiss the possibility of the divine.

Indeed, in Wilder's *The Alcestiad,* Hercules entertains serious doubts about his own widely acknowledged divinity. Because of his apparently superhuman feats, people have good reason to see him as more than man, but Hercules says that this overlooks how hard his labors are: "You see, Admetus, everyone says I am the son of Zeus and therefore my labors must be easier for me than for another man. If I have the blood and the heart and the lungs of Him (*pointing upward*) in me, shouldn't they be easy? But, Admetus, they are not easy. The Hydra!" (*CP,* 407). Partly this is pique; by underestimating his difficulties, people slight his achievements. His victory over the Hydra is achieved with immense effort and serious suffering, and rather than singing a *Te Deum* he wants the credit for it. But like Caesar, Hercules also wonders about the role of the gods in his life. Admetus reassures him that "God or man, Hercules—god or man, all men honor and are grateful to you," but Hercules persists, "But I want to know. Some days I feel that I am the son of Zeus. Other days I am . . . I am a beast, Admetus, a beast and a brute" (*CP,* 407). In Euripides' *Alcestis,* Hercules does not suffer from doubts, and he acts as a Hellenic gentleman ought to: because Admetus has treated him with hospitality, he will rescue the wife of his host. Wilder's Hercules rejects this classical virtue: "Hospitality is for guests not brothers" (*CP,* 409). Wilder's Hercules acts from love of Alcestis and Admetus and with hope, but his faith is shaky at best.

In *The Eighth Day,* Frank Rudge wonders if Miss Doubkov comprehends the reasons for Ashley's escape and the survival of the family at the Elms: "I don't think you realize how many mysterious things lie back of this thing. Who organized the rescue? [. . .] Who's behind the boardinghouse?" (*ED,* 72). His explanation is that Ashley must have rich friends; only wealthy patrons could pull off the rescue and subsidize the boardinghouse. The alternative, that a despised religious sect and a young girl are responsible, does not lessen the mystery. The Deacon of the Covenanters regards the same events as mysterious: "Your father did not lift a finger to save himself, but he was saved. That is strange. Your father had no friends, he says, but friends saved him. Your mother never left her house; she had no money; she was dazed. But a child who never held a dollar in her hand sustained a house. Is that not strange?" (*ED*, 377). The Deacon's answer differs from the private investigator's: "The sign of God's way is that it is strange" (*ED*, 377). The benevolent Bishop also knows that the world cannot be reduced to facts; he tells Roger, "Life is surrounded by mysteries beyond the comprehension of our limited minds. Your dear parents have seen them; you and I have seen them. We transmit (we hope) fairer things than we can fully grasp" (*ED*, 221). Again, denying the mysterious is a form of reductionism, and to avoid reductionism, tolerance must be extended to human belief. The limitations of the hard-headed mining directors in *The Eighth Day* are apparent when John works to bring a priest, over Mr. Smith's objections, to the mine high in the Andes. He informs John, "Roman Catholicism is childish superstition at best; in Chile it's beneath contempt" (*ED*, 153). John responds, "I think we're all bad judges of what goes on in other people's minds about God, Mr. Smith. It's a bad thing to force a God on a man who doesn't want one. It's worse to stand in the way of a man who wants one badly" (*ED*, 154). The priest, when he arrives, is a rigorous ascetic and clearly of a type superior to Smith. John is not a Catholic, nor even ostensibly a Christian, but he knows that the miners and their beliefs cannot be dismissed out of hand.

In *Theophilus North*, Ted, who we know has not believed in God from the age of seventeen, reads from Bishop Berkeley, a resident of the second city of Newport (the eighteenth-century city), to Dr. Bosworth, a member of the wealthy sixth city of Newport but with links to the scholarly fifth city of the nineteenth century, about Berkeley's controversy with Halley, when the astronomer had claimed that the doctrines of Christianity were inconceivable. Berkeley had countered that much of Newton was "obscure, repugnant and precarious": "'What are these fluxions . . . these velocities of evanescent increments? They are neither finite quantities, nor quantities infinitely small, nor yet nothing. May we call them the ghosts of departed quantities?' Crash! Bang! The structure of the universe, like the principles of the Christian faith—according to the Bishop—were perceived only by the intuition" (*TN*, 91). As I argued in an earlier chapter, this view is held also by Pascal and Goethe, an insistence that some knowledge, even of the most important kind, is not quantifiable. Ted seeks to avoid reductionism in any form.

That the world has more in it than can be expressed quantitatively is something that he knows from personal experience. He possesses "a certain gift for soothing, for something approaching mesmerism—dare I say for "driving out demons?" Nevertheless, Ted avoids, for the most part, either using this gift or even letting other people find out about it; "It is inseparable from a certain amount of imposture and quackery" (*TN,* 3). To use the gift not only restricts others, it traps Ted himself: "I want to engage in life in the spirit of play, not in leading others by the nose, nor in rendering others ridiculous in my own eyes" (*TN,* 280). He recognizes how his gift can be used, and he asserts that an engagement with life is the value that must trump all others. Ted openly admits his inability to comprehend all faiths, as is shown in his friendship with Eloise, who plans to be a nun: "She was disattaching herself from love of her family—and naturally from friendship—in order to encompass us all in a great offering that I could not understand" (*TN,* 187). Nevertheless, he respects her oblation because he loves her as she loves her family and God. He refuses to dismiss either Berkeley's or Eloise's faith or deny his own gift; to do any of the above would be as false as to accept simpleminded notions of religious faith. Granville Hicks summed up the complexity of Ted's character through an analysis of his name: "His first name proclaims that he is a lover of God, but we see him as one who loves his fellow man which—as Leigh Hunt observed—may be the same thing. As for the second name, it may be a reminder of the cold wind of skepticism."[5]

A sense of mystery is the perquisite for understanding the religious element in Wilder's postwar works. In the previous chapter I argued that *The Seven Ages of Man* for the most part indicates how we are trapped in our development as biological organisms, and that *The Seven Deadly Sins* shows how we trap ourselves. In the same cycles, however, Wilder presents plays that offer a more hopeful vision of development and sin. That is, experience cannot be reduced to biological determinism or to an all-encompassing sin: mysteriously, development leads to growth and sin to repentance. Ultimately, *The Seven Ages of Man* was to "give the impression of an unfoldment."[6] Man in the aggregate is not determined by biology. Writing to Amos about *The Seven Deadly Sins,* Thornton explains: "Anyway, I've got some of the virtues glimmering through the cracks of their janus-faced vices."[7] Sin itself can prompt the first steps toward holiness.

Development is a slow process, particularly in nature. Tom explains to his mother, Mrs. Carter, in "The Rivers Under the Earth," how sand dunes that form a point of land in the lake finally turn into woods: through a process of slow accretion of humus, soil is provided for grass, followed by bushes, then white pines, and finally red pines. A recurring theme in Wilder, the passing of civilizations, is mentioned in connection with the point of land in the lake (which to anyone who has lived in Madison, Wisconsin, is going to suggest Picnic Point on Lake Mendota): "We were told that this point had been some sort of Indian ceremonial campground . . . and a burial place, I suppose. Your father used to find arrow heads here" (*CP,* 638). Time, whether biological or cultural, changes things slowly, but the tone here is meditative rather than despairing. After all, the play is about parents and children. And the aging of parents is a part of the process of nature, regretted by both parties, perhaps, but not "tragic."[8]

Patience and faith combine in Wilder's works to allow time for development. In *Theophilus North,* Ted borrows from his alter ego's (Thornton's) life to talk about archeology and his year at the American Academy in Rome:

> We dug and dug. After a while we struck what was once a much traveled road over two thousand years ago—ruts, milestones, shrines. A million people must have passed that way . . . laughing . . . worrying . . . planning . . . grieving. I've never been the same since. It freed me from the oppression of vast numbers and vast distances and big philosophical questions beyond my grasp. I'm content to cultivate half an acre at a time. (*TN,* 373)

This passage echoes, whether consciously or not, a remark by Carl Jung. In *Symbols of Transformation* (first published in 1912 and first translated into English in 1916), Jung, praising Freud for his work on the unconscious and the Oedipal complex, claims that understanding Freud is similar "to the uncanny feeling which would steal over us if, amid the noise and bustle of a modern city street, we were suddenly to come upon an ancient relic": "Suddenly we remember that on this spot where we now hasten to and fro about our business a similar scene of life and activity prevailed two thousand years ago in slightly different forms; similar passions moved mankind, and people were just as convinced as we are of the uniqueness of their lives."[9] Continuity exists, and that frees Ted from the need to work toward radical transformations, since, after all, they are probably not possible, granted the underlying basis of human nature.[10] He escapes the terror of immensity that troubled Tennyson in *In Memoriam.*

Like Keats's Grecian urn, the human race is the product, if not of silence, at least of slow time. Moreover, it is difficult to determine when development occurs because of our inability to understand our own thought processes. Mrs. Carter associates fireflies with an old horse and tells Tom: "There are many associations like that one can't explain" (*CP,* 636). Tom is inclined to dismiss these reactions, but his mother thinks that they are significant: "No—all those quirks, as you call them, are like wrecks at the bottom of the sea. They mark the place where there was once a naval battle—or a storm" (*CP,* 637). Tom "learns about old age," according to his father, Mr. Carter, when another boy, meaning a different woman entirely, says that his mother is too old to sing. That his mother could age is not something that he has ever thought about. He is attracted to a girl named Violet because, when he was two, his mother had a "violet" phase, wearing violet-colored clothes and violet-scented perfume. There are unpredictable positive developments from these random associations. Tom decides to become a doctor to treat the problems of aging because of the misunderstanding about his mother. Mr. Carter decided to become a lawyer while thinking of the Indian initiation ceremonies that took place on the point. The virtues and practices that come with adulthood are set in motion by the forces that move the characters. Francesca, Tom's sister, recounts the story of the boy calling Mrs. Carter old: she knows this to be "mean" and says so when talking to her father. Her honesty cannot reach the unstated underlying cause: jealousy of her mother, because, just as Tom is closer to his mother, she is closer to her father. That recognition may come later. Francesca is, after all, very young. Still, honesty and humility, the mature awareness of one's weaknesses and, indeed, of the limitations of rationality, are ultimately essential to a meaningful life.

Ultimately, there are both pragmatic and religious elements to the plays of development. Pragmatically, one needs to be aware of the perils of faulty development. But faith is required to believe that there is a point to it all, that humanity is moving toward some greater good, as it seems to in "The Rivers Under the Earth." Similarly, even sin can be the impetus to development. While "Avarice," "Wrath," and "Pride" in *The Seven Deadly Sins* leave characters imprisoned in the tomb of self, as I argued in the previous chapter, other plays in the cycle portray an awareness of sin as the beginning of reform.

In "A Ringing of Doorbells (Envy)," Mrs. Beattie is a crippled widow whose daughter died young. Mrs. Kinkaid and Daphne are swindlers who cadge money from Army widows for fictitious voice lessons and whom Mrs. Beattie agrees to see even though her housekeeper, Mrs. McCullum, has warned her about them. Mrs. Beattie, *"proud, stoical and every inch the 'General's Widow'"* (*CP,* 520), is nonetheless consumed with envy:

> MRS. BEATTIE (*Her eyes on Mrs. McCullum with a sort of sardonic brooding*): Think of how full their lives must be!—Full . . . occupied!
> MRS. McCULLUM (*With a start*): What? What's that you said, Mrs. Beattie? *Occupied!*—But what they're doing is immoral.
> MRS. BEATTIE: I'd exchange places with them *like that.* (*CP,* 523)

Mrs. Beattie is no longer impressed with moral conventions and longs for any kind of activity. She seems tired of her dignity and of the insincere role that she has played for years. She also envies Mrs. Kinkaid, because the latter has still her daughter, who poignantly resembles Mrs. Beattie's own dead child:

> MRS. BEATTIE: Look!—She's studying her notes.—Yes, the girl— there is a resemblance . . . Isn't it strange . . . (*Broodingly, with a touch of bitterness*) Young . . . and beautiful . . . occupied . . .
> MRS. McCULLUM: And wicked!

MRS. BEATTIE (*Dismissing this*): Oh! . . . Alive . . . (*Starting to hobble off*) Alive and together. (*CP,* 524)

Solitude and inactivity are a negative state; Mrs. Beattie's envy is portrayed sympathetically.

Surprisingly, Daphne is the instigator of the confidence game, and her mother goes along because her daughter is more strong-willed than she. Daphne, too, is consumed with envy. When she sees the picture of Mrs. Beattie's daughter, she spits on it and says, "She had everything she wanted. She didn't know what it was to know *nobody,* to have to spend all your time among common vulgar people, to skimp—" (*CP,* 528). Daphne is not merely criminal, she is emotionally blind. She snarls at the crippled woman when Mrs. Beattie makes it clear that she knows they are swindlers: "(*Beginning with low contempt*): Oh, you can talk. You don't know what other people's lives are like. Our lives are just awful. You've got everything you want and you've always had everything you want. You don't know what it is for me to see my mother treated just like dirt by people she shouldn't have to speak to" (*CP,* 531). Daphne possesses youth, health, and beauty, while Mrs. Beattie can barely move and has for company only an unimaginative and dim housekeeper. Both envy the other.

Wilder did not finish the play, but it echoes and perhaps rejects the relatively unhopeful ending of "Cement Hands." In "A Ringing of Doorbells," Mrs. Beattie tells Mrs. McCullum to allow Daphne and Mrs. Kinkaid to speak, but Daphne silences her mother and tries to leave:

DAPHNE: [. . . .] And what right did you have to a life like that? None at all. You were born into the right cradle. That's all you did to earn it.
MRS. BEATTIE (*Firmly but not sharply to Daphne*): *Have* you a remarkable voice?
DAPHNE: No.
MRS. KINKAID: Daphne! (*CP,* 532)

As Hamlet tells Polonius, treat every man as he deserves and who shall 'scape whipping? No one controls into which family they were born, and to envy those who have position is as useful as envying those who are left-handed. The position of neither character is really enviable, and yet they imprison themselves bitterly through their envy. But possibly both have learned something. Mrs. Beattie seeks information and Daphne, apparently to her mother's surprise, tells the truth. In short, honesty at least suggests for both characters an acceptance of what cannot be changed and a movement toward a fuller realization of self. Sin does not end the possibility of self-realization unless the individual rejects self-examination.

In "The Wreck of the Five-Twenty-Five (Sloth)," the transition to repentance has already begun. Mr. Hawkins is a misanthrope. "All windows are the same," he tells the Rotary Club in a speech recounted by his friend: "You know how crazy people look when you see them through a window—arguing and carrying on—and you can't hear a word they say? He says that's the way things look to him. Wars and politics . . . and everything in life" (*CP,* 513). When the preacher describes the catastrophe of the atom bomb, Hawkins, according to his daughter, told him, "suppose the atom bomb didn't fall, what would we do then?" (*CP,* 510). Every work day he returns from the city on the same train: "There we sit for twenty years playing cards on the five-twenty-five, hoping that something big and terrible and wonderful will happen—like a wreck, for instance" (*CP,* 510). Hawkins sees himself as trapped in a world of façades. He tells his wife and daughter what he sees from the train: "Those people—those cars—that you see on the streets of Bennsville—they're just dummies. *Cardboard.* They've been put up there to deceive you. What really goes on in Bennsville— inside those houses—*that's* what's interesting" (*CP,* 536). Dishonesty characterizes his relations with his friends: "We're so expert at hiding things from one another—we're so cram-filled with things we can't say to one another that only a wreck could crack us open" (*CP,* 516). In short, he yearns for an apocalypse because it will provide a revelation of the truth of human behavior and relations. The misanthropy lies in his conviction that everyone is a hypocrite.

He is, of course, mistaken. Mrs. Hawkins's judgment is the sounder: "Minnie, the world is full of people who think that everybody's happy except themselves. They think their lives should be more exciting" (*CP,* 512). Hawkins plays on this when he tells his family that they should go to Bennsville: "They're happy there, aren't they? No, not exactly happy, but they live it up to the full. In Bennsville, they kick the hell out of life" (*CP,* 515). Again, sin isolates the individual in a penitentiary of the mind: "It's as though he thought he were in a kind of jail or prison" (*CP,* 508).

But until the time of the play he does nothing. The play begins with the mother and daughter contemplating what he might like for dinner. When the daughter notes that he did not complain about pork chops, Mrs. Hawkins says with exasperation, "He doesn't ever say anything. He eats what's there.—Oh, Minnie, men never realize that there's only a limited number of things to eat" (*CP,* 507). She wishes that he would complain. The catalyst for change in their household is a bequest from a woman who has told Hawkins that he needs to stand outside his own window and look in. He does so with difficulty: "It took me a whole hour to get up the courage to go and stand" (*CP,* 517). The challenge makes him nearly suicidal; in fact, he watches with a gun in hand. The similarity to Burkin in *Heaven's My Destination* cannot be missed: both men are looking at other people from a position of superiority, as if other people were merely specimens in a lab.

And that is not the way you look at people you care about. "People who've known one another as long as you and I have are not supposed to *see* one another," says his wife: "The pictures we have of one another are inside." Objectively everyone looks silly. Marriage is an action and to freeze it is to kill it, a sort of murder to dissect. Nevertheless, Hawkins has been jarred from sloth and will take up an active role in his life, first by taking his family out to dinner: "There is no 'away.' . . . There's only 'here.'—Get your hats; we're going out to dinner.—I've decided to move to 'here.'" How long Hawkins has been consumed by sloth, oblivious to reality, is made immediately apparent. His wife tells him that women no longer wear hats: "That was in your mother's time" (*CP,* 518). While comical, this dramatizes the years of sitting and eating what is put in front of him without complaint. Hope comes with the smallest of steps: going out to dinner.

And sin can even be a spur to virtue. In "Someone from Assisi (Lust)," Father Francis's song to Lady Poverty was originally sung to

Mona to seduce her. This is not merely an expression of lust. G. K. Chesterton writes insightfully about Saint Francis's relationship to the troubadours of southern France: "There was a strain in the southern romance that was an excess of spirituality, just as the pessimist heresy it produced was an excess of spirituality."[11] The paradoxical relationship between carnal and spiritual love so characteristic of religious literature in the medieval period is only part of what Wilder is dramatizing here. John the troubadour sought something beyond the merely physical, and so does Francis, precisely because the physical has so profound an attraction to him. Virtue is active, not simply a renunciation of sin, and always an ongoing process. Mother Clara and Pica treat Father Francis as if he were already a saint, but he knows that he needs their prayers. He urges Sister Clara to bless him after he has blessed her: "Say after me; God bless you Brother Francis, and God forgive you the load of sins with which you have offended him" (*CP,* 555). Despite his claim that Lady Poverty has freed him from his cowardice, he clearly fears to eat food with saffron or even to dine with the sisters of the order because he knows the pull that the flesh has for him. Moreover, he knows "how beautiful she [Lady Poverty] is! And . . . and (*Lowering his voice*) how severe. Sometimes I almost offend her!" (*CP,* 560). Despite his ecstatic union with Lady Poverty, he finds the world a grim place: "Who can measure the suffering—the waste—in the world? And every being born into the world—except One—has added to it" (*CP,* 558). He repeatedly urges Clara to come pray with him in the chapel as a way to flee the world.

But he had apparently forgotten Mona. Now mad, chased from her daughter's house every morning, and kicked and stoned by the boys of the town, she believes that a king, either Solomon or the king of "France" (the country of origin of Francis) is coming for her: "And I shall say: Oh, King, change the hearts of the world" (*CP,* 554). Near the end of the play, when she enters with half her face covered with blood, she confronts Francis:

> MONA (*She stares at Francis somberly*): Who are you? What's your name?
> FRANCIS: I was christened John.

MONA: John!—Do you know who John was?

FRANCIS (*In a small voice*): Yes.

MONA: You stand there—idle as a log—and *do* nothing. If all the men in world named John would join themselves together and be worthy of their name, the world would not be like *that*. (*CP,* 562–63)

The reference here is presumably to John the Baptist, who is to "make straight the way of the Lord" (John 1:23). Francis must not retreat to the chapel to pray; he must take action. Wilder dramatizes this vividly: "*As though overcoming a powerful repulsion, Francis applies the wet cloth to Mona's forehead*" (*CP,* 563). The play ends with Francis taking Mona by the arm and escorting her off the stage to her home. He leads away the victim of his sins, thus providing her with his protection. Desire was the impetus for Francis's behavior as courtier and as husband of Lady Poverty. Now he must do what he does not desire: touch the woman he seduced and walk with her. The consequences of sin remain even after one has renounced it.

Nowhere in *The Seven Deadly Sins* is it made clear what deity the sinner offends; sin mostly represents an absence of good. One must look elsewhere for something beyond the merely natural, the mysterious something that Caesar and Francis seek or sin against. Caesar proposes for discussion at Clodia's banquet the topic of whether poetry is inspired by the gods. Asinius Pollio obediently repeats something like the traditional Platonic arguments that it must be. Clodia responds that men are then doubly unhappy because men are not gods (and thus doomed to suffer) and the poets are liars, who portray a Golden Age that will never come. Further, they are deluded and, indeed, mentally ill from some childhood disorder, so they seek consolation in "their feverish dreams" (*Ides,* 81). Thus, even if the gods exist, they harm men by communicating through poets. Catullus' answer is the story of Alcestis, versions of which Wilder had been working on for many years, and which would subsequently become the first act of *A Life in the Sun* (1955).[12]

Alcestis seeks in the play "certain answers to the most important questions that can be asked." She desires to be more than a wife and mother, who, like Mrs. Antrobus, is "bound by that furious love that tigresses feel for their cubs": "She felt that there was more to be obtained from life than being the instrument of its forces and that that *more* could be obtained at Delphi" (*CP,* 82). That is, the life of humans, in the absence of the gods, differs little from animals, in that it is a product of instinct. Admetus, usually a self-reliant man, does not see the problem; he had felt the presence of Apollo when he yoked a lion and a boar together and drove them around the city. In his view, the divine has signalled that Alcestis should marry him, but she rejects such evidence: "It is just such stories which have increased the confusion in which all men live" (*Ides,* 84). The rejection by Alcestis of someone else's miracle is an interesting point that deserves exploration. Writing to Amos on October 13, 1940, Thornton expresses his own doubts about supernatural events: "You remember my formula for all supernatural phenomena, Yeat's table-rapping and all 'Seeing the XVIII Century,' and so on: *Fascinating but not interesting.* Atavistic pleasurable shudder but not assimilable knowledge."[13] Strikingly, even if one had evidence of the supernatural, that evidence does not translate to knowledge.

In a sense, Alcestis' rejection of such travelers' tales is similar to Eliot's: "Signs are taken for wonders"; the marvelous is not unequivocal evidence for the divine in that no general principle follows from the marvelous.[14] Admetus may have been the beneficiary of a miraculous intervention, but it does not follow that any obligation accrues to Alcestis, nor can his certainty create certainty for her. Then, Tiresias arrives to tell them that Apollo is manifest in one of five herdsmen at the gate who must serve Admetus for a year. Tiresias stresses that he, though a prophet, has no further information so questions are pointless. Just as Admetus is sure of the presence of the god in his dream, so Tiresias is sure that Apollo is here, and he warns Admetus to treat the herdsmen justly, which he would have done anyway, being Admetus the Just and Hospitable. In other words, Tiresias' knowledge does not generate a larger field of recognition or duty. Neither Admetus' miraculous performance nor Tiresias' prophetic voice can help Alcestis, who must find the god for herself. These events only increase confusion.

Alcestis goes to stand before the herdsmen and asks Apollo "to speak to her in His own person, to emerge from that hiding in which the Gods delight, and to give her an answer to the questions that were her very life" (*Ides,* 85). Alcestis seeks a personal god. The five herdsmen are not ordinary: one is a healer, one never loses his way however dark the night, one is an inventor, one is a poet, and one is a philosopher whose "interest is to inquire into the nature of the Gods— whether they exist and in what ways we find them" (*Ides,* 87). But they are all imperfect. The healer will let a child die so he himself can sleep; the inventor's wonders "don't mean" anything in that neither he nor anyone else can figure out what to do with them; the navigator cannot stop drinking even in the presence of Alcestis. Worst of all, the poet "loses joy in the thing he has made and is in labor to fashion another. That is enough to assure me that he is not a God, nor even a messenger of the Gods, for the Gods cannot be thought of as despising their handiwork" (*Ides,* 87). The philosopher's tale is interrupted by Caesar falling into an epileptic fit, so Catullus' tale is not completed, but there is no need to explain why philosophers cannot be Apollo: their answers are always unsatisfactory, at least to those who are not philosophers.

Catullus' answer to Clodia's nihilism through the Alcestis myth is twofold. The first is that an imperfect messenger, such as an immature or deluded poet, is not evidence either that the gods do not exist or that they mean ill to man. An argument proposed by a politician may be a good argument whatever the motivations of the politician; the purpose of the argument is irrelevant to the soundness of the argument. Clodia's argument of the imperfections of poets is therefore a version of the genetic fallacy. The herdsmen represent something that transcends their time and place: for example, the healer remains a source of knowledge whatever his personal limitations may be. That the poet is not satisfied with his work means that he can see beyond his own limitations. The failings of Catullus therefore are not germane to whether or not Catullus is inspired. And the second response is implicit in the collapse of Caesar, who elsewhere writes that he can sense the divine during his fits. Catullus now sees "greatness humbled in insanity [and] wrote no more stinging epigrams against him" (*Ides,* 88).

Caesar is no ordinary man, yet he, too, has the failings of his physical form, just as Catullus' greatness as a poet comes from a critical error, if not flaw: his love for the utterly unworthy Clodia. Again, Eliot's "Gerontion" is pertinent: virtue can cause vice, and vice versa.

But the real question of the Alcestis story is explored more fully in the play. If *The Ides of March* is fundamentally an exploration of personal freedom, which must be established in the face of religions that limit the individual, then *The Alcestiad* is an expression of personal freedom as itself a religious statement. Since the gods and man are incommensurate, how could either communicate with the other in the first place?[15] In *The Alcestiad,* the herdsman asks Alcestis: "But if they did exist, these gods, how would they speak to us? In what language would they talk to us? Compared to them, we are diseased and dying and deaf and blind and as busy as clowns. Why, there are some who even say they love us. Could you understand that? What kind of love is that, Princess, when there is so great a gulf between the lovers?" (*CP,* 387). Would there not be something strange about gods who would waste their time on something as far beneath them as men? Death tells Apollo to leave men alone: "They will never understand your language. The more you try to say something, the more you drive them distraught" (*CP,* 373). Tiresias says sourly, "If the gods didn't love men, we'd all be happy; and the other way round is true, too: if we men didn't love the gods, we'd all be happy" (*CP,* 383). However, this happiness of men and gods would be torpor, a contentment untroubled by aspirations. The divine exists to stir men out of their content, but divine love faces inherent difficulties in expressing itself. An acute reviewer of the play for *The Times* of London laid out the fundamental difficulty of Apollo: "If he reveals himself in his glory, he must provoke abasement, but abasement is not love. If he hides his divine attributes, it would be an act of condescension, and love does not admit of condescension."[16]

The problem of incommensurability exists in the nature of things. But sometimes the difficulty is that the divine can no longer be seen through the veil of institutionalized religion. Dying religions and exhausted religious practices recur in Wilder's works from the beginning. The theme of the exhaustion of the Roman and Greek mythol-

ogy presented in *The Cabala* turns up again in *The Eighth Day*. Dr.
MacKenzie explains the Greek pantheon as an embodiment of different kinds of people: "They put themselves on the altar" (*ED*, 147).
But, as in *The Cabala*, Dr. MacKenzie, a type of Saturn, knows that
those types are not the only ones possible and that they no longer have
sacred energy: "We're shorn. We're decayed. It's an awful thing, Mr.
Tolland, to be robbed of one's divinity—awful! There's nothing left
for us to do but enjoy ourselves in our miserable way" (*ED*, 149). Indeed, the Greek pantheon may be actively harmful. The thief taker
Wellington Bristow is a type of Hermes, the conductor of souls to
Hades, and his "thoughts ran on deathbeds, coffins, and funerals" (*ED*,
166). Bristow's discovery of John drives John from a useful life to
death at sea.[17]

The Greek pantheon is not the only exhausted religious system
that Wilder addresses in his later works. In *The Eighth Day*, the Kangaheelas, the original inhabitants of the area around what became
Coaltown, regarded themselves as the chosen people and believed that
the All-Father "has singled out the Kangaheelas from among them
[humanity]. He will return. Let them BLAZE THE TRAIL against
that day. The race of men will be saved by a few." However, the Kangaheelas no longer exist as a tribe, and "professors estimate that there
were never more than three thousand Kangaheelas alive at one time"
(*ED*, 21). The tone here is not dismissive, but that does not alter the
fact that they were mistaken about their importance to the transformation of man.

The deity or deities that remain in Wilder's postwar work,
whether in decline or ascension, are not the omniscient, omnipotent
God of Christianity, Judaism, or Islam. Nor is this outside the mainstream of twentieth-century American thought. William James, in
A Pluralistic Universe, originally given as a series of lectures in 1909,
regards religious experience as a fact, much as does Caesar after his
epileptic fits:

> Those who have such experiences distinctly enough and often
> enough to live in the light of them remain quite unmoved by criti-
> cism, from whatever quarter it may come, be it academic or scien-
> tific, or be it merely the voice of logical common sense. They have

had their vision and they *know*—that is enough—that we inhabit an invisible, spiritual environment from which help comes, our soul being mysteriously one with a larger soul whose instruments we are.

Granted the irreducible reality of religious experience, James is left with a problem: in his view, the pantheistic vision of God as a monist entity is incoherent; that is, philosophical problems such as evil genuinely are unsolvable in a monist system. As opposed to the "all-form" of reality, he offers the "each-form" of pluralism, which is compatible with either monotheism or polytheism, and where God is at the top of a ladder of consciousness: "Having an environment, being in time, and working out a history just like ourselves, he escapes from the foreignness from all that is human, of the static timeless perfect absolute." One of the advantages of this view is that it makes spirituality compatible both with empiricism—we are no longer obligated to explain away the multiple forms of experience as illusions, as we are with idealistic pantheism—and with evolution, where, in the absence of "principles of unity," elements of consciousness are, according to James, "represented as summing themselves together in successive stages of compounding and re-compounding, and thus engendering our higher and more complex states of mind."[18]

These thoughts bear some resemblance to Amos Wilder's repeated insistence in his works that the Incarnation must be taken seriously: Jesus is both God and man in a specific place and time in history. As a consequence, Amos argues on numerous occasions that it is understandable that biblical interpretation has frequently "been absorbed with the subjective and personal aspects of salvation": "But his [Jesus'] all-encompassing mission had to do with a new Israel, a new temple; and the heavenly symbols he used for these should not blind us to the corporate renewal of God's people that was involved."[19] Hence, the apocalypse was immanent rather than imminent, an ongoing process in time leading to the renewal of the Christian congregation in this world.

But James's idea of God as existing in time also bears some similarity to the ideas of Goethe, which occupy so prominent a place in Wilder's work, as well as to the necessity for development, a spiritual evolution, in Wilder's postwar works. In *Theophilus North,* Ted paraphrases Goethe to Miss Elspeth, who has "nightmares of being caged" (*TN,* 292): "Nature wishes every living thing to be a perfect example of its kind and to rejoice in the gift of life" (*TN,* 290). Ultimately, the divine has to do with life as lived. In *The Ides of March,* the Rites of the Good Goddess, according to Caesar, affirm "life itself, all mankind and the creation" (*Ides,* 153). And, drawing on Goethe, Wilder has Caesar place the divine in growth and change: "It is my opinion, however, that it is the law of life that all things grow and change, casting aside the husks that protected their origins and emerging into fairer and nobler forms. It is so that the Immortal Gods have ordained it" (*Ides,* 150).[20] What Caesar regards as problematic about the Rites of the Good Goddess, and which he wants excised, is "the elimination of obscenity"; by this, he means presumably the vestigial remnants of fertility cults that hinder the development of higher forms of mentality: "Let us at least say of religion that it means that every part of the body is infused with mind, not that the mind is overwhelmed and drowned in body" (*Ides,* 155).

Caesar, at first, hopes to purify the rites to regenerate the women of Rome. And, at the very least, hope of regeneration or purification answers the dream of the void. The herdsman in *The Alcestiad,* who is responsible for the mortal wound of Admetus, also believes that his death will give his own life purpose: "For if the gods exist, that is their sign: that whatever they can do is an unfolding—a part of something larger than we can see. Let me die this death, Princess—for it would save me from that other death which I dread and which all men dread: the mere ceasing to be; the dust in the grave" (*CP,* 396). Worse than death is a meaningless universe: being used as a part of the divine purpose sanctifies death and makes it something to be sought by the herdsman. And purpose, direction toward something, justifies suffering. On the simplest level, hardship builds character. Wilder writes to his aunt Charlotte on October 21, 1955: "But then I believe, with Toynbee, that every aspect of human activity is invigorated from having to cope with natural forces, even though they present themselves as destructive."[21] This rather Whiggish view of history implies that the survivors of pestilence, famine, and natural disasters are in some way strengthened by the experience. But Wilder is not naïve about suffering, as demonstrated by the comments of his alter ego Ted in *Theophilus North:* "There's a vast amount of suffering in the world—a small, but important, part of it, unnecessary" (*TN*, 315).

Thornton writes to Amos that "Schopenhauer said sourly that all the philosophy in the world was at the mercy of a toothache. Seneca said otherwise. I don't have to remind you of Von Hügel on the uses of pain; I've stowed it away for my agôn when it comes."[22] For Schopenhauer, pain is as dehabilitating as the tyranny of the will, and a Stoic such as Seneca thinks that the true philosopher can rise above it. Baron Friedrich von Hügel's essay "On the Preliminaries to Religious Belief and on the Facts of Suffering, Faith and Love" denies both. The essay was written to a woman "on the death, after a long illness, of her little daughter of eighteen months, in answer to the question, 'how such suffering could be permitted by a God said to be all-good and all-powerful.'"[23] Von Hügel dismisses pantheism, Epicureanism, and Stoicism because we cannot flee or deny suffering, "since pain, suffering, evil are not fancies and prejudices, but real, very real."[24] But he nevertheless affirms "that it is precisely the deepest, the keenest sufferings, not only of the body but of mind, not only of mind but of heart, which have occasioned the firmest, the most living, the most tender faith."[25] While von Hügel's explanation of the mystery is specifically Christian, his conclusion that we are penetrated by "God, the Ultimate Reality and Truth, the Ultimate Lover and Goodness"[26] at such times is applicable to Wilder's postwar works even in the absence of Christianity: "What makes us, in the midst of it all, persist in believing, indeed persist in acting (with great cost) on the belief, that love and devotedness are utterly the greatest things we know, and deserve the sacrifice of all our earthly gifts, of our very life?"[27] The fact, in von Hügel's view, of our response is mysterious, but that mystery is itself a source of faith in something that transcends suffering.

In Act Three of *The Alcestiad*, Epimenes cannot offer a prayer when he returns in disguise from exile and sees the suffering in the city: "The God turned his face away. My father killed. My brother and sister killed. Myself sent away by night to live among strangers. My mother a slave—or dead. And the land under pestilence and the dead bodies lying unburied under the sun. To whom do I make a prayer?" (*CP,* 415–16). Cheriander, Epimenes' friend, argues passionately that one cannot surrender to despair: "Are you the first man to have suffered? Cruelty, injustice, murder, and humiliation—is it only here that those things can be found? Have you forgotten that we came here to establish justice? That you yourself said that men of themselves could never have arrived at justice—that it was planted in their minds by the gods?" (*CP,* 416). Some vestige of higher things is planted in men's minds; suffering is a test that draws us to the mysteries of faith. Alcestis tells the usurping tyrant Agis that people ask the wrong gifts of the gods: "We ask of them health . . . and riches . . . and our happiness. But they are trying to give us something else, and better: understanding. And we are so quick to refuse their gift" (*CP,* 424). She warns Agis after the death of his daughter of "the last bitterness of death": "It is the despair that one has not lived. It is the despair that one's life has been without meaning. That it has been nonsense; happy or unhappy, that it has been senseless" (*CP,* 428). The leap of faith is to affirm meaning and purpose in the face of suffering, because not to do so is worse: suffering continues but is not redemptive. Alcestis chides Epimenes for being too much like her youthful self and too little like his father: "Great happiness was given to me once, yes . . . but shall I forget that now? And forget the one who gave it to me? All that has happened since came from the same hands that gave me happiness. I shall not doubt that it is good and has a part in something I cannot see" (*CP,* 420). This recalls Wilder's novel *The Woman of Andros,* in which the title character praises all things bright and dark.

Even disbelievers feel obligated to pass on hope to the young. *The Eighth Day*'s title comes from a quasi-evolutionary speech by Dr. Gillies. He tells his wife, "Well, maybe NATURE after hundreds of millions of years has begun selecting for intelligence and mind and spirit. Maybe NATURE is moving into a new era. Breed out the stupid; breed in the wise" (*ED,* 279). The term "selection" here is the key. The problem that Darwin represented for religious belief was not evolution per se. What Darwin explained was a random, rather than directional, process. As Thomas Kuhn has explained, Darwin's theory was revolutionary because it suggested "a process that moved steadily from primitive beginnings but *toward* no goal."[28] Certain random mutations turned out to have survival advantages: a bear born with white fur at the beginning of an ice age, for example, as a matter of luck may have had a better chance of sneaking up on its prey. It might therefore survive and reproduce, whereas a bear with brown fur might not. This does not really imply a "better" bear, or "progress" in the essence of bearness. Indeed, at a time of global warming the white fur of the bear may turn out to be a disadvantage. The bear has not changed or "regressed." Because of a random mutation, one bear survives and reproduces and the other does not. What Dr. Gillies, on the other hand, is proposing is not merely that "intelligence and mind and spirit" have greater survival characteristics; he implicitly thinks those are an improvement in the human race, that these are the essence of a higher type of humanity. That would imply an idea of progress that gives evolution a direction toward what people should be and a capacity to step outside the material fact and make a judgment about what is valuable about people. Such a concept of progress would be outside the materialism of biology.

Dr. Gillies, when he gives his speech about what will happen in the twentieth century, says that "creation has not come to an end": "In this new century we shall be able to see that mankind is entering a new stage of development—the Man of the Eighth Day" (*ED*, 22–23) When "Mind and Spirit" educate the race, we will move "from the self-enclosed, self-favoring life into a consciousness of the entire community of mankind" (*ED*, 25). Dr. Gillies claims for the young people in his audience that there are developmental goals as a process of natural selection. In short, this is not really about Darwin because progress, rather than random process, guides evolution—a biologist would regard this as a teleological fallacy. Of course, the progress is not infallible; Wilder writes to his sister Janet, a zoologist, that *The Eighth Day* shows "how down through families and cultures and centuries the destructive elements in one generation can produce good elements in the next; and how the good elements in one generation could produce bad effects in the next—a sort of birds' eye view of a hundred years" (*SL*, 574). Mrs. Wickersham, with the gray eyes of Athena, quotes Keats to John: "He said that life is a 'vale of soul making.' He might have added that it's a 'vale of soul-unmaking,' too. We go up or we go down—forward or back" (*ED*, 181). This is a fundamentally religious attitude toward the world. The ultimate goal of this process for Wilder is "the Man with Head Raised."[29] That the species itself, through the individual, can be transformed for the better, shedding old destructive forms, becomes a kind of ongoing revelation for the Wilder brothers. Amos Wilder claims that this is something people know *a priori:* "All men know in their bones that man is a creature that is to be surpassed! That there is a door in the great wall somewhere!"[30]

The narrator of *The Eighth Day* asks about the Ashleys in general and John in particular, "Are humiliation, injustice, suffering, destitution, and ostracism—are they blessings?" (*ED*, 17). María Icaza tells John about his hardships, "There is no happiness save in understanding the whole. You are a creature who God loves—particularly loves. You are being born" (*ED*, 122). If one posits that crisis is something that nature itself can adapt to and consequently improve the type, and that this improvement can be passed down, then suffering becomes explainable: it is the necessary stress that frees the individual or the species to adapt and develop. As early as 1938, Wilder was writing to Isabel about his sympathy for people suffering "small troubles" and how "cold-hearted" he was about "big ones": "They're deeply embedded in life, and nothing can be done about them and they have to be fought out and lived through alone. And it's a privilege and a necessity. And they're their [*sic*] to weed out the weak from the strong."[31] Whatever conduces to change creates at least the possibility of change for the better. Not always, of course: Sophia is broken by her suffering. But she saves her family, which allows Lily and Constance to develop.

Religion, then, is to have faith in the developmental possibilities, in an evolutionary sense, of the human race and its works. Virtue acts upon that faith, and the two other Christian virtues of hope and love sustain it. John, as a man of faith, rejects materialism and is certain "that one small part of what is given us is free. [He] explore[s] daily the exercise of freedom." Thus, John works because he thinks that the universe is not entirely determined, and as such his efforts have theological significance: "There is no creation without faith and hope.

There is no faith and hope that does not express itself in creation" (*ED*, 99). Wherever he goes he improves the life of those around him, whether in Coaltown or in the Andes. His freedom, guided by faith and hope and expressed in work, negates through his own actions the vision of nothing. After his conviction and before he is rescued, he explains the great "as if" to Roger and Sophia: "We cannot understand now what has happened to us. Let us live as though we believed there were some meaning in it" (*ED*, 145).

Of course, the religious view that I am ascribing to Wilder may not look like religion at all to a contemporary believer; it is, however, not an anomaly in twentieth-century thought. George Santayana, in *The Life of Reason,* dismisses the supernatural from any religion held by a thinking person: "rational religion has these two phases: piety, or loyalty to necessary conditions, and spirituality, or devotion to ideal ends." In other words, religion allows us to accept what must be accepted, while also representing our aspirations. Thus, religion is about the here and now: "True religion is entirely human and political, as was that of the ancient Hebrews, Romans, and Greeks. Supernatural machinery is either symbolic of natural conditions and moral aims or else is worthless."[32] Another example of a twentieth-century non-believer who nevertheless thinks that we must posit "ultimate terms" to transcend "the dialectical wrangle" is Kenneth Burke. This allows us to imagine an "ultimate design."[33] One could say that for Burke and Santayana, religion exists even in the absence of God.

Dr. Gillies, who lacks faith and hope, nevertheless recognizes an ethical obligation not to kill them in others: "It is the duty of old men to lie to the young. Let them encounter their own disillusions. We strengthen our souls, when young, on hope; the strength we acquire enables us later to endure despair as a Roman should" (*ED*, 24). One can only achieve stoic resignation if hope has not been prematurely blighted. That is, whether or not hope is justified, it forms the character that allows young people to endure the random misfortunes of life. Youthful idealism in particular is the leading edge of the moral aims of the species and thus represents devotion to "ideal ends." The Maestro, Lily's voice teacher, too, repudiates belief in the gods as real, numinous presences. He asks Roger, "Who can count the prayers that have ascended to gods who do not exist? Mankind has himself created sources of help where there is no help and sources of consolation where there is no consolation." Nevertheless, "the representations of such beings are man's greatest achievement" (*ED*, 235). The aesthetic response to the divine, whether the divine exists or not, leads to art, "the only satisfactory products of civilization" (*ED*, 234). "Heaven," the Maestro tells his daughter, in an obviously Freudian explanation, "is the memory of infancy" (*ED*, 352).³⁴ Unlike Freud, he does not denigrate religious belief because of what it has produced, and he, too, works to see that music in general and religious music in particular are performed as well as can be.

Ultimately for Wilder, the Christian virtues are reimagined as the foundation of spiritual evolution. Hope is "irrational" but sustained by "the marvelous" (such as the rescue of John Ashley) but especially by love: "It is doubtful whether hope—or any of the other manifestations of creativity—can sustain itself without an impulse injected by love. So absurd and indefensible is hope. Sophia's was nourished by love of her mother and sisters, but above all by love of those two distant out-casts, her father and brother" (*ED*, 57). The trouble is that Sophia becomes starved for love. Dr. Gillies sees the problem but can do nothing about it: "'She's starved for something,' he said to himself. 'She misses her father and her brother.' There was a lack of affection in the air at 'The Elms.' Each of the Ashleys lived apart from the others" (*ED*, 76). In the absence of her father and brother, Sophia is an example of what Joan of Arc would be without the love of God (Roger refers to So-phia's "Domrémy look" in the novel). Beata's love is absorbed by John and Roger, Lily's eyes are fixed on her future, and Constance is too young. Finally, Sophia is institutionalized in a permanently child-like state, and Dr. Gillies can only regard her as a kind of devolution: "Some people go forward and some go back" (*ED*, 94). In a sense here, Paul's 1 Corinthians 13:13 is portrayed in its negation: "And now abideth faith, hope, love, these three; but the greatest of these is love." Without love, hope cannot be sustained, and the townspeople who mock Sophia, the sisters who cannot help her, the mother who is ir-ritated by her, and even the absent father and brother leave wisdom to fade. The Christian virtues still represent an important statement of what is necessary for a life worth living, but they are presented in an evolutionary framework where their absence hinders progress.

And evolution takes multiple paths, some fruitful and some not. In 1964, Wilder writes to his aunt Charlotte about the religious function of John Ashley in *The Eighth Day:* "He is not aware of having any religious beliefs at all; but the reader has known that he is a *man of faith* being born!! His instinct precedes his 'wits.' Without knowing it he is constantly 'making straight in the desert the highway. . . .'"[35] The reference to John 1:23 emphasizes religion as an ongoing process: John Ashley is a type of John the Baptist who recognizes himself as a type of Isaiah.[36] The dim apprehension of the mysterious enables the capacity for work of John Ashley and the other admirable characters in the novel. John himself, according to Olga, "was chosen. He was a sign" (*ED,* 69). Olga, a seamstress Dostoyevsky, inspires George with tales of Mother Russia: "Russia is the Christ-bearing country. She is the Ark that will save the human race when the great Floods come" (*ED,* 300). The hospital orderly Peter Bogardus is a Buddhist who believes that the enlightened will slowly bring the cosmos to purification: "They move among us now, in disguise, aiding us to ascend that mighty ladder" (*ED,* 193). These are all ambiguous guides. Although Wilder does not mention it, Polish Romantics in the nineteenth century regarded Poland as the Christ of nations, and Russia as a source of their redemptive suffering. Another orderly, Old Clem, dismisses Bogardus because of the latter's ignorance of the great books: "A man who tried to understand anything without knowing THOSE BOOKS would just be a feathered kangaroo. Like Pete Bogardus" (*ED,* 197).

On one level these beliefs fulfill the traditional religious task of consolation. John's grandmother, a member of a fringe evangelical sect, also has faith in a grand design: "Her thought turned always on God's plan for the universe. She asked to be shown her part in it." At the same time, "she consoled herself and the congregation by the conviction that God converts even our shortcomings to His own ends" (*ED,* 135). Olga knows that Dr. Gillies does not believe his own speech about the development of humanity and does not care: "'Dr. Gillies didn't believe a word of it,' she said. 'I did. I believed every word of it. And so did my father. I couldn't walk straight if I didn't'" (*ED,* 25).

The central metaphor of *The Eighth Day* is that of the tapestry. The Deacon shows Roger an old rug: on one side a "mazelike design in brown and black could still be distinguished." But, "No figure could be traced on the reverse. It presented a mass of knots and of frayed and dangling threads" (*ED,* 376). The Deacon explains: "These are the threads and knots of human life. You cannot see the design" (*ED,* 377). All of the seekers are like the threads of the tapestry and hence are examples of the pluralism of the novel. The Deacon's religion is a curious amalgam of Buddhism and Christianity. After showing Roger a picture of the Tree of Jesse, he says to him, "It has been a mistake of the Jews and Christians to believe that there is only one Messiah. Every man and woman is Messiah-bearing, but some are closer on the tree to a Messiah than others" (*ED,* 376). He wonders if Roger, as the son of John, is a part of a Messiah-bearing line. But the novel as a whole suggests that John, Roger, Constance, Mrs. Wickersham, and others are all making straight the way toward a better world. The traditional metaphor for America, from Israel Zangwill's play of 1914, was "the melting pot," where ethnic and religious differences were melted away and a single alloy emerged. Arthur Miller uses the same metaphor in *The Crucible* to account for the Salem witch trials, where diversity must be destroyed by being burned away. Here, Wilder substitutes the idea of a tapestry.

In *Thornton Wilder and His Public* (1980), Amos Wilder mentions Malcolm Cowley's puzzlement over the lack of truly substantive studies in the United States of Wilder's work.[37] To some extent this gap has been filled, but a great deal remains to be done, particularly in the area of Wilder's relation to intellectual currents of the twentieth century. I have argued that prior to World War II his career moves from a perception of the exhaustion of Christianity in the twentieth century, to an examination of the social injustice of America particularly in the 1930s, to an assertion of the value of piety in the face of the Great Depression and the looming disaster of the war. Further, I have attempted to describe what I believe to be an intellectual dichotomy present in most of his postwar works, between existential man in an absurd universe, and man seeking faith through an evolutionary model that may ultimately lead to a higher type of the species. Above all, I have tried to understand his oeuvre as existing in an implicit dialogue with the scholarly writings of his brother Amos. Many other interpretive models could and should be applied to Wilder's work, for as literature they persistently invite rereading.

I hope, however, that other critics will look at Thornton Wilder as a writer responding to the history and to the intellectual, economic, and spiritual currents of his time, rather than attempt to evade the historical issues with an appeal to "universal human values." Such values may exist, but they can only do so in a particular scene built from the materials of the time. Wilder's best work, far from being a portrait of an ideal America, is a somber contemplation of our longing for something sacred in a world where the numinous seems to recede ever more rapidly. His characters seek a satisfactory life in a world where traditional models of the proper end for a man or woman have been emptied of their vitality. The common tendency to see Wilder as the literary equivalent of Norman Rockwell is false, not because Rockwell is a bad painter—he is a very fine craftsman—but because their aims are utterly different. Rather, Wilder's artistic brothers are Cervantes and Updike, whose characters also struggle to find a satisfactory expression of their spiritual desires.

Notes

Introduction: Brothers in Arms

1. In a letter to his grandmother, Elizabeth Lewis Niven, for which the editors of *Selected Letters* suggest a date of 1915, Wilder writes from Berkeley, California, where he went to high school, that after a year at Oberlin and three years at Yale, he would like to spend two years studying at Harvard in George Pierce Baker's postgraduate playwrighting course, a further indication of his awareness of his vocation; *The Selected Letters of Thornton Wilder,* ed. Robin G. Wilder and Jackson R. Bryer (New York: Harper, 2008), p. 43.

2. *Thornton Wilder: An Intimate Portrait* (New York: Saturday Review Press/E. P. Dutton, 1975), pp. 264–65. Wilder himself wrote to Goldstone: "I've been telling you for years that I'm not the kind of author that you understand" and urged him not to do a biography of him; *Selected Letters,* pp. 661–63.

3. *Thornton Wilder and the Puritan Narrative Tradition* (Columbia and London: University of Missouri Press, 2006), p. 9.

4. "Thornton Wilder in Berlin," in *Conversations with Thornton Wilder,* ed. Jackson R. Bryer (Jackson and London: University Press of Mississippi, 1992), p. 10.

5. *Thornton Wilder and His Public* (Philadelphia: Fortress Press, 1980), p. 49.

6. "Thornton Wilder and the *Perennial Philosophy:* A Legacy of Goodness as Represented by His Five Affirmations, First Enunciated in the Early Plays of *The Angel That Troubled the Waters,*" in *Thornton Wilder: New Essays,* ed. Martin Blank, Dalma Hunyadi Brunauer, and David Garrett Izzo (West Cornwall, CT: Locust Hill Press, 1999), pp. 109, 111.

7. "Berdyaev's Eschatological Vision in Wilder's Last Works," *Renascence* 35 (Spring 1983): 154–66.

8. *Myth and Modern American Drama* (Detroit: Wayne State University Press, 1969), pp. 200–224.

9. Lifton, *"Vast Encyclopedia": The Theatre of Thornton Wilder* (Westport, CT: Greenwood Press, 1995), pp. 139–67; Haberman, *The Plays of Thornton Wilder* (Middleton, CT: Wesleyan University Press, 1967), pp. 41–53.

10. Yale Collection of American Literature, Beinecke Rare Book and Manuscript Library (hereafter YCAL), Thornton Wilder MSS 108, Folder 1260.

11. By this I mean that Wilder was in favor of the bold experimentation in literary form that characterized, for instance, James Joyce. It is, of course, possible to have ideas that are the product of twentieth-century intellectual currents and yet use traditional literary methods to express them (as in the realist novels of Sinclair Lewis, for example) or to have ideas that would have been regarded as conventional in the nineteenth century or earlier and yet feel that these ideas require a new expression (the poetry of T. S. Eliot). In other words, there is more than one kind of modernism. For a very instructive examination of an author who similarly is trying to find a new expression for traditional values, see Peter A. Huff, *Allen Tate and the Catholic Revival: Trace of the Fugitive Gods* (New York: Paulist Press, 1996), particularly pp. 34–37.

12. (New York: Coward-McCann, 1933), p. 262.

13. The allusion is to the story of Francesca and Paolo in Canto 5 of *The Inferno*. They are seduced by reading a romance about Lancelot: "That book, and he who wrote it, was a pander. / That day we read no further." Trans. John Ciardi.

14. YCAL Thornton Wilder MSS 108, Folder 2942 contains Wilder's undergraduate themes.

15. *The Shores of Light: A Literary Chronicle of the 1920s and 1930s* (New York: Farrar, Straus & Giroux, 1952), pp. 376–77 and 384–91.

16. *In Search of Lost Time,* trans. C. K. Moncrieff and Terence Kilmartin, rev. D. J. Enright (New York: Modern Library, 2003), vol. 2, pp. 62 and 186.

17. *The Shores of Light,* p. 433.

18. I quote the King James version here because the Revised English Bible's translation implies something quite different from what Wilder seems to have in mind: "I send you out like sheep among wolves; be wary as serpents, innocent as doves."

19. Gilbert Harrison describes Wilder's meeting with Freud in *The Enthusiast: A Life of Thornton Wilder* (New York: Fromm, 1986), pp. 139–40.

Wilder's letter about his conversation with Freud in 1935 describes him as "really a beautiful old man"; *Selected Letters,* p. 303.

20. *The Basic Writings of Sigmund Freud* trans. and ed. Dr. A. A. Brill (New York: Modern Library, 1995), p. 895.

21. Trans. and ed. James Strachey (New York and London: W. W. Norton, 1961), p. 55.

22. *Selected Letters,* p. 182. Many years later, Wilder mentions in a letter to his brother Amos in August 1967 that he had previously read all of *The Golden Bough:* YCAL Thornton Wilder MSS 108, Folder 4415.

23. (Mineola, NY: Dover Publications, 2002), p. 712.

24. *The Poetical Works of Tennyson,* ed. G. Robert Stange (Boston: Houghton Mifflin, 1974), p. 164.

25. (Mineola, NY: Dover Publications, 1997), p. 177. Amusingly, Dashiell Hammett in his modernist detective story *The Dain Curse* (1929) has one set of crooks, the Haldorns, establish a cult, the Temple of the Holy Grail: "They brought their cult to California because everybody does, and picked San Francisco because it held less competition than Los Angeles" (New York: Vintage Books, 1989), p. 103. The Continental Op, the protagonist of *The Dain Curse,* like Hammett, does not believe in the supernatural.

26. Roger Finke and Rodney Stark, *The Churching of America, 1776–2005* (New Brunswick, NJ, and London: Rutgers University Press, 2nd ed. 2005), pp. 275–83 in particular.

27. Two reviewers of *The Angel That Troubled the Waters* thought that Wilder's willingness to acknowledge religious themes was unusual. In *The Times Literary Supplement* (November 8, 1928), p. 826, the plays "are pleasant to read . . . partly because they are concerned with spiritual subjects which it is a refreshment to rediscover in contemporary fiction." E. R. R., in *The Bookman* 75 (December 1928): 187–88, wrote that Wilder's success is "one of the most hopeful signs in modern literature; for in all his work he has a preoccupation with religion, and a sense of values which is quite contrary either to the worship of success, of nature, or of self."

28. (New York: Grove Press, 1972), p. 25.

29. YCAL Thornton Wilder MSS 108, Folder 43.

30. *The Brothers Karamazov,* trans. Constance Garnett (New York: Dell Publishing, 1956), p. 137.

31. Trans. W. Montgomery, intro. James M. Robinson (New York: Macmillan, 1973), pp. 398–99, 401.

32. *Selected Plays: George Moore and Edward Martin,* "chosen, with an introduction by David B. Eakin and Michael Case" (Washington, DC: The Catholic University of America Press, 1995), p. 209.

33. Wilder writes to his father on January 12, 1917, to say that "I won't discuss Sterne or Moore any further. Read the book when I send it." On the "Second Sunday in March" in 1917 he writes: "I have been reading a book of George Moore that is quite disgusting." Much of Moore's work was borderline scandalous, so it is impossible to determine what in particular he was reading. The letters are contained in YCAL Thornton Wilder MSS 108, Folder 48. Wilder writes in a letter to his mother, also from 1917, that he feels a special affinity for Moore, although he praises him for his "tone" and his "mood"; *Selected Letters,* pp. 93–94.

34. *The Diary of Søren Kierkegaard,* ed. Peter Rohde (New York: Citadel Press, 1987), p. 151.

35. *The Education of Henry Adams* (New York: Modern Library, 1931), p. 34.

36. *Anxious Decades: America in Prosperity and Depression, 1920–1941* (New York and London: W. W. Norton, 1992), p. 194.

37. *The Protestant Ethic and the Spirit of Capitalism,* trans. Talcott Parsons (Mineola, NY: Dover Publications, 2003), p. 183.

38. Trans. Thomas Common (Mineola, NY: Dover Publications, 1999), pp. 55–56.

39. Trans. Walter Kaufmann (New York: Vintage Books, 1989), pp. 69–70.

40. *H. L. Mencken on Religion,* ed. S. T. Joshi (Amherst, NY: Prometheus Books, 2002), pp. 32 and 53.

41. (Mineola, NY: Dover Publications, 1994), pp. 196–210 in particular.

42. *The Profits of Religion* (1918; Amherst, NY: Prometheus Books, 2000), p. 94.

43. (Mineola, NY: Dover Publications, 1999), pp. 289–90.

44. (New York: Signet Classics, 1967), p. 233.

45. (New York: Penguin Books, 2001), p. 451.

46. (New York: Carroll & Graf, 2004), p. 203.

47. (New York: Farrar, Straus & Giroux, 1991), pp. 372–77.

48. (New York: Vintage Books, 1990), pp. 487, 365.

49. (New York: Library of America, 2003), p. 734.

50. YCAL Thornton Wilder MSS 108, Folder 51.

51. YCAL Thornton Wilder MSS 108, Folder 53.

52. YCAL Thornton Wilder MSS 108, Folder 13.

53. YCAL Thornton Wilder MSS 108, Folder 15.

54. YCAL Thornton Wilder MSS 108, Folder 17.

55. YCAL Thornton Wilder MSS 162, Folder 121.

56. YCAL Thornton Wilder MSS 108, Folder 13.

57. *Ahead of All Parting: the Selected Poetry and Prose of Rainer Maria Rilke,* ed. and trans. Stephen Mitchell (New York: Modern Library, 1995), p. 193.

58. Abr. by Helmut Werner, English abr. prepared by Arthur Helps, trans. Charles Francis Atkinson (Oxford: Oxford University Press, 1991), pp. 207–8.

59. YCAL Thornton Wilder MSS 108, Folder 13.

60. *Science and the Modern World* (New York: The Free Press, 1967), p. 188.

61. *The Travel Diary of a Philosopher,* trans. J. Holroyd Reece (New York: Harcourt, Brace & Company, 1925), vol. 2, p. 333.

62. To treat the playlets as a parable, as does Izzo, would require some explanation of what the formal characteristics of a parable are: the term is not self-explanatory, especially in twentieth-century biblical studies, where the import of the parables has been a much debated subject. See, for instance, Amos Wilder's *Early Christian Rhetoric: The Language of the Gospel* (1962; Cambridge: Harvard University Press, 1971), pp. 71–88.

63. *"Vast Encyclopedia": The Theatre of Thornton Wilder,* p. 15. Indeed, Lifton sees Romantic Neoplatonism as present in Wilder's work throughout his career.

64. (New York: Scribner, 2003), p. 67. Wilder writes to his sister Isabella on November 28, 1926, that Hemingway was "wonderful. It's the first time I've met someone from my generation whom I respect as an *artist*"; *Selected Letters,* p. 195.

65. *Poetry, Tales, and Selected Essays* (New York: Library of America College Editions, 1996), p. 1358.

66. *Tragic Sense of Life* (1921; Mineola, NY: Dover Publications, 1954), p. 16.

67. YCAL Thornton Wilder MSS 108, Folder 53.

68. Nelvin Vos has previously argued for the importance of Amos Wilder's work as an aid to understanding Thornton's in "Thornton Niven Wilder and Amos Niven Wilder, Siblings: Point and Counterpoint," in *Thornton Wilder: New Essays,* pp. 31–49.

69. For an overview of the achievements of Amos Wilder see John Dominic Crossan, *A Fragile Craft: The Work of Amos Niven Wilder* (Atlanta: Scholars Press, 1980).

70. As a student at Oxford from 1921 to 1923, Amos Wilder studied under C. H. Dodd. He was also Albert Schweitzer's secretary at Mansfield College at Oxford in 1922.

71. See "Chronology of Amos N. Wilder's World War I Service," in Amos Wilder, *Armageddon Revisited: A World War I Journal* (New Haven: Yale University Press, 1994), pp. xi–xii.

72. *The Spiritual Aspects of the New Poetry* (New York: Harper & Brothers, 1940), p. 28.

73. *The New Review of Books and Religion* (November 1977), p. 3. A similar reaction is apparent in Hemingway's memoir of life in Paris in the 1920s, *A Moveable Feast,* when he recalls the poet Blaise Cendrars, with whom Hemingway would drink on occasion: "In those days we did not trust anyone who had not been in the war, but we did not completely trust anyone, and there was a strong feeling that Cendrars might well be a little less flashy about his vanished arm." Cendrars's ostentatious display of his disability smacks too much of a prewar view of heroic sacrifice. (New York: Scribner, 2003), p. 82. Hemingway's suspicion is an expression of his dissatisfaction with the genteel lies told by society about war.

74. *Armageddon Revisited,* p. 125.

75. YCAL Thornton Wilder MSS 108, Folder 50.

76. *Armageddon Revisited,* p. 51.

77. Ibid., p. 64.

78. Ibid., p. 131.

79. Ibid., pp. 102–3.

80. Ibid., p. 103.

81. Ibid., p. 150.

82. YCAL Thornton Wilder MSS 108, Folder 4409.

83. *The Spiritual Aspects of the New Poetry,* p. xviii.

84. A recording of the documentary is in YCAL Thornton Wilder MSS 108, Folder 3862.

85. *The Spiritual Aspects of the New Poetry,* p. xix.

86. YCAL Thornton Wilder MSS 108, Folder 40.

87. "Religion and Literature: Reminiscences and Observations," Harvard Divinity School Library, Amos Wilder Papers b MS 641/2, p. 6.

Chapter One. Historical Religious Crises in Wilder's Early Novels

1. *The Cabala; and, the Woman of Andros* (New York: HarperCollins, 2006), pp. xxi, xv. Niven is by no means unusual in her view of the novels as ahistorical. Malcolm Cowley, for instance, says that despite, or perhaps because, of Wilder's training in archeology, "what he sees at the end of a vista is what the archeologist often sees; that is, fragments of a finished pattern of life, in many ways similar to our own. It is not what the historian tries to see: a living community in a process of continual and irreversible change"; "The

Man Who Abolished Time" (1956), rpt. in *Critical Essays on Thornton Wilder,* ed. Martin Blank (New York: G. K. Hall & Co., 1996), p. 35. Mary Ellen Williams also sees Wilder as affirming "the existence of all time in one time," specifically in *The Cabala* but also in his novels in general; *A Vast Landscape: Time in the Novels of Thornton Wilder* (Pocatello: Idaho State University Press, 1979), p. 8.

2. This was recognized by the novel's initial reviewers. Gilbert Thomas, for instance, describes it as "a study of Christianity blossoming before its time," in *The Spectator* (March 22, 1930): 503.

3. Wilson, *The Shores of Light,* pp. 444–45.

4. The captain is an echo of Captain Alvarado in *The Bridge of San Luis Rey.* Significantly, the character from Christian, eighteenth-century Peru in the earlier novel is able to endure his loss, while the classical avatar goes insane.

5. *The Greek Experience* (New York: Mentor Books, 1957), p. 71.

6. *Theology and Modern Literature* (1958; Cambridge: Harvard University Press, 1967), p. 66.

7. Introduction to *Kerygma, Eschatology, and Social Ethics* (1954; Philadelphia: Fortress Press, 1966), p. 14.

8. *Early Christian Rhetoric,* p. 6.

9. *The Symposium* in *The Republic and Other Works,* trans. B. Jowett (Garden City, NY: Anchor Books, 1973), p. 345.

10. *American Characteristics and Other Essays,* ed. Donald Gallup (New York: Harper & Row, 1979), p. 152.

11. *Selected Letters,* trans. Leonard Tancock (London: Penguin Books, 1982), pp. 30, 84, 226, 196, 59.

12. YCAL Thornton Wilder MSS 108, Folder 70.

13. Linda Simon suggests that the Abbess is modeled after Thornton's aunt Charlotte, chair of the International Committee of the YWCA, in *Thornton Wilder: His World* (Garden City, NY: Doubleday & Co., 1979), p. 51.

14. YCAL Thornton Wilder MSS 108, Folder 51.

15. Abr. and ed. A. S. Pringle-Pattison (Oxford: Clarendon Press, 1924), p. 277.

16. *Pensées,* trans. Honor Levi (Oxford: Oxford University Press, 1995), p. 178.

17. Ibid., p. 148.

18. Ibid., p. 153.

19. Ibid., p. 35.

20. Ibid., p. 158.

21. *Maxims and Reflections,* trans. Elizabeth Stopp, ed. Peter Hutchinson (London: Penguin Books, 1998), pp. 161–62.

22. *Conversations of Goethe with Johann Peter Eckermann,* trans. John Oxenford, ed. J. K. Moorhead (1930; n.p.: Da Capo Press, 1998), p. 139.

23. *Theopoetic: Theology and the Religious Imagination* (Philadelphia: Fortress Press, 1976), p. 75.

24. *Eschatology and Ethics in the Teachings of Jesus* (1950; Westport, CT: Greenwood Press, rev. 1978), p. 117.

25. (N.p.: Book of the Month Club, 1995), pp. 50–51. In conversation with John E. Pember in 1929, Wilder mentions *Death Comes for the Archbishop* in connection with Proust, Joyce, and *Orlando* as examples of modernism; see *Conversations with Thornton Wilder,* p. 7.

26. Or, as the devil tells Ivan in *The Brothers Karamazov,* "proofs are no help to believing, especially material proofs. Thomas believed, not because he saw Christ risen, but because he wanted to believe, before he saw." Trans. Garnett, p. 396.

27. In his attempt to convert the Chinese, Ricci borrowed some Chinese terms ("Lord of Heaven" for God) and practices (such as veneration of the dead) to make Christianity compatible with their existing beliefs. He was attacked as heretical by Franciscan and Dominican missionaries. See Joseph Brucker, "Matteo Ricci," *The Catholic Encyclopedia,* vol. 13 (New York: Robert Appleton Company, 1912), from http://www.newadvent.org/cathen/13034a.htm.

28. *The Spiritual Aspects of the New Poetry,* p. 223.

29. (London: Oxford University Press, 1969), pp. 396–97.

30. YCAL Thornton Wilder MSS 108, Folder 14.

31. YCAL Thornton Wilder MSS 108, Folder 51.

32. YCAL Thornton Wilder MSS 108, Folder 13.

33. *Thornton Wilder* (New York: Ungar, 1986), p. 40.

34. *The Spiritual Aspects of the New Poetry,* p. 216.

35. (New York: Charles Scribner's Sons, 1937), pp. 9, 197.

36. YCAL Thornton Wilder MSS 108, Folder 35, letter dated December 14, 1966.

37. (New York: Image Books/Doubleday, 2001), p. 162.

38. (Mineola, NY: Dover Publications, 2005), pp. 241–42.

39. *Grace Confounding: Poems by Amos Niven Wilder* (Philadelphia: Fortress Press, 1972), p. 51.

40. Rex Burbank points out that Samuele has much in common with Henry James's naïve American travelers in Europe; *Thornton Wilder* (New York: Twayne Publishers, 1961), p. 36.

41. Or, as Rilke writes in Sonnet VII of the "Sonnets to Orpheus," "Praising is what matters! He was summoned for that, /and came to us like ore from a stone's / silence. His mortal heart presses out /a deathless, inexhaustible wine." *Ahead of All Parting,* p. 423.

Chapter Two.   Coming Home to America

1. *New York Times,* December 11, 1926, p. 15.

2. *The Art of Thornton Wilder* (Lincoln: University of Nebraska Press, 1965), pp. 32–33.

3. *Thornton Wilder: The Bright and the Dark* (New York: Thomas J. Crowell, 1972), pp. 38–39.

4. *Thornton Wilder and the Puritan Narrative Tradition,* p. 69.

5. (Mineola, NY: Dover Publications, 2004), pp. 242–43.

6. YCAL Thornton Wilder MSS 108, Folder 5.

7. YCAL Thornton Wilder MSS 108, Folder 12.

8. YCAL Thornton Wilder MSS 108, Folder 62.

9. YCAL Thornton Wilder MSS 108, Folder 46. The editors of *Selected Letters* suggest the fall of 1916 as a probable period for the letter (pp. 87–88).

10. YCAL Thornton Wilder MSS 108, Folder 13.

11. The script from the American Laboratory Theater production of the play (a copy of which Tappan Wilder kindly allowed me to examine) has Magnus forgiving all the sinners, while Dabney in particular cannot forgive himself. If anything, this script privileges personal judgment over any institutional or historical standard even more so than the original. I have decided, however, not to include a lengthy discussion of the acting script since it is a collaborative enterprise, while the *Yale Literary Magazine* version of the play is Wilder's alone.

12. "Wilder: Prophet of the Genteel Christ," in *The New Republic* (October 22, 1930): 267.

13. Ibid.

14. Ibid.

15. "Communist Criticism," *The Nation* 131 (1930): 583–84.

16. (New York: Macmillan, 1933), pp. 257–92.

17. "Our Critics, Right or Wrong," *The Nation* 141 (October 23, 1935): 468–72.

18. Rpt. in *The Shores of Light,* p. 503.

19. Wilder was aware of the changing attitudes toward his works and was not particularly troubled by them. He writes to Sibyl Colefax on

November 2, 1932: "Myself have dwindled to the least fashionable of authors. Few book reviews come out without a passing disparagement of my work. But I don't mind. I have a rather low opinion of my books myself, but am fairly conceited about the next ones"; *Selected Letters,* p. 257.

20. See *The Long Christmas Dinner and Other Plays in One Act* (New York: Bard, 1980).

21. *Why I Am Not a Christian* (New York: George Allen & Unwin, 1957), p. 33.

22. *Eschatology and Ethics in the Teachings of Jesus,* p. 70.

23. Ibid., p. 69.

24. (New York: Coward-McCann, 1939), p. 46.

25. (New York: Coward-McCann, 1934), p. 189.

26. I agree with Rex Burbank's claim in *Thornton Wilder* (New York: Twayne Publishers, 1961), p. 97, that *The Matchmaker* belongs with the works of Wilder's earlier career. Wilder himself refers to *The Matchmaker* as a "revival" in a letter to Joseph Still on December 15, 1953; YCAL Thornton Wilder MSS 162, Folder 72.

27. *Playboys & Killjoys: An Essay on the Theory & Practice of Comedy* (New York: Oxford University Press, 1987), p. 25.

28. It should be mentioned that in an interview in 1955, Wilder denied that the play has any "special message"; see "Wilder Says Humor His Only Message," in *Washington Post,* December 6, 1955, p. 36.

29. Thus, in *Indiana Jones and the Last Crusade,* Dr. Jones (Sean Connery) can say to his son (Harrison Ford) about his affair with a much younger woman, "I have the same desires as the next man." When his son responds, "Dad, I was the next man," the audience reacts only with laughter. In a different movie, this could be the subject of tragedy, but here in context it is simply funny. Still, the movie is about the difficulties that fathers and sons have in communicating as well as about the underlying competition for respect and affection that threatens reconciliation between them.

30. As E. F. M. in a review for the *Christian Science Monitor* wrote, "It is a gentle plea for a happier and perhaps a trifle more adventurous world—in the playful sense of the word. Of adventure in its sterner aspects there is an abundance at present"; December 13, 1938, p. 14.

31. YCAL Thornton Wilder MSS 108, Folder 68.

32. *The Spiritual Aspects of the New Poetry,* p. 84.

33. YCAL Thornton Wilder MSS 108, Folder 35, December 14, 1966, to Kay.

34. George's inability to act like "one of the guys" or even to participate easily in casual conversation is actually evidence for his saintliness. As an anal-

ogy, Galahad, in T. H. White's *The Once and Future King,* is despised by Arthur's more worldly knights, and Lancelot explains the irrelevance of such judgments: "People talk far too much. Where I have been, where Galahad is, it is a waste of time to have 'manners.' Manners are only needed between people to keep their empty affairs in working order. Manners makyth man, you know, not God. So you can understand how Galahad may have seemed inhuman, and mannerless, and so on, to the people who were buzzing and clacking around him"; (New York: Berkeley Publishing, 1966), p. 461.

35. (New Brunswick, NJ: Transaction Publishers, 2006), p. 19.

36. *New York Times,* January 2, 1935, p. 23.

37. Some readers thought that George was inspired by Wilder's friend, the heavyweight champion Gene Tunney. See Linda Simon, *Thornton Wilder: His World,* p. 112.

38. In a letter from Amos to Thornton dated January 13 but without a year, Amos writes, "My conviction is that all illness is [a] superficial symptom of some major process of readjustment going on in the deeper self. Rilke says the same thing interestingly, in one way, in one of his letters to that young poet." YCAL Thornton Wilder MSS 108, Folder 4410.

39. YCAL Thornton Wilder MSS 108, Folder 1712, March 13, 1960.

40. *The Autobiography of St. Ignatius Loyola with Related Documents,* trans. Joseph F. O'Callaghan, ed. John C. Olin (New York: Harper Torchbooks, 1974), pp. 46–47.

41. YCAL Thornton Wilder MSS 108, Folder 26, letter to Amos dated March 2, 1953.

42. YCAL Thornton Wilder MSS 108, Folder 3064.

43. Miguel de Cervantes, *Don Quixote,* trans. Edith Grossman (New York: HarperCollins, 2003), pp. 249, 251.

44. *The Tragic Sense of Life,* trans. J. E. Crawford Flitch (1921; Mineola, NY: Dover Publications, 1954), p. 315. Wilder refers repeatedly to Unamuno in his notes on *Don Quixote;* see YCAL Thornton Wilder MSS 108, Folders 3064 and 3065.

45. Cervantes, *Don Quixote,* p. 43.

46. *The Tragic Sense of Life,* p. 90.

47. *The Diary of Søren Kierkegaard,* ed. Peter Rohde (New York: Citadel Press, 1987), pp. 165, 164.

48. Even here, Wilder's affection for his characters is apparent. Previously to *Heaven's My Destination,* the most famous Roberta in American literature would have been Theodore Dreiser's Roberta in *An American Tragedy.* She, too, is a farm girl who gets pregnant. But George marries his Roberta, and Dreiser's Clyde allows his to die. Distinguishing Wilder from

his contemporaries, Bernard Grebanier observes that Wilder, unlike, for instance, Sinclair Lewis, "loves his fellow Americans and, not blind to their faults, sees them with the charity with which we view those we love"; *Thornton Wilder* (Minneapolis: University of Minnesota Press, 1964), p. 27.

49. "Don Quixote in the American Scene," *Anglican Theological Review* 25, no. 3 (July 1943): 273.

50. *Thornton Wilder,* trans. Frieda Schutze (New York: Frederick Ungar, 1971), p. 54.

51. H. J. Rose, *A Handbook of Greek Mythology* (New York: E. P. Dutton & Co., 1959), p. 109.

52. Amusingly enough, Wilder admits in a letter to his sister Janet's husband Toby that he is reading "*The Cruise of the Beagle*" [*sic*] for the first time in 1975; see YCAL Thornton Wilder MSS 108, Folder 5, letter dated. January 14, 1975.

53. *The Varieties of Religious Experience* (New York: Penguin Books, 1982), p. 358. In a letter to Amos, Thornton called *Varieties of Religious Experience* "a great book"; YCAL Thornton Wilder MSS 108, Folder 4407, letter dated October 16, 1916.

Chapter Three.   Piety, the Individual, and the Community

1. "Thornton Wilder," *The English Journal* 28 (January 1939): 6–7.

2. *Theology and Modern Literature,* p. 33.

3. Ibid., p. 32.

4. "Heirs of Newfoundland," in *Yale Review* 21 (Winter 1931): 403. The reference to stanzas 22 and 23 of *Sir Gawain* is an acute one; the beauty of the description of the yearly cycle is enhanced by its parallel to Sir Gawain himself: in the springtime of his life he must prepare for the likely death that awaits him on his quest, just as the year ends in winter.

5. *American Characteristics and Other Essays,* p. 36.

6. Ibid., p. 35.

7. One can see an embodiment of the claim in W. H. Auden's "In Praise of Limestone" where a region "Of short distances and definite places" creates a genial community that believes in a merciful God easily pacified by a good poem. *Collected Poems,* ed. Edward Mendelson (New York: Random House, 1976), p. 414.

8. Wilder's one-acts were so original that many of the initial reviewers regarded them as either slight or essentially undramatic or both. Walter

Prichard Eaton in the *New York Herald Tribune* said that the plays "lack any real dramatic bite"; December 13, 1931, p. 19. *The Times Literary Supplement* claimed that "Mr. Wilder leaves an impression of being more interested in experimental forms than in the substance of his dramas, with the consequence that, in his hands, experiment, which may be vitalized by the compulsion of the subject, wears often a *dilettante* air of being indulged for its own sake"; December 10, 1931, p. 1001. The reviewer for *Theatre Arts Bookshelf* wrote that the plays "are hardly more than studies in dramatic material and statement"; *Theatre Arts Monthly* 16 (February 1932): 175. The plays "seem better designed for reading than for the stage," according to Robert Littell in the *Saturday Review of Literature,* December 12, 1931, p. 366. Subsequent productions of these plays have shown their dramatic power.

9. "A Novelist as Playwright," in *The Christian Century,* March 2, 1932, p. 293.

10. "Thornton Wilder, the Real, and Theatrical Realism," in *Realism and the American Dramatic Tradition,* ed. William W. Demastes (Tuscaloosa: University of Alabama Press, 1996), pp. 139–55.

11. Trans. Andrew R. McAndrew (New York: Signet Classics, 1962), p. 40.

12. Camus represents an example of the nihilism that Dostoyevsky predicted. In a letter to Amos dated June 13, 1946, Thornton encloses an interview with Camus and comments, "His favorite novel in the world is Dostoievski's The Possessed, centering on the character of Kirillov: the instant of consciousness before suicide is the only valid viewpoint in the world!!"; YCAL Thornton Wilder MSS 108, Folder 20.

13. *The Life of Reason* (Middlesex: Echo Library, 2006), pp. 317 and 318, originally published in 1905 and 1906.

14. Gertrude Stein, *Writings, 1903–1932* (New York: The Library of America, 1998), p. 5.

15. *Orthodoxy,* p. 2.

16. "A Preface for 'Our Town,'" *New York Times,* February 13, 1938, p. 155.

17. Strikingly, an audience of five hundred sightless persons "saw" the play with great success in its initial run; see "500 Blind Attend Play Without Scenery: Find Imaginations Fill In Details Easily," *New York Times,* March 21, 1938, p. 32.

18. *Conversations with Thornton Wilder,* p. 112.

19. For the steady rise in GNP per capita from the early 1930s to the second half of the 1930s and then the frightening reversal, see John

McClymer's *The Birth of Modern America, 1919–1939* (Maplecrest, NY: Brandywine Press, 2005), p. 158.

20. *Conversations with Thornton Wilder,* p. 33.

21. Rpt. in *Readings on Thornton Wilder,* ed. Katie de Koster (San Diego: Greenhaven Press, 1998), p. 133.

22. *Our Town: An American Play* (Boston: Twayne Publishers, 1989), p. 93. The idea is not uncommon; it is found in authors as disparate as Nietzsche and Tennyson.

23. "How They Used to Live," *New York Times,* February 13, 1938, p. 155.

24. Achilles makes no such speech in Homer, Euripides, Ovid, Quintus Smyrnaeus, Racine, or Kleist.

25. *The Odyssey of Homer,* trans. Richmond Lattimore (New York: Harper Colophon Books, 1965), p. 180.

26. "The Skin of Whose Teeth," *Saturday Review of Literature* 25 (December 19, 1942): 3. The charge that Wilder was guilty of plagiarism was easily refuted by Edmund Wilson in "The Antrobuses and the Earwickers," *The Nation,* January 30, 1943, pp. 167–68. Wilder actually wrote a refutation of the plagiarism charge and sent it to his sister Isabel to forward to the *Saturday Review.* The editors of *Selected Letters* suggest that his attorney and family talked him out of replying on the grounds that he should not dignify the charges; see *Selected Letters,* pp. 412–15.

27. Wilder's letters offer an example of how this might function in the creative realm. He writes Isabel in 1934 about a movie project: "Charles Lederer and I have been working for two days on a movie. Terms same as Joan of Arc. Two weeks = 35 page story. Even if they don't like it I get $1500. About how a girl dressed as a boy joins Shakespeare's Globe theatre company and creates the great heroines. Lousy?" YCAL Thornton Wilder MSS 108, Folder 85. This idea floated in the ether until the 1990s, when it was embodied in the film *Shakespeare in Love* (1998).

28. According to Leonard Lyons, "Wilder was about to be commissioned into the Army when he finished writing this scene. He quickly read the Dialogues of Plato, his 'Laws' and 'Symposium,' but could find no appropriate quotations. And so he wrote something which sounded as if it were a quotation from Plato, put the philosopher's name to it—and went off into the Army"; "Broadway Gazette," *Washington Post,* May 18, 1943, p. 10.

29. *The Letters of Gertrude Stein & Thornton Wilder,* ed. Edward M. Burns and Ulla E. Dydo with William Rice (New Haven: Yale University Press, 1996), p. 306.

Chapter Four.   The Appetite for Destruction and the Obstacles to Growth

1. *Night,* trans. Stella Rodway (New York: Bantam Books, 1960), p. 32.

2. *Ethics Preceded by On the Improvement of the Understanding,* ed. James Gutman (New York: Hafner, 1949), p. 6.

3. For example, in Samuel Johnson's *Rasselas,* a philosopher exhorts his listeners to "arm themselves against the shafts of malice and misfortune, by invulnerable patience, concluding, that this state only was happiness, and this happiness was in everyone's power." When next Rasselas sees the philosopher, he is mourning for his daughter. Rasselas reminds him of the resources of reason and patience. But, "What comfort, said the mourner, can truth and reason afford me? Of what effect are they now, but to tell me, that my daughter will not be restored?" Johnson does not expect the reader to judge the philosopher harshly for his inconsistency: rather, he expects the reader to learn, as does the philosopher, the inadequacy of rationalism in the face of sorrow for any feeling human being: *Samuel Johnson, Rasselas, Poems, and Selected Prose,* 3rd ed., ed. Bertrand H. Bronson (New York: Holt, Rinehart, & Winston, 1971), pp. 645 and 646.

4. Consider Chris's reflections on the deaths of his soldiers in Arthur Miller's postwar play, *All My Sons* (1947): "Everything was being destroyed, see, but it seemed to me that one new thing was made. A kind of . . . responsibility. Man for man. . . . And then I came home and it was incredible. I . . . there was no meaning in it here; the whole thing to them was a kind of a—bus accident"; rpt. In *Modern Drama: Selected Plays from 1879 to the Present,* ed. Walter Levy (Upper Saddle River, NJ: Prentice Hall, 1999), p. 525.

5. See, for instance, his extraordinary misreading of Faulkner's *Light in August* in *The Journals of Thornton Wilder 1939–1961,* selected and ed. Donald Gallup (New Haven: Yale University Press, 1985), pp. 18–19; or his letter to Isabel on July 22, 1949, where he dismisses Graham Greene's chilling *Brighton Rock* as a "most sordid book and really all phony contrived morbid psychology"; YCAL Thornton Wilder MSS 108, Folder, 120.

6. *Reflections on the Revolution in France* (Oxford: Oxford University Press, 1999), p. 96.

7. In a letter to his father of "Tuesday 27/28, 14" he gleefully quotes negative passages from Mrs. Thrale about Burke (YCAL Thornton Wilder MSS 108, Folder 45). In a letter dated October 25, 1916, he reports to his father that he is astonished that Professor Wager (whom Wilder liked very much) admires Burke (YCAL Thornton Wilder MSS 108, Folder 47).

8. Interestingly, Wilder corresponded with Cary Grant on a possible film version of *Gulliver's Travels,* which Howard Hawks was to direct. Wilder declined to work on the script, but he proposed that it should not be treated as a fantasy, but rather "as dead-pan sober-serious travel-experience"; *Selected Letters,* pp. 473–75.

9. *A Connecticut Yankee in King Arthur's Court* (New York: Harper & Row, 1965), p. 74.

10. For example, in Roger Daltrey and the Who singing "Hope I die before I get old," a song roughly contemporaneous with the composition of "Youth."

11. *Conversations with Thornton Wilder,* p. 14.

12. Trans. and ed. James Strachey (New York: W. W. Norton, 1989), p. 82.

13. All references to *The Seven Ages of Man* and *The Seven Deadly Sins* are cited in the text as *Collected Plays.*

14. Or as Wordsworth mourns in the "Ode on Intimations of Immortality": "At length the Man perceives it die away, / And fade into the light of common day."

15. (New York: Harper & Brothers, 1955), p. 15.

16. Or as Drummond, the lawyer representing the schoolteacher Cates in Jerome Lawrence and Robert E. Lee's *Inherit the Wind* (1955), a play about the Scopes Monkey Trial, says about his own pie-in-the-sky (the rocking horse Golden Dancer), "Bert, whenever you see something bright, shining, perfect-seeming—all gold, with purple spots—look behind the paint! And if it's a lie—show it up for what it really is"; *Selected Plays of Jerome Lawrence and Robert E. Lee,* ed. Alan Woods (Columbus: Ohio State University Press, 1995), p. 60. Lawrence and Lee are not as simpleminded as this passage might sound: Drummond exits the play carrying a copy of Darwin and the Bible. But certainly anyone who insists on a fundamentalist interpretation of the Bible is portrayed as a danger to intellectual and social progress.

17. For instance, both brothers admired Goethe, who has the Lord tell Mephisto: "I never hated those who were like you; / Of all the spirits that negate, / The knavish jester gives me least to do. / For man's activity can easily abate, / He soon prefers uninterrupted rest; / To give him this companion hence seems best / Who roils and must as Devil help create." *Faust,* trans. Walter Kaufmann (New York: Anchor Books, 1990), p. 88.

18. *Theology and Modern Literature,* p. 35.

19. YCAL Thornton Wilder MSS 108, Folder 14.

20. YCAL Thornton Wilder MSS 108, Folder 4417.

21. *The Bible and the Literary Critic* (Minneapolis: Fortress Press, 1991), p. 89.

22. *Journal of Religion* 40, no. 3 (July 1960): 160.

23. YCAL Thornton Wilder MSS 108, Folder 4416. Ultimately, Papajewski wrote a book about Wilder; *Thornton Wilder* (Frankfurt am Main: Athenäum Verlag, 1961).

24. YCAL Thornton Wilder MSS 162, Folder 69.

25. From "The Encounter with Nothingness," in *The Philosophy of Jean Paul Sartre,* ed. and intro. Robert Denoon Cumming (New York: Vintage Books, 1965), pp. 128, 129.

26. *No Exit and Three Other Plays* (New York: Vintage Books, 1961), p. 51.

27. Ibid., p. 122.

28. *An Introduction to Existentialism* (New York: Dover Publications, 1962), p. 87.

29. YCAL Glenway Westcott MSS 134, Folder 1710. Brooks Atkinson, for instance, called *The Ides of March* "a bookish novel. Mr. Wilder's ideas about life seem not to spring from life directly"; "Wilder's Roman Fantasia," *New York Times,* February 22, 1948, p. 30. On the other hand, Paul Jordan Smith, writing in the *Los Angeles Times,* calls Caesar "warm and alive" and says that Wilder "has sympathy and a rare imaginative sense": February 22, 1948, p. D4. Fanny Butcher praised the novel as "a bonfire to the mind" because of its philosophical wisdom; *Chicago Daily Tribune,* February 22, 1948, sec. 4, p. 3. On the whole, reviews were respectful, if not glowing.

30. YCAL Thornton Wilder MSS 108, Folder 22.

31. YCAL Thornton Wilder MSS 108, Folder 24.

32. Ibid.

33. YCAL Thornton Wilder MSS 108, Folder 19.

34. YCAL Thornton Wilder MSS 162, Folder 67. For the Catholic position on man's free will, see *The Catechism of the Catholic Church* (New York: An Image Book, Doubleday, 1995), pp. 481–82.

35. Monroe C. Beardsley, *Aesthetics from Classical Greece to the Present* (University: University of Alabama Press, 1966), p. 216.

36. *Mere Christianity* (New York: HarperCollins, 2001), p. 37.

37. Lawrence Jasper, "Edward Sheldon," in *American Playwrights, 1880–1945: A Research and Production Sourcebook,* ed. William W. Demastes (Westport, CT: Greenwood Press, 1995), p. 382.

38. See George B. Bryan's entry in *The Dictionary of Literary Biography 7,* ed. John MacNicholas (Detroit: Gale Research, 1981), part 2, pp. 228–31.

39. Goldstone, *Thornton Wilder: An Intimate Portrait,* pp. 36–37.

40. In a letter to Amos dated October 8, 1970, Wilder mentions that he has been unlucky in his close male friends: "one (in the clergy who you know well) ceased growing; Bob H got involved in coils and coils; Lauro de Bosis lost his life heroically; Ned Sheldon invalided, but abundant in spirit, died"; YCAL Thornton Wilder MSS 108, Folder 4415.

41. YCAL Thornton Wilder MSS 108, Folder 6.

42. Letter dated October 11, 1946; YCAL Thornton Wilder MSS 108, Folder 20.

43. Wilder's Caesar is a compulsive teacher, particularly of young women, for instance; in this way he recalls the Caesar of George Bernard Shaw's *Caesar and Cleopatra*. A further point of similarity between the two works is the boyish infatuation of Caesar with Cleopatra. In a letter to Maxwell Anderson in 1956, Wilder mentions another source: "For a Caesar I was richly fed by a great admiration for the thousands of pages of Simón Bolivar's correspondence: a lofty smiling half-sad unshakenness in the face of the betrayal of friends and beneficiaries"; *Selected Letters*, p. 544.

44. *The Golden Bough*, p. 46. Of course, Caesar was also condemned for those qualities for which Frazer (and apparently Wilder) admired him. In Henry Fielding's *Jonathan Wild*, a history of a "great man," "when the mighty Caesar, with wonderful greatness of mind, had destroyed the liberties of his country, and with all the means of fraud and force had placed himself at the head of his equals, had corrupted and enslaved the greatest people whom the sun ever saw, we are reminded, as an evidence of his generosity, of his largesses to his followers and tools, by whose means he had accomplished his purpose, and by whose assistance he was to establish it"; (London: Penguin Classics, 1986), p. 41. This, of course, is Catullus' view of Caesar in Wilder's novel. See, for instance, Document LX: "Our fathers died to acquire those liberties of which One Man now is robbing us. . . . Death to Caesar. For our country and our Gods" (*Ides*, 212–13).

45. *On the Nature of the Universe*, trans. R. E. Latham (New York: Penguin Books, 1951), p. 177. Briefly, Lucretius' position on the argument from design—the universe shows design and consequently there must be a designer—is that one can attribute no further perfection to the designer than one can see in the design (Hume made a similar argument in the eighteenth century). That is, if we saw a house, we would infer the presence of a builder; but we could assume no perfection in the builder if we saw flaws in the house. Since we see numerous flaws in the universe (at least from the human point of view), it follows that if there is a god, he is either not omnipotent, or the universe was not created by him, or it was created without man in mind. Moreover, Lucretius can explain the creation of the universe to his

own satisfaction with atomistic philosophy, so there is no need to invoke any deity at all.

46. *The Journals of Thornton Wilder 1939–1961,* p. 237.

47. Cumming, ed., *The Philosophy of Jean Paul Sartre,* p. 133.

48. *The New Man* (New York: Farrar, Straus & Giroux, 1999), p. 101.

Chapter Five.   *Mystery, Pluralism, and Evolution*

1. Caesar's language echoes that of Dostoyevsky's Prince Myshkin, who, in his epileptic fits, finds that "his mind and heart were flooded with extraordinary light: all torment, all doubt, all anxieties were relieved at once, resolved in a kind of lofty calm, full of serene harmonious joy and hope, full of understanding and the knowledge of the ultimate cause of things"; *The Idiot,* trans. Henry and Olga Carlisle (New York: Signet Classics, 2002), p. 236.

2. "Riddles, Silence, and Wonder: Joyce and Wittgenstein Encountering the Limits of Language," *English Literary History* 57, no. 2 (Summer 1990): 459–84; rpt. in *Critical Essays on James Joyce's A Portrait of the Artist as a Young Man,* ed. Philip Brady and James F. Carens (New York: G. K. Hall, 1998), p. 249.

3. For an alternative view, that Caesar's assassination is the emblem of his failure because of his mistreatment of women, see Donald Haberman's "The Myth of the Good Goddess in *The Ides of March,*" in *Thornton Wilder: New Essays,* ed. Blank et al., pp. 247–57.

4. *The Wasteland and Other Poems* (New York: Harvest Books, 1962), pp. 20–21.

5. *New York Times Book Review,* October, 21, 1973, p. 16.

6. Letter from Wilder to his sister Charlotte on November 4, 1962; YCAL Thornton Wilder MSS 108, Folder 4426.

7. YCAL Thornton Wilder MSS 108, Folder 4411.

8. The tone here is close to Asagai's affirmation of faith in Lorraine Hansberry's *A Raisin in the Sun* (1959). Beneatha tells Asagai that life is an endless recurring cycle of misery, and he tells her, "It isn't a circle—it is simply a long line—as in geometry, you know, one that reaches into infinity. And because we cannot see the end—we also cannot see how it changes. And it is very odd but those who see the changes—who dream, who will not give up—are called idealists . . . and those who see only the circle—we call *them* the 'realists'!" (New York: Signet Books, 1988), p. 134. Because change is not immediately apparent, some deny its existence. Asagai regards that as

evidence of immaturity because the development of humanity, politically and socially, is a lengthy process.

9. *The Basic Writings of C. G. Jung,* ed. Violet Staub De Laszlo (New York: Modern Library, 1993), p. 8.

10. In a letter to Robert Penn Warren, Wilder mentions Jung's theory that the Greek and Roman pantheons "are perfections of ourselves"; YCAL Robert Penn Warren MSS 51, Folder 1540.

11. *St. Francis of Assisi* (Garden City, NY: Doubleday & Co., 1924), p. 98.

12. As early as February 7, 1939, Wilder writes to Sibyl Colefax that he is "wrestling" with the play; see *Selected Letters,* p. 364.

13. YCAL Thornton Wilder MSS 108, Folder 4410.

14. *The Wasteland and Other Poems,* p. 19.

15. C. S. Lewis writing within a couple of years raises the same issue in his novel *'Til We Have Faces:* "I saw well why the gods do not speak to us openly, nor let us answer. Till that word [the honest though ugly expression of ourselves] can be dug out of us, why should they hear the babble that we think we mean? How can they meet us face to face till we have faces?" (New York: Harcourt Brace Jovanovich, 1956), p. 294. Orual in Lewis's novel is jealous of Psyche and therefore angry at the gods for taking her, but she is only aware of this at the end. Until then she conceals from herself her anger through grief. In Lewis, the queen's refusal to face herself and her motives honestly makes it impossible for God to show himself clearly, and hence the novel's title: How can we face God until we have faces?

16. August 23, 1955, p. 4.

17. Wilder's presentation of the Greek pantheon as no longer a useful mythology finds a parallel in Robert Graves. At an early stage in the composition of *The Eighth Day,* on March 21, 1961, Thornton writes to Amos, "You can't deny that Robert Graves with his immense if eccentric learning is always great fun"; YCAL Thornton Wilder MSS 108, Folder 4412. Graves sees a perversion of the Greek pantheon as emblematic of the problems of the modern world: "Though the West is still nominally Christian, we have come to be governed, in practice, by the unholy triumvirate of Pluto god of wealth, Apollo god of science, and Mercury god of thieves." *The White Goddess* (1948; New York: Farrar, Straus & Giroux, 1966), p. 476. Apollo has created the atom bomb, and Pluto and Mercury are warring over the material world. However much one may be amused by Graves's literal lunacy—he believed that the white goddess of, among other things, the moon was the source of all true poetry and that any society that resisted her was profoundly unbalanced—he suggests the hold, perhaps destructive, that earlier religious ideas maintain on the modern imagination.

18. (Lincoln: University of Nebraska Press, 1996), pp. 307–8, 318, 185.

19. *New Testament Faith for Today,* p. 139.

20. In "Metamorphose der Pflanzen," Goethe explains that nature begins with "the dry kernel [that] holds and protects the dormant life." Ultimately, this is an expression of the goddess Nature herself: "Every plant announces, to you now, the laws eternal / Every flower louder and louder is speaking with you. / You but decipher here the holy glyphs of the Goddess, / Everywhere, though, you see her in even their changing itself." Trans. Frederick Turner and Zsuzsanna Ozsváth, *Kronoscope: Journal for the Study of Time* 6, no. 2 (2006): 255. In Goethe's poem, contemplating nature inspires higher faculties, such as love.

21. YCAL Thornton Wilder MSS, Folder 7.

22. Letter apparently from 1942, YCAL Thornton Wilder MSS 108, Folder 17.

23. *Essays and Addresses on the Philosophy of Religion* (New York: E. P. Dutton & Co., 1921), p. 98.

24. Ibid., p. 111.

25. Ibid., p. 109.

26. Ibid., p. 115.

27. Ibid., p. 114.

28. *The Structure of Scientific Revolutions,* 2nd ed. (Chicago: University of Chicago Press, 1970), p. 171.

29. See "Culture in a Democracy," in *American Characteristics and other Essays,* ed. Gallup, p. 73.

30. "The Reality of the Life of Faith," *Harvard Divinity Bulletin,* October 1964, p. 20.

31. Letter dated March 22, 1938, YCAL Thornton Wilder MSS 108, Folder 88.

32. *The Life of Reason,* p. 359. Robert W. Corrigan has also suggested that Wilder is indebted to Santayana in "Thornton Wilder and the Tragic Sense of Life" (1961), rpt. in *Critical Essays on Thornton Wilder,* p. 80.

33. *A Rhetoric of Motives* (1950; Berkeley: University of California Press, 1969), particularly pp. 181–88.

34. In *The Future of an Illusion,* Freud says that heaven has "an infantile prototype"; (New York: W. W. Norton, 1989), p. 21.

35. Letter dated May 1, 1964, YCAL Thornton Wilder MSS 108, Folder 9.

36. Lincoln Konkle demonstrates that Puritan typology recurs frequently in Wilder's works in *Thornton Wilder and the Puritan Narrative Tradition* (Columbia and London: University of Missouri Press, 2006).

37. (Philadelphia: Fortress Press, 1980), p. 16.

Index

Christopher J. Wheatley

is Ordinary Professor of English at the Catholic University of America.

CPSIA information can be obtained
at www.ICGtesting.com
Printed in the USA
LVOW10s0741290618

582194LV00001BA/129/P